MUSKETS & APPLEJACK

MUSKETS & APPLEJACK

SPIRITS, SOLDIERS, AND THE CIVIL WAR

MARK WILL-WEBER

REGNERY
HISTORY

Regnery History™ is a trademark of Salem Communications Holding Corporation; Regnery® is a registered trademark of Salem Communications Holding Corporation

Cataloging-in-Publication data on file with the Library of Congress

ISBN 978-1-62157-509-2
e-book ISBN 978-1-62157-559-7

Published in the United States by
Regnery History
An imprint of Regnery Publishing
A Division of Salem Media Group
300 New Jersey Ave NW
Washington, D.C. 20001
www.RegneryHistory.com

Manufactured in the United States of America

10 9 8 7 6 5 4 3 2 1

Books are available in quantity for promotional or premium use. For information on discounts and terms, please visit our website: www. Regnery.com.

Distributed to the trade by Perseus Distribution
www.perseusdistribution.com

In memory of the battles fought and hardships endured by General J. K. Robison and the men of the Sixteenth Pennsylvania Cavalry.

CONTENTS

PREFACE

As historical lightning rods go, one might be hard pressed to find a nineteenth-century figure of greater conductivity than Daniel Edgar Sickles. He was a Tammany Hall politician, Union general, and the first man to successfully plead temporary insanity in an American courtroom after he shot to death his wife's ill-fated lover in Washington's Lafayette Square in February of 1859.

Born in 1819,* Sickles—despite losing a leg at the Battle of Gettysburg in 1863—lived to ninety-four years of age, apparently confirming the old proverb that "only the good die young" (some of his enemies referred to him as "Devil Dan"). Sickles could strike a roguish pose with great conviction. One contemporary said the general "looked like a Spanish brigand that we see represented on a stage of a theatre, with his huge mustache, plumes and boots."

---

* There are discrepancies on the exact date of Daniel Sickles's birth, as some historians claim Sickles himself—near the end of his life—said he had been born in 1825.

Although Sickles did and said many controversial things (he once purposely insulted the Queen of England by refusing to stand for a toast to Her Majesty), he spoke very emphatically about the role of alcohol in watering the seeds of secession that led to the Civil War:

> The War of the Rebellion was really a whiskey war. Yes, whiskey caused the Rebellion! Congress was "whiskey in the morning"…then whiskey all day; whiskey and gambling all night. The fights…the angry speeches…were all whiskey.

At first glance, it seems a most outrageous claim—the very idea that *whiskey* was the major cause in launching the war that swept away more lives of American soldiers (approximately 620,000, but with some estimates as high as 750,000) than were lost in all other U.S. wars combined from the Revolutionary War up to and including World War II.

But was alcohol at least a contributing factor to the fermentation of hostilities? That's certainly an easier argument to make. Sickles may have exaggerated the cause-and-effect relationship, but examination of various incidents in the lead-up to the war reveals that "Devil Dan" (who was quite fond of drinking himself) was not completely off target.

In fact, at several crucial pre-war incidents—the Brooks-Sumner caning controversy, various acts of violence in "Bleeding Kansas" (including the "Sack of Lawrence"), the squelching of John Brown's slave rebellion at Harpers Ferry, and the publishing of Harriet Beecher Stowe's *Uncle Tom's Cabin*—alcohol was involved in one way or another.

The brutal attack by South Carolina representative Preston Brooks upon Charles Sumner, staunch abolitionist senator from

Massachusetts, understandably draws much attention. In fact, the Brooks-Sumner affair would be conspicuous by its absence if omitted from any history of pre–Civil War events.

On May 22, 1856, Brooks—brooding and "very likely tipsy with drink"—entered the Senate chambers. Armed with a hefty gutta-percha walking stick, the South Carolinian planned to teach the unsuspecting Sumner a harsh lesson. Brooks's motivation for what he saw as justifiable revenge came from an anti-slavery speech in which Sumner had recently insulted both South Carolina in general and Senator Andrew Butler, Brooks's older cousin, in particular.

Brooks ambushed Sumner, whose long legs were initially stuck under his desk as his attacker's blows rained down upon him with a savage rapidity. So merciless was the beating that the stunned Yankee senator "bellowed like a calf" (Brooks's own words, *sans* remorse).

Sumner eventually managed to free himself from his desk but collapsed on the floor. Brooks had shattered his gold-headed cane on his victim's skull and body, reducing Sumner to a blood-soaked and unconscious heap. Colleagues—initially held at bay by Southern politicians in cahoots with Brooks—rushed to assist Sumner, but it would be three years until he would return to the U.S. Senate, and he never fully recovered to a robust state of health.

One of the more recent treatments of this controversial incident can be found in the historian Rachel Shelden's book *Washington Brotherhood: Politics, Social Life, and the Coming of the Civil War*. While some examinations of the Brooks assault touch lightly or not at all on the role of Demon Alcohol, Dr. Shelden asks a compelling question in her work:

> Perhaps the worst political mistake of all was letting alcohol influence one's behavior in and out of Congress. Drinking both the evening before and the morning of the caning no doubt influenced Brooks's actions.... If Brooks had been sober, might he have struck Sumner only once or twice rather than thirty times?

Without question, the incident further inflamed tensions between Northerners and Southerners—though Shelden notes that relations between regional politicians in Washington, perhaps surprisingly, returned to normal rather quickly. Newspapers and critics in the North blasted Brooks, but in Dixie he was lionized; some admirers even sent him new canes as gifts to salute what they saw as a decisive and necessary act.

Just a day before the Brooks-Sumner affair, pro-slavers sacked the town of Lawrence, Kansas. Thomas H. Gladstone—an Englishman who wrote about his travels through the U.S. during "Bleeding Kansas"—noted the pro-slavery horsemen were "maddened by drink" when they burned Governor Charles Robinson's hilltop residence in Lawrence. The raiders then fled east, flush with both plunder and whiskey. Gladstone described meeting these Missouri "border ruffians" soon after:

> Their thirst knew no bounds; and when a barrel of Bourbon or Monongahela, or Double Rectified was accessible, they forgot even in some instances the politics of its possessor. Thus through the day they sustained their turbulent fury, and when night came, it found them prepared for any excesses.

So the pro-slavery factions from Missouri gained a reputation for whiskey swilling long before a cannon was ever aimed at Fort Sumter. But surely not all the "Jayhawkers"—the "Free State" counterattack to the "Border Ruffians"—were non-drinking deacons, either. After all, Kansas in the mid-nineteenth century was essentially a rough frontier territory that would not achieve statehood until 1861 and, in such an era, drinking was quite commonplace.

Notably, alcohol was present again when John Brown's slave revolt was crushed at Harpers Ferry, Virginia, in mid-October of 1859. Alcohol did *not* play a role in Brown's plan to capture the armory, take hostages, and rally the slaves into a rebellious force—as he, like most abolitionists, railed against the evils of liquor. But the militiamen who trapped Brown and his disciples in the engine house apparently had far more booze than discipline. As a Maryland militia captain (who arrived late and sober on the scene) described it:

> Every man had a gun and four-fifths of them were under no command. The military had ceased firing, but men who were intoxicated were firing their guns in the air, and others at the engine house.

Fortunately, a troop of Marines under the command of Colonel Robert E. Lee (still in a U.S. uniform—as was his top lieutenant on the scene, J. E. B. Stuart) arrived the next day. Lee, noting that numerous militiamen were obviously under the influence, immediately closed all the saloons. Many a commander—especially ones like Lee who had seen firsthand the difficulties of directing intoxicated troops during the Mexican War—would attempt to use this same, basic tactic during the Civil War. Lee's Marines stayed sober and successfully stormed the engine house on October 18. Wounded during the attack, John Brown was captured and eventually hung for his failed "rising" in December.

The evils of alcohol even made an appearance in the most important novel of the decade—*Uncle Tom's Cabin*, written by abolitionist Harriet Beecher Stowe. No small influence on Northern sensibilities and political thought, Stowe's book sold an estimated 300,000 copies in 1852. Predictably, it also received some angry rebuffs from Southern journalists and steeled Southern resentment against "Black Yankees" attempting to trudge upon the traditional ways of life below the Mason-Dixon Line.

It was probably no coincidence that Simon Legree—the infamous arch-villain and slave master of Mrs. Stowe's fictional story—indulges in hard liquor. To make her villain even more despicable, Stowe had Legree force alcohol on his female slaves to make them more pliable for his sexual advances. As the dialogue between two of Legree's slaves reveals:

> "He wanted me to drink some of his hateful brandy," said Emmeline, "And I hate it so—"
>
> "You'd better drink," said Cassy. "I hated it, too, and now I can't live without it. One must have something;—things don't look so dreadful when you take that."
>
> "Mother used to tell me never to touch any such thing," said Emmeline.
>
> "*Mother* told you!" said Cassy, with a thrilling and bitter emphasis on the word mother. "What use is it for mothers to say anything? You are all to be bought and paid for, and your souls to whoever gets you. That's the way it goes. I say *drink* brandy; drink all you can, and it will make things come easier."

Legree also supplied his male slaves with liquor when he was bored, "…warming them up with whiskey [to] amuse himself by setting them to singing, dancing or fighting, as the humor took him."

Like many abolitionists, Mrs. Stowe also embraced the temperance cause and, in fact, had written about the scourge of Demon Alcohol prior to her crusades against slavery. It would have been a logical inclination for Mrs. Stowe to make alcohol contribute to Legree's depravities and to the brutalities practiced on his slaves.

Whatever alcohol's influence may have been in the crucial events leading up to the Civil War, it certainly proved to be front and center in all its various guises *during* the war. Drink was a tonic to soothe nerves both pre- and post-battle, and also an attempt to celebrate the holidays of home in some sort of makeshift imitation. Alcohol also served as one of the soldiers' first choices as a boredom killer around camp, and dovetailed nicely with other soldierly vices such as gambling and (when possible) womanizing.

Demon Alcohol also caused much consternation and outright havoc during wartime, including occasional incidents that can only be described as atrocities. Soldiers were punished, guardhouses were filled, and even high-ranking officers made mistakes of booze-induced brashness or, conversely, drank to the point of lethargy.

And as the diaries and letters of Civil War soldiers and officers on both sides show, alcohol—the consumption of it and the seemingly endless pursuit to acquire it—sometimes supplied a rare-but-welcome bit of comic relief. German and Irish soldiers are often the participants—or butts—of these humorous anecdotes, a phenomenon also reflected in the social and cultural commentary about the war.

But perhaps most important were the *practical* applications of alcohol; hard liquor (whiskey, brandy, and applejack leading the charge) was the primary treatment for sheer pain and terror when a soldier was wounded in battle. Additionally, small doses were often prescribed to combat various illnesses (mixed with quinine to combat mosquito-borne diseases, for example), inclement weather conditions, and just general fatigue. Laudanum, a mixture of opium with alcohol, was an effective painkiller when available. Just having a small flask of brandy, whiskey, or laudanum could provide at least *some* bit of comfort for a soldier going into harm's way.

GREAT GRANDDAD'S DILEMMA

Near the end of the war—a mere two days before Lee's surrender at Appomattox, in fact—Col. John Kincaid Robison of the Sixteenth Pennsylvania Cavalry took a Confederate bullet in his upper leg while leading a saber charge at Farmville, Virginia. As a devout Presbyterian and, therefore, presumably not much of a drinker, perhaps the cavalry colonel arrived at a temporary "truce" with alcohol—at least until battlefield surgeons could gouge out the rebel slug embedded in the colonel's thigh. J. K. Robison, who will make some brief cameo appearances in this book, happens to be this writer's great-grandfather.

There *were* examples (notable for their rarity) of wounded soldiers or officers who refused the use of any alcohol in their treatment. Perhaps the best example was General Robert McAllister (a very religious man) who was badly wounded in the Peach Orchard on the second day at Gettysburg. He was adamant in his refusal of any intoxicants, but a clever battlefield surgeon—eager to combat his patient's inevitable pain—surreptitiously mixed a few ounces of whiskey into the general's milk.

Alcohol as treatment was one thing, and as a habitual recreational pursuit, quite another. When the Sixteenth Pennsylvania Cavalry mustered out in June of 1865, Colonel Robison advised them in his farewell speech to abandon any "bad habits" they might have acquired while serving in the ranks. He wanted them to be good citizens once they returned home. No doubt that transition was easier for some men than others.

WHICH SIDE DRANK MORE?

In my pursuit of this interesting but unusual history, I found that one of the most frequently asked questions from curious acquaintances was: "Well? Which side drank more?"

Some of the more recognizable names of the Confederacy were surprisingly temperate, even leaning decidedly toward abstinence. The names in that camp that come readily to mind include General Robert E. Lee, General Thomas "Stonewall" Jackson, and General J. E. B. Stuart.

In the opposite drinking camp, however, fell notable individuals like General Ulysses S. Grant, General Philip Sheridan, and General William Tecumseh Sherman—not to mention the likes of General Joseph "Fighting Joe" Hooker, General Dan Sickles, or General Ambrose Burnside. Hooker's Army of the Potomac headquarters in 1863, for example, was once infamously described by Captain Charles Francis Adams Jr. of the Massachusetts cavalry as "a place no self-respecting man would go, and no decent woman could go...a combination of bar-room and brothel."

But despite the apparent disparity when it came to the drinking habits of "top brass," the only real answer (after wading through dozens and dozens of Civil War journals, diaries, and memoirs of both officers and enlisted men) is this: *both* armies drank a lot, and probably more than most of us might have imagined.

One amusing anecdote particularly comes to mind regarding which side managed to guzzle down more alcohol. Although President Abraham Lincoln did not indulge in any real drinking himself (he ranks as one of, if not *the* most temperate of all our chief executives), he nevertheless occasionally had to deal with anti-alcohol crusaders. When he did, one of Lincoln's favorite defensive foils against the "holier-than-thou" crowd was a good sense of humor.

A prime example comes down to us courtesy of Lincoln's secretary John Hay. Hay's diary entry of September 29, 1863, recorded this amusing mission to the White House from a "cold-water" contingent (i.e., abstainers of alcohol):

Today came to the Executive Mansion an assembly of cold-water men & cold-water women to make a temperance speech at the President & receive a response. They filed into the East Room looking blue & thin in the keen autumnal air, Cooper, my coachman, who [was] about half tight, gazing at them with an air of complacent contempt and mild wonder. Three blue-skinned damsels personated Love, Purity & Fidelity, in Red, White & Blue gowns. A few Invalid soldiers stumped along in the dismal procession. They made a long speech at the President in which they called Intemperance the cause of our defeats. He could not see it as the rebels drink more & worse whiskey than we do. They filed off drearily to a collation of cold water & green apples, & then home to mulligrubs.

Given that the Federals had won major victories at both Gettysburg and Vicksburg just several months prior to the "cold-water" visit chronicled by Hay, Lincoln must have felt that the war effort—with whiskey or without—was finally headed in the right direction.

1861

*"A sailor and a soldier will do almost anything
for a glass of grog."*

—*George E. Stephens*

CHAPTER 1

RUMBLINGS OF WAR AND EARLY DAYS
1861

FORT SUMTER: "A PRELUDE TO CERTAIN WAR"

In mid-April of 1861, William Howard Russell, the much-acclaimed war correspondent for the *Times* of London, rushed from Washington down to Charleston, South Carolina. Russell was quite sure that the latest developments at Fort Sumter—Confederate cannons blasting away at the ramparts and the Stars and Stripes above them— were destined to ignite historic events: "The act seemed to me," Russell wrote of the bombardment, "a prelude to certain war."

Part of Russell's journey south involved a leg on a steamship from Baltimore to Norfolk, Virginia. Although the portly and gourmandizing Irish-born journalist was by no means unacquainted with alcohol, even he was a bit taken aback by the "gentlemen" passengers nonchalantly knocking back cocktails mere minutes after the sun spread its morning rays across the Chesapeake Bay.

In the matter of drinks, how hospitable the Americans
are! I was asked to take as many as would have rendered
me incapable of drinking again; my excuse on the plea
of inability to grapple with cocktails and the like before
breakfast, was heard with surprise, and I was urgently
entreated to abandon so bad a habit.

But Russell's steamship experience probably was a fairly representative sketch of "drinking America" in the mid-nineteenth
century. And so it provides some context that might make it easier
for modern aficionados of history to comprehend *why* John Barleycorn held such sway in both armies during the Civil War.

The imbibing on the vessel proved to be suitable preparation
for what awaited the reporter when he reached Charleston. Russell
arrived in the city a few days after a thirty-three-hour shelling had
forced Major Robert Anderson to surrender the harbor fortress to
his former West Point artillery student, General Pierre G. T. Beauregard. Beauregard held Anderson in high regard, as reflected in a
gift he sent to Sumter in the weeks before the bombardment: the
Confederate general offered a supply of cigars and claret to the
Union officers, though—by some accounts—Anderson refused
these luxury items.

What Russell found when he reached Charleston was an armed
and frenzied citizenry (and numerous rebels from other Southern
states) intoxicated on the secessionist movement, though the par-
taking of various alcoholic drinks undoubtedly served to elevate
their martial mood to a fever pitch. It was as if Russell had stumbled upon a weird wedding reception that had degenerated into a
drunken brawl.

Russell was mildly amused by a few of the monikers adopted
by the various units—"The Live Tigers" and "Yankee Smashers"
and such—but probably not surprised by the overflowing amounts
of available alcohol (literally buckets of booze in some tents) and

the "roistering" rebels' willingness to share it with the journalist they had only just met.

> In every tent were hospitality, and a hearty welcome to all comers. Cases of champagne and claret, French *pâtés* and the like...In the middle of these excited gatherings I felt like a man in complete possession of his senses coming in late to a wine party. "Won't you drink with me, sir, to the—(something awful)—of Lincoln and all Yankees?"

Russell, however, soon found that the Southerners displayed instantaneous indignation at even the slightest suggestion that war with the more populated and industrial North might end badly for all, but particularly for the South. No doubt the wine, whiskey, and assorted punches were at least partly responsible for the blind faith of the so-called "Fire-Eaters"—Dixie's most ardent secessionists—and possibly of many of the common Southerners who fell in line behind them. Four years later, of course, it would prove to be an incredibly disastrous analysis.

But Russell was not completely alone in his opinion of how the war might end for the South. Mary Chesnut, the wife of James Chesnut (a former U.S. Senator from South Carolina who became a top Confederate) concurred with Russell's risk assessments concerning war with the North. By the first autumn of the war, an exasperated Mary Chesnut—with an accusatory glare flashed toward alcohol's role in the South's mirage of war glory—wrote in her diary:

> "Ideas preserved in alcohol"; wild schemes, exaggerated statements—inflamed and irrational views of our might and the enemy's weakness! If "*In Vino Veritas,*" God help us! I care no more for alcoholized wisdom than I do for the chattering of blackbirds. But the great statesmen

and soldiers deliberately drink down their great inheritance of reason, and with light hearts become mere gabbling geese. Alcohol! Pfaugh!

Although Mary Chesnut and Union General Daniel Sickles were obviously on opposite sides of the war, their conclusions concerning the intoxicating accelerants that helped ignite it proved to be strikingly similar. Sickles's statement ("Yes, whiskey caused the Rebellion!") perhaps sings with embellishment, but it gains credibility when dovetailed with Chesnut's own observations.

In those heady days prior to actual war, an eccentric-but-colorful character—and certainly one well known to W. H. Russell, Mary Chesnut, and Sickles—was one Louis Trezevant Wigfall. A transplanted Texan born into the plantation culture of South Carolina, Wigfall was not only a "Fire-Eater" but also a deep imbiber of "firewater." The latter habit stretched back to his teenage years and no doubt intensified his zealous actions in regards to the former. In short, if one wanted to back up Sickles's seemingly incredible proclamation that whiskey started the war (or Mrs. Chesnut's milder complaint, for that matter), then Louis T. Wigfall might well have served as a poster boy.

Quick to react to insults (real or imagined, alcohol-inspired or not), Wigfall once fought a duel with none other than Preston Brooks. The two hotheads managed to wound each other, but not mortally.

Given his affinity for alcohol and confrontation, it is not impossible that the excitable Wigfall was under the influence on April 13, when—without any official orders from General Beauregard—he had two slaves and a private row him out to Fort Sumter. The sky was still thick with whistling projectiles and smoke from the rebel batteries, but Wigfall—intent on his grandiose, self-assigned mission—arrived with a flag of truce (a white handkerchief attached to a sword) and demanded that Major Anderson surrender the fort. When Anderson floated a white bed sheet to serve as a surrender flag, the bombardment abruptly ceased. The general's aides arrived, thinking they would present surrender terms to the Union commander, but they were surprised to find Wigfall—the rogue ambassador—had pre-empted them. Essentially the same terms held, however—that the Yankees could salute their flag, abandon the fort, and leave on Union ships.

Predictably, Wigfall was quite eager to re-enact his mission for Russell's benefit when—a few days after the fall—he accompanied the journalist out to the fort. True to form, Wigfall was blatantly intoxicated during his encore performance, as Russell documented:

> I am sorry to say, our distinguished friend had just been paying his respects *sans bornes* to Bacchus or Bourbon, for he was unsteady in his gait and thick in speech; but his head was quite clear, and he was determined that I should know all about his exploit.

Wigfall clearly reveled in the unfolding of historical events and his place in them. In fact, Mary Chesnut described the infamous Fire-Eater during the days of the Sumter siege as the only "thoroughly happy person I see."

Meanwhile, the recently inaugurated President Abraham Lincoln, both sober and somber, called up 75,000 volunteers in response to the attack.

JOHN BARLEYCORN AND THE "CALL UP"

The surrender of Fort Sumter produced jubilation in most of the South. Virginia—key to the aspirations of the fledgling Confederacy—finally left the Union on May 23. Virginia's departure was precisely what the Fire-Eaters had hoped would happen once the hot cannons had shelled Sumter into submission. The Northern states answered President Lincoln's call and rushed to mobilize. Perhaps Abner Small, a young officer from Maine, best captured these far-reaching consequences when he wrote: "When the rebels fired on Fort Sumter, their shells traveled remarkable distances; one flew north and exploded under me. I landed in the ranks of the 3rd Maine."

In Paris, France, Philip Kearny—a wealthy man fond of French cuisine and wine—heard the news and said: "My God! They've all gone mad!" A West Point graduate and officer with both Mexican War and frontier experience, Kearny took steps to head immediately back to his native New Jersey.

Edmund Ruffin—a wealthy plantation owner and one of the most fervid of the Fire-Eaters (he fired one of the first shots against Fort Sumter)—was so over the moon about his native Virginia's secession from the Union that he temporarily dropped his staunch temperance stand. "I departed from my usual abstinence," he wrote, "so far as to drink a glass of ale and another of wine."

For the average citizen-soldier, John Barleycorn swaggered at the head of the column in those early days. Alcohol was sometimes part of the recruiting process and it certainly appeared frequently on the troop trains and in the boot camps of both armies.

"Substitutes"—paying someone to take your place in the draft— eventually became part of the scenario, too. Immigrants proved to be convenient fodder for raising an army, and sometimes alcohol lubricated the process. Some devious practitioners ran scams dubbed "Running a Mick"—essentially getting an Irish immigrant drunk and signed up as a substitute and then keeping the bounty.

Charles Haydon of Michigan, who joined the Kalamazoo Light Guards just days after Fort Sumter's surrender, provided some detailed insights into early mobilization and camp life in his Civil War diary—a journal in which alcohol is often a prominent part of the narrative. Haydon, himself a moderate drinker who eventually rose to the rank of lieutenant, would later in the war make this simplistic observation about controlling soldiers: "There is seldom any difficulty so long as you can keep them away from liquor and women, but there always is if you do not."

But that goal was, of course, easier stated than applied. In fact, Haydon's opening entry, dated April 30, 1861, documents that some men—befuddled by booze—never even made it to boot camp: "Left Kalamazoo in the Kalamazoo Light Guard for Detroit.... At Mirengo we threw off James McEvoy for drunkenness and insubordination." As for keeping the soldiers away from the opposite sex, Haydon rapidly received a dose of reality when his unit hit boot camp in Detroit. On May 6, 1861, he sardonically scribbled: "Some rain last night, weather fair this morning. If the men pursue the enemy as vigorously as they do the whores they will make very efficient soldiers."

While certain commanders and units were more successful than others in limiting alcohol abuse, the basic rule was to enforce abstinence or to strictly limit alcohol to measured medicinal doses for sick or wounded soldiers. Soldier laborers—trench diggers, or those assigned the repugnant task of burial duty—also were frequently rewarded with "commissary" whiskey, delivered in relatively small allotments of a "gill" (about four ounces).

But enterprising soldiers would sometimes cajole, buy, or swap for gills from non-drinkers and soon became "tight"—or worse. While there are many anecdotes of soldiers cleverly corralling extra whiskey gills, this one (witnessed by Dock Owen, a CSA private in the Holcombe Legion of South Carolina) strikes some humorous notes in contrast to the brutal realities of the war:

> We had two men in our company that never drank, John Pinson and Jesse Lomax. Two of the boys caught on and after they got their share came back with a cup each and told Captain Smith these men were broke down and wanted theirs. He told me to let them have it. Captain Smith was getting gentlemanly groggy. The boys saw a

chance to lay in a supply, and when we were busy would call for Pinson and Lomax's ration. Finally Captain Smith said "Durn Pinson and Lomax. I sent whiskey enough to Company F to kill a mule and still they want more." The boys had half a gallon each.

The ingenuity of the Civil War soldier to obtain liquor is a thread woven through the diaries, memoirs, and letters of that era. The temperate and religious Lieutenant George E. Stephens—an African-American soldier and journalist in the Fifty-Fourth Massachusetts—was repulsed by some of the incidents he witnessed in the first year of the war:

> A sailor and a soldier will do almost anything for a glass of grog. One fellow discovered that his musket barrel would hold just one pint, he straightaway gets a pass, has himself and his musket filled, and comes into camp, and fills a famished comrade. Another nearly fills a stone jar, covers the top of it with butter, and passes in. Another buys a sack of potatoes, half of which prove to be whiskey-skins, and so they go, resorting to every device whereby the baneful beverage can be obtained.

"Rifle barrel whiskey" was not unknown to the Southern soldiers, either. As a Georgia soldier noted in his memoirs: "In the early days of the war men would bring liquor into camp in their gun barrels, a convenient stopper being inserted in the muzzle."

Eventually, of course, the provost guards became a bit wiser. Seemingly mundane items that attracted an inordinate amount of attention were suspect. Peddlers with a wagon full of pickles, for example, once approached the Fifteenth Massachusetts camp, and soon there seemed to be a rambunctious scrum of soldiers jostling for a prime position to purchase ... pickles? Of course, closer examination by provost guards soon revealed that for every jar of pickles on that wagon there were *five* jars of whiskey.

BRAXTON BRAGG AND THE PENSACOLA BLUES

Pensacola, Florida, was a "hot spot" in prewar and early war activities. The Union forces were holed up in Fort Pickens on Santa Rosa Island, and there were periodic cannonade exchanges with Rebel batteries on the mainland.

Pensacola people, in fact, argue that the first shots of the Civil War were actually fired *there*. In January 1861, long before shells burst over Fort Sumter, a handful of Floridian militia men appeared menacing enough to draw a few bullets from U.S. soldiers, as the Yankees abandoned Fort Barrancas for the superior Fort Pickens on Santa Rosa.

The Federals were understandably a bit jumpy; at one point there were less than one hundred soldiers manning Fort Pickens. But by mid-April, with Lincoln in the White House and war all but inevitable, reinforcements of 1,000 men and some heavy guns arrived to relieve the outnumbered garrison under Lieutenant Adam Slemmer. The Johnnies had squandered their opportunity to capture the most important fort guarding the Pensacola harbor.

But when Confederate General Braxton Bragg, a graduate of West Point and an officer demanding discipline from his men, first arrived at Pensacola in March, he might have been tempted to declare John Barleycorn his primary adversary. In fact, Bragg (sometimes described as humorless) once groused: "We have lost more valuable lives at the hands of whiskey sellers than by the balls of our enemies."

In April of 1861, Bragg wrote to his wife, admitting how problematic it was to control the notorious Louisiana troops, especially if they could rustle up some rum or whiskey and get to the deplorable state of what soldiers commonly deemed "fighting drunk":

The night before last…many of them assembled in the village [got] drunk, and a free fight commenced and for a while things looked badly. By the use of the bayonet and handcuffs on the *Zouaves* of New Orleans, they were soon quelled. I…declared martial law and commandeered the grog shops…The air is yet redolent with the odor of whiskey. I captured enough to have kept the army drunk for two months.

Alcohol issues would haunt Bragg for most of his Civil War tenure. More than a few times he would accuse some of his sub-officers of over indulging. Whether any of those particular situations ever influenced the actual outcome of a battle or campaign is debatable.

There were some minor engagements during the Pensacola campaign—the Battle of Santa Rosa Island (with a few hundred casualties on both sides) and heavy artillery barrages a few days after the New Year—but nothing of true significance. As for Pensacola, the Confederate troops abandoned it after the Union took New Orleans in the spring of 1862. With dramatic engagements unfolding in the mid-Atlantic states, it was obvious that the soldiers might be more useful elsewhere. When the Johnnies departed, the amount of alcohol consumed in Pensacola presumably took a dramatic plunge.

TRAINS, TROOPS, AND WHISKEY

Transporting troops long distances by train or by ship often proved to be high-risk opportunities for soldiers to get drunk. Knowing that it was unlikely they would be required to march or fight for some hours, the most inspired often managed to obtain—and pound down—alcohol. Sutlers (merchants who followed after army camps) seemed always ready to sell booze to the boys, despite orders against it. Some officers, such as the teetotaler and highly religious General Oliver Otis Howard, would punish illegal whiskey-sellers at railroad stops by taking them dozens of miles down the tracks and booting the offenders off in the middle of nowhere. The violator then faced a long trudge back to his home base, there to contemplate either reform or an improved sales plan.

But even well-meaning citizens would sometimes be tempted to treat the lads to a drink or two as they passed through town en route to the front. On one occasion, during a brief layover by rail in Washington, D.C., the 149th New York Volunteers managed to get hold of "a great deal of poor whiskey"—smuggled to them by a unique, if simple, ruse:

> Women by the scores hovered around the train and supplied the soldiers with whisky which they concealed under their skirts…[Every] man that desired was supplied with what he wanted to drink and a full canteen besides…

Then again, the 149th previously had recorded a weird incident not long after they were formed in central New York. Leaving Geneva, New York, the regiment embarked on several steamships to cross Lake Seneca. Some of the men had over-imbibed on a train prior to reaching Geneva, and the voyage was an opportunity to rest up and steer back toward a shore of semi-sobriety. Yet there was, predictably, an exception:

> On one boat, however, an intoxicated man belonging to Co. D., while the steamer was proceeding, climbed up and road [sic] astride the walking beam in motion. Col. Strong ordered him down, but what cared he for military orders? He had no reverence for shoulder straps, and as for compelling him, where was the man that dared climb up and remove him from his perilous position? When he tired of the amusement, he faced about and came down in safety.

Photo showing the Louisiana Tigers. *Courtesy of the Library of Congress.*

TIGERS ON THE TRAIN

Transporting drunken soldiers continued to be an occasional problem for both sides throughout the war, but in the first year of the war, two notorious incidents—both involving Louisiana troops—stood out above most others.

The Louisiana Tigers were involved in a potentially deadly incident on June 1. The Tigers—en route to Virginia from mosquito-infested Pensacola, Florida, where their commander General Braxton Bragg had effectively hindered alcohol consumption by his soldiers—stopped near Montgomery, Alabama, for their troop train to re-supply. Perhaps seeking a break from lording over their motley and often unruly troops, the officers foolishly opted to ride in the rear "officers only" car. Nothing if not resourceful, the Tigers uncoupled the caboose from the rest of the train, then forced the engineer to take them straight to Montgomery. Marooned on the tracks, it took some hours before the officers could muster up another engine and race after their breakaway bayou boys.

Despite their flashy zouave uniforms, the Tigers were tough customers, mostly foreign dockworkers of Irish, German, and Creole descent (or "wharf rats," as their detractors would sniff), apt to settle even their most petty disputes with Bowie knives or a set of brass knuckles. Alcohol only aggravated their savage traits.

So when the officers finally arrived in Montgomery, they were not shocked to find the untamed Tigers on the verge of tearing up the town. Determined to keep up a good head of steam, the Tigers had broken into liquor stores, consumed much of their contents, and, in some cases, were poised to break into private homes. The First Georgia Regiment, meanwhile, had scrambled out and stood by with bayonets, warily weighing the tense situation and perhaps the consequences of tackling the surly and besotted lot.

But fortunately the Louisiana officers arrived by backup train and sprang into action. As one Captain Thomas Cooper De Leon described it:

> The charge of the Light Brigade was surpassed by those irate Creoles. With the cars still in rapid motion they [the officers] leaped off, revolver in hand; and charged into the quarter where their drunken men were still engaged in every sort of excess.

In a flurry of French curses and flailing pistol handles cracking down upon thick heads, the brass finally brought the intoxicated Tigers to bay. When the hung-over Tigers moved north, no doubt the denizens of Montgomery were happy to bid them *adieu*.

But the other incident involving Louisiana troops did not end so well. On August 2, boxcars packed with troops headed north, bound for Virginia, and stopped at Grand Junction, Tennessee, where the Confederates had a supply depot. Given that many of the Louisiana soldiers (a multi-ethnic mix of Irish, Polish, Germans, Italians, and Creoles listed as the Thirteenth Louisiana Volunteers) were already intoxicated from some "bust head" whiskey they had managed to snag in Mississippi, responsible officers attempted to prevent them from getting more. The officers tried, with only partial success, to close down some liquor-selling "groceries" and peddlers, but as evening approached, fights broke out between drunken soldiers and a general riot erupted. When some of the relatively sober fled to the Percy Hotel, the intoxicated troops broke in doors and windows with rifle stocks and axes—smashed up furniture and shook out drawers—and then even attempted to set the hotel ablaze. A civilian described them as "like a mob of infuriated devils."

Desperate to restore some order, the Polish-born Colonel Valery Soulakowski waded into the rioters and shot a few of his own soldiers. Two died immediately and a half dozen more at least suffered mortal wounds, but Soulakowski finally suppressed the donnybrook, with the help of other officers and a group of sober soldiers. When an account of the affair was published in the *Memphis Daily Appeal*, a grateful citizen was quoted as saying, "Great credit is due Col. Soulakowski and Maj. York and men of the Armstrong Guards for quelling the riot and saving the town from destruction."

CRIME AND PUNISHMENT

Soldiers were routinely punished for their alcohol-inspired missteps—some of which were mere shenanigans and others much more serious violations, such as desertion, stealing, sleeping on picket duty, or threatening the life of an officer. Robert Sneden, a soldier and artist with the Fortieth New York Volunteers—known as the "Mozart Regiment"—described the place of confinement at their 1861 camp very near Alexandria, Virginia:

> The 40th Regiment have built a log guard house for delinquents at the entrance of the camp at Post No. 1. The only light is admitted to the inside by a narrow slit in the flat roof…so all have a holy horror of being put there. Sometimes the drunken soldiers who are put there have to be put in irons. They yell and make the air blue with curses all night.

And, as Sneden noted, the so-called "hard cases" would sometimes be "bucked and gagged"—a common practice used to subdue drunk and unruly soldiers. For a solider to be "bucked and gagged," he must be placed on the ground in a sitting position, his stretched-out arms tightly bound to his lower legs, with a wooden stick or rod placed directly under the knees and above the arms. The gag might be a handkerchief or piece of rag cloth, wrapped around a rod, small stick, or even a bayonet, and stuffed in the offender's mouth and tied to his head.

In June of 1861, Haydon—in a fairly typical diary entry for him—wrote: "One man drew a revolver on the guard and was tied neck and heels and dragged to the guard house. Several others were arrested, cause whiskey in every case."

Other punishments included hanging a soldier by his thumbs, or forcing the captive to "wear the barrel suit"—the prisoner was fitted inside a hollowed out barrel (holes cut for arms, legs, and head) and made to lug it around camp. The barrel suit served the dual purpose of subjecting the offender to much ridicule and functioning as a stark reminder to would-be rogues and ruffians of what might occur if they flaunted military rules.

Despite these harsh punishments, the guardhouses rarely lacked for "lodgers." As Sneden attested:

> The men get on sprees while in Alexandria on few hours' leave, and fill the guard house on their return to camp. An officer can go to Washington, see the sights and have a good time at Willard's Hotel or elsewhere. The privates must stick to the Virginia mud. Many fights take place between the men belonging to different regiments while returning to camp in a semi drunken condition. Sometimes a whole company in camp have to be turned out armed to march and quell and arrest the rioters. The 40th New York guard house is generally full of prisoners.

Fighting between different regiments—in both the Rebel and Yankee armies—proved to be not unusual, and alcohol almost always helped make it happen. A noteworthy case in rebel ranks involved the Louisiana Tigers. Camped in Virginia, the Tigers went prowling for soldiers from the Twenty-First Georgia regiment, claiming that the latter had stolen whiskey from them. Only the intervention of a Georgian officer—wielding both a pistol and a peace offering of drinks around—seemed to momentarily diffuse the potentially volatile situation. The Louisiana men did thank him kindly for the drinks, but when they departed the Tigers left a threat hanging in the air that they could "clean out" the Twenty-First Georgia anytime they chose to do so.

The early days of the war were full of many such misadventures, as each side struggled to get their full military might in gear; but soon the battles would begin in earnest—and alcohol would be right there along the battle lines.

CHAPTER 2

BULL RUN HANGOVERS AND TROOP TROUBLE

1861

"COLONEL MILES, YOU ARE DRUNK."

The first major battle of the Civil War took place on July 21 (a very hot Sunday), near a railroad junction at Manassas, or, as the Union troops came to call it, "Bull Run"—named for a rather modest river that gurgled along in northern Virginia. The Federal force in this first major battle was formidable in size (more than 30,000 men under General Irvin McDowell), but lacking in experience. In a clever move by rail, the Confederates were able to shift a large amount of troops under General Johnston from western Virginia to support General Beauregard (riding his much-vaunted celebrity after the capture of Fort Sumter) to turn back the Yankee attack.

Alcohol was part of the Bull Run story, from the few days just before the battle through several days immediately after it.

Print showing the First Battle of Bull Run. *Courtesy of the Library of Congress.*

On the eve of the battle, John C. Tidball, a Union artillery officer, stumbled upon a gathering of officers in General Louis Blenker's regiment. The vast majority of them were German, and whether they were conversing in their native tongue or simply in English butchered both by their accents and by the free-flowing lager, Tidball admitted that they were difficult to understand. The setting itself resembled something of an impromptu *Hofbrauhaus*, with a table thrown together by piling empty wooden crates on top of each other—upon the highest of which the officers had placed their glasses of beer. As Tidball observed:

> When not drinking…all talked at once, each endeavoring to gain attention by elevating his voice above the rest, and gesticulating more violently.… The only moment of silence that anyone allowed himself was when he was

drinking. In their vehemence they thumped the table with their sword scabbards and shook their fists in the air as though striking at Jefferson Davis in person. There was not much time lost between drinks, and as they drank the more eager they became for the fight.

General Blenker himself was at the center of this Teutonic tornado. Earlier in the day, Blenker supposedly had ridden down to Bull Run, glared across the water at the Confederate positions, and on the strength of this reconnaissance emphatically declared that— if only the proper orders would come down from his superiors—he would "clean dem fellows out like von streak of lightening!"

Still riding the "one Southerner can whip three Yankees" belief (a myth that would only gain momentum after Manassas with the Battles of Wilson's Creek and Ball's Bluff), the Confederates, too, prepped themselves for battle—and not without some spirited encouragement. As one soldier from the Fourth South Carolina Volunteer Regiment wrote home to his wife:

> When we are not drilling the time is pretty much taken up by drinking popskull [whiskey], frying pan cakes, and bruising around generally.... Most of the boys here think that we are just going to have a frolic.

Alcohol of a far more aristocratic line than either German lager or "popskull" also appeared at Bull Run. Champagne and claret bottles arrived in the picnic baskets of would-be revelers and elegant observers (including some members of the U.S. Congress), as hundreds of the Washington elite travelled out in coaches and buggies. They were already somewhat buzzed with the heady idea that the glittering Union army would quickly crush the traitors and chase them back to Richmond on this hot and sultry Sunday. Why not witness such a spectacle through a spyglass with a few glasses of fine French wine?

This interest in watching the upcoming joust between North and South raised havoc with the prices of top-shelf alcohol in Washington. W. H. Russell groused: "The French cooks and hotel-keepers, by some occult process of reasoning, have arrived at the conclusion that they must treble the prices of their wines and of the hampers of provisions which the Washington people are ordering to comfort at their bloody Derby." Despite the seller's market, the thirsty journalist managed to secure one flask of light burgundy and a second of brandy before he ventured out to report on the battle.

Alcohol at Bull Run, in fact, led to one of the first full-blown scandals of the war. The incident involved Colonel Dixon S. Miles, a West Point graduate and a veteran of the Mexican-American War. In command of the left flank of the Union attack, Miles looked quite bizarre in that he was wearing *two* straw hats (though, in his defense, some officers who had served in Mexico or the Southwest sometimes resorted to two hats for protection from the sun), and he appeared to be acting strangely as well. Colonel Israel B. Richardson (a.k.a. "Fighting Dick") of the Michigan regiments soon confronted Miles, and upon seizing command from him near Blackburn Ford, bluntly proclaimed: "Colonel Miles, you are drunk."

Miles protested both the loss of his command and what he saw as Richardson's impertinence, but other officers—including General McDowell—supported Miles's removal. Three weeks later—with the Union loss at Bull Run under full scrutiny—Miles faced a court-martial on charges of drunkenness in the field. Colonel Richardson held firm on what he and others that day had witnessed: Colonel Miles had been intoxicated. Miles admitted that he had been drinking brandy, but explained that he had been ill and that his physician had prescribed the treatment.

In a display of either irony or desperation, or perhaps both, Miles called General Blenker as one of his character witnesses. Blenker basically testified that, in his opinion, Miles was by no means a heavy drinker. But many a soldier and officer knew he could usually find alcohol for sale at the German camp, and perhaps Blenker felt obligated to vouch for a frequent customer.

Nevertheless, the charges were upheld. Miles was forced to take several months of leave, and eventually was reassigned to guard the arsenal and fort at Harpers Ferry. He died there in 1862 when General Thomas "Stonewall" Jackson's men laid siege to the fort (and, upon the fort's surrender, took thousands of prisoners and captured heaps of supplies), and there were rumors that Miles was intoxicated during his final battle. As Colonel Charles S. Wainwright, an artillery officer in the Army of the Potomac, recalled that "disgraceful surrender" in his diary:

> Everything indicates that Colonel Miles was at his old practices and drunk, or else that he was a fool if not a coward. Ten thousand men in such a position certainly should have been able to hold out for forty-eight hours, in half of which time they would have been relieved; or his whole command might have cut their way out...

CHAOS IN THE CAPITAL: "A PERFECT PANDEMONIUM"

The Union Army's intentions at Bull Run had been to rout the rebels, surge on to Richmond, and strangle the infant Confederacy in its cradle. The shocking reality, however, was an undignified "skedaddle" back to Washington, a discouraged army in disarray, licking its wounds—not to mention panicky picnickers mucking up the retreat. Liquor proved to be a convenient and readily available balm for this embarrassment, if one of dubious value.

Months before General George B. McClellan would be promoted to supreme commander of the Union Army, he was in Washington and observed firsthand the appalling aftermath of the debacle. A moderate imbiber himself, one can nevertheless sense

McClellan's disgust when he described Washington a few days after
Bull Run:

> I found no preparations whatever for defense, not even
> to the extent of putting the troops in military positions.
> Not a regiment was properly encamped, not a single
> avenue of approach guarded. All was chaos, and the
> streets, hotels, and bar-rooms were filled with drunken
> officers and men absent from their regiments without
> leave—a perfect pandemonium.

Amazed that the Confederates had not followed up their victory on the battlefield with a march on the capital, the dapper
McClellan stated: "There was really nothing to prevent a small
cavalry force from riding into the city." McClellan was not alone
in his fears that Washington was in an extremely vulnerable situation. Frederick Law Olmsted (famed architect and journalist)
wrote to his wife on July 29: "Why Beauregard does not attack I
cannot imagine." The lost opportunity was not missed entirely by
some with Confederate sympathies either. In her August 8 diary
entry, Mary Chesnut wrote:

> A friend in Washington writes me that we might have
> walked into Washington any day for a week after Manas-
> sas, such was the consternation and confusion there. But
> the god Pan was still blowing his horn in the woods.
> Now she says Northern troops are literally pouring in
> from all quarters...And she thinks we have lost our
> chance forever.

Chesnut's mythological nod ("Pan was still blowing his horn
in the woods...") seems to suggest that the Confederates were too
busy enjoying their initial success to follow up with what might
have been a knockout blow.

In support of Mary Chesnut's accusations, the diary of Lieutenant George Campbell Brown suggests that the celebrating Confederates *did* spend an inordinate amount of time in a victory dance (in lieu of invading the vulnerable Union capital) and perhaps alcohol was part of this euphoric moment. As Brown remembered, an officer renowned for his singing was summoned to General Richard Ewell's crowded and festive headquarters to belt out a popular new tune called "My Maryland":

> I had lost sight of Beauregard & Longstreet both, when some one attached my attention to the former who was joining in the chorus with a will, while the latter as it ended, mounted a bench and *encored* lustily ... This was all the foundation for a story current at the time that all at the dinner all had gotten drunk & that Longstreet had danced a jig on the table among the plates (a pretty figure, his, for jigs!) & Beauregard had jumped on a bench & sung the *Marseillaise*—or "My Md.", I don't know which.

"JOYFUL" EXCHANGE ON THE PICKET LINES

Since much of the war in northern Virginia was fought along rivers and streams—often forming natural picket lines—soldiers on both sides were always aware that their counterparts were sometimes less than a mere hundred yards away. With rare exceptions, both armies seemed to establish and follow rules of "no sniping" against soldiers assigned to picket line duty. Fraternization, of varying degrees, developed even in the first months of the war, and exchanges quickly followed suit. Humorous insults were fired back and forth on a semi-regular basis, and some bartering of truly desired items—coffee, tobacco, alcohol, and even newspapers—was quite common.

Shortly after Bull Run a soldier from the Eleventh Pennsylvania Volunteer Infantry wrote home to his local newspaper (the *Democrat*

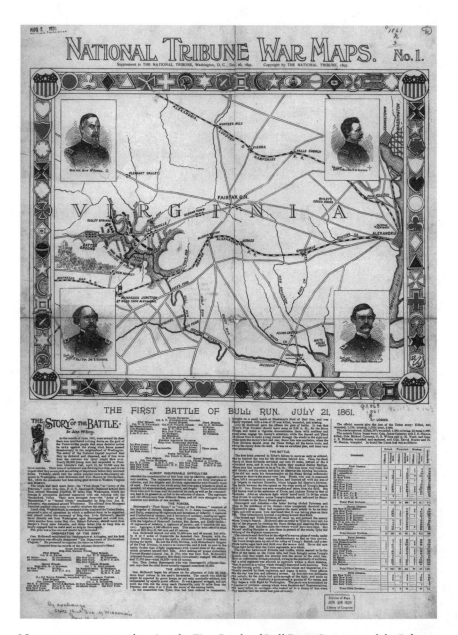

Newspaper war map showing the First Battle of Bull Run. *Courtesy of the Library of Congress.*

& *Sentinel* in Cambria County) and described a typical "friendly" incident with the Johnnies (probably men from the Thirty-fourth Virginia) across the way: "A number of our boys swam across by special invitation to take a smile of 'O be joyful,' at the time offering a toast to the Union which a Lieutenant in the rebel army considered extremely bold."

Another soldier took the plunge "at the solicitation of a couple of Virginia's fair daughters" and—after seeking permission—presented them with a big smooch before coming back across the Potomac for the presumably less pleasant company of his fellow soldiers.

ROLLICKING REBS: THE GOREE LETTERS

The abject Union failure at Bull Run may have brought greater scrutiny on the habits of Yankee officers of high rank (such as the disgraced Dixon Miles), but a letter in the first fall of 1861—from Thomas J. Goree to his mother—leaves little doubt that the victorious Confederates also had to deal with alcohol problems, too— and not just with rank-and-file soldiers.

Goree, who started as a wet-behind-the-ears lieutenant on General James Longstreet's staff, penned a lengthy letter to his mother in early November. Writing from the rebel camp near Centreville, Virginia, he made certain to assure mom (or, as he addressed her, "My Dearest Mother") that his *own* drinking habits were in rapid reform:

> There are many temptations thrown in the way of a young man in the army, but I think I can resist them. When I first came here, I thought that an occasional drink would be beneficial for my health, and would take one sometimes, but I found out...that I always felt better without it than with it.

Goree then proceeded to laud General J. E. B. Stuart, noting that the daring and dashing cavalry officer "does not touch a drop, neither does he smoke or chew." But Goree switched to a different tone concerning some generals. Several commanders passed muster, while Goree obviously found the alcohol habits of others both appalling and potentially hazardous to "the Cause."

> I wish that all the officers in our Army were half so abstemious, but it is not the case. Generals Johnston and Beauregard, Major General Gustavus W. Smith, Kirby Smith, Van Dorn, Longstreet and Jackson are comparatively temperance men, but Brigadier Generals Elzey, Evans and Wigfall are always more or less under the influence of liquor, and very often real drunk, and for that reason they are not safe generals, for no man, when under the influence of liquor, can or will act with discretion.

General Nathan "Shanks" Evans in particular drew much attention for his fondness for ardent spirits, including the fantastic charge that he had an aide whose main purpose was to follow Evans about, be it in camp or on the battlefield, with a small keg of whiskey. As General G. Moxley Sorrel confirmed in his *Recollections of a Confederate Field Officer*: "Evans was difficult to manage…He had a Prussian orderly, with a wooden vessel holding a gallon of whiskey always strapped on his back and there was the trouble."

When Sorrel had to find Evans to countermand an overly aggressive attack order that "Shanks" had issued (most likely while under the influence), he later recalled: "I proceeded to hunt up Evans, finding him under a tree, too close to his '*Barrelita*,' as he liked to call his whiskey holder. But he had to listen and comply [to the counter orders]…"

Although certainly one of the heroes of the First Manassas (despite rumors he was slightly snookered during that battle and also at Ball's Bluff), Evans eventually had to be phased out of any crucial decisions in the Virginian theater. Most believed that whiskey was at the root of it. Certainly Goree (like Sorrel) did, writing: "Genl. Evans is one of the bravest men I ever saw, and is no doubt a good officer when sober, but he is unfortunately almost always under the influence of liquor."

BALL'S BLUFF AND A WOUNDED LIEUTENANT

In the first months of the war, both armies showed their inexperience—but the Union seemed to do so in even grander style. The Battle of Ball's Bluff, fought on October 21, was a typical example. A modest Union force of about 300 men initially crossed the Potomac on a reconnaissance mission, but this misadventure soon escalated into a serious engagement—with the Yankees tediously ferrying across support and the Johnnies bringing up a rather sizeable force to repulse the invasion.

If the Confederate commander Nathan "Shanks" Evans was intoxicated, as was the rumor, it did not greatly hinder the overall rebel effort. The boys in gray inflicted heavy casualties on the retreating Yankees, and killed U.S. Colonel Edward Baker—a sitting U.S. Senator from Oregon—in the process. The Yankees suffered about 1,000 casualties in dead, wounded, captured, and even a few men who drowned in the river in the chaotic retreat back across the Potomac. Rebel forces incurred less than 200 casualties. Among the Union casualties there was a young lieutenant and recent Harvard graduate named Oliver Wendell Holmes Jr. with the Twentieth Massachusetts Volunteer Infantry. Holmes, who wisely carried a painkilling substance in his jacket, as did most officers, provided a captivating glimpse inside the mind of a wounded soldier in his diary:

Shot through the lungs? Lets see—and I spit—Yes—
already the blood was in my mouth…

What should I do? Just then I remembered and felt in
my waist coat pocket—Yes, there it was—a little bottle
of laudanum which I had brought along—But I won't
take it yet; no see a doctor first—It may not be as bad as
it looks—At any rate wait till the pain begins.…

Fellow soldiers finally got Holmes back across the Potomac and
to a field hospital where the hospital steward ("a cockeyed Dutchman who afterwards stuck me certain shekels for his services")
took over Holmes's care:

[He] looked at my wound and conjectured the true state
of affairs—bound me round with an infernal bandage…
having first rammed plugs of lint into the holes, and then
left me exceedingly joyful, for he had told me I should
live—I could have hugged him for that—After this—whiskey—lightheadedness—laudanum…

The "cockeyed" Dutchman was right; Holmes survived Ball's
Bluff and, later in the war, two more wounds at Antietam and
Chancellorsville respectively. In fact, a terrible case of dysentery
actually knocked Holmes out of action for the longest stint.

His war wounds—and the whiskey and laudanum he used to
treat them—apparently did the officer no lasting harm. Holmes
returned home to Boston to pursue a career in law. In 1902, Holmes
was appointed by President Theodore Roosevelt to the U.S. Supreme
Court and served until 1932.

FIRING SQUADS

Near the end of 1861, two separate incidents—with alcohol
playing a major role in both—occurred in the Confederate ranks.

The first, in late fall, happened at Winchester, Virginia, under the command of General Thomas "Stonewall" Jackson, when a soldier named James Miller was court-martialed for shooting Captain John Henderson of the Jefferson County Cavalry. According to a local newspaper account:

> Drunkenness was the only plea, in extenuation; but [Miller] was only one or two degrees in liquor at the time he committed the offence—excited, but not drunk, in the general acceptation of the term.

Miller was sentenced to death by firing squad and the unbending Jackson—not a man to view any degree of intoxication in the ranks as mitigating circumstances—denied pleas for a less severe punishment. However, word did reach President Jefferson Davis in Richmond and Davis moved to overrule the execution.

But in an ironic outcome, the messenger chosen to relay the stay-of-execution to Jackson's camp himself got drunk, and by the time he arrived to deliver Davis's reprieve, Miller had already been executed on November 26.

In December, a similar situation arose after the already infamous Louisiana Tigers became embroiled in a slew of drinking incidents. As he noted in his memoirs, General Richard Taylor (the son of President Zachary Taylor and a plantation-class aristocrat) had with great reluctance found the pugnacious and hard-swilling "wharf rats" placed under his command:

> So villainous was the reputation of this battalion that every commander desired to be rid of it; and General Johnston assigned it to me, despite my efforts to decline the honor of such society. He promised, however, to sustain me in any measures to enforce discipline, and but a few hours elapsed before the fulfillment of the promise was exacted.

After some intoxicated Tigers were tossed in the guardhouse—not a rare occurrence—several of their comrades (also under the influence) brazenly attempted to spring them by storming the jail. It proved to be a futile—and fatal—act. They ended up in irons for the night and subsequently faced a court martial. General Taylor, looking to set an example, sentenced two alleged ringleaders, Michael O'Brien and Dennis Corcoran, to death, and also decreed that the soldiers assigned to carry out the order would come from the ranks of the Tigers.

An impassioned plea for leniency from the colorful and popular Tiger leader—Major Roberdeau Wheat—was rejected. On December 9, O'Brien and Corcoran—by some accounts after reading a statement warning their fellow Tigers of what the evils of alcohol might lead to—were dispatched by a firing squad. As a private in the Sixteenth Mississippi (writing to his "Dearest Ma") noted:

> They were shot on Tuesday. Our brigade was ordered out to see them executed. I was standing fifteen steps from them when they were shot. They seemed to be perfectly reckless in regard to their fate. I heard a man say when they got in the wagon to go to the place of their execution, one of them danced all over his coffin and said they would show them how Louisianans could die.

A POST-BATTLE TOAST

The Battle of Belmont in Missouri on November 7, 1861, fea-tured Ulysses Simpson Grant in command. Grant brought his Union forces down the Mississippi River from Cairo, Illinois, and landed at Belmont where he surprised and initially overran the rebel camp. The Confederates, reinforced by troops from Columbus,

Kentucky, launched a spirited counterattack, and the Yankees withdrew by riverboats.

In comparison to Bull Run (and many battles yet to come) the casualties were not particularly high, at just over 600 on each side. Still, a CSA surgeon remarked that the bodies of dead and wounded soldiers on the field seemed as thick "as pumpkins in a patch" when he arrived on a moonlit evening to treat the sufferers using what would be some of the standard medicinal supplies of his trade—brandy, opium, and water.

In the aftermath of the battle, Grant agreed to meet with rebel commanders—Leonidas Polk (an Episcopalian minister turned rebel warrior), Benjamin Franklin Cheatham, and others—to arrange for a truce to bury the dead on both sides and also to exchange prisoners. A series of these "flags" took place on riverboats in mid-November, and the talks were marked by courtesy, a modest amount of jocularity, and apparently more alcohol than would have been deemed necessary for ceremonial toasts.

Cheatham and Grant—both generals who would be dogged by rumors throughout the war of being overly fond of strong drink—found they shared a keen interest in horse racing. A suggestion was floated that perhaps the regional differences might be settled by a horse race along the banks of the great and muddy river. Grant reportedly chuckled at the suggestion and admitted that he wished it might be that simple.

At one of these champagne-hoisting "flag of truce" affairs, the Union cavalry General John Buford (an old friend of Polk's) proposed a mutual toast to: "George Washington, the Father of our Country!"

But before the glasses could even be clinked, Polk ingeniously adjoined: "*And* the first Rebel!"

At that, the Yankee officers could only shrug and begrudgingly acknowledge Polk's point. In this particular case, they had no answer to the Confederate's clever counterattack.

HOLIDAY CHEER

Even in the first year of the war, holidays conjured up a strange brew of reflection and wistfulness for most soldiers. A year prior, most men were pursuing "normal" occupations and lives—and perhaps a local sweetheart. The comforts of home and hearth were rudely replaced by the rigors of camp life. Somewhat suddenly, their new daily reality was facing an enemy and a lot of uncertainty on the opposite riverbank.

Alcohol consumption played a weirdly dual role for them during the 1861 holidays—first, as a connection to past rituals, and second, as a way to numb their homesickness. When one delves into the diaries and letters of Civil War veterans, holiday entries very rarely pass without references to either an abundance or absence of alcohol. For example, Charles Haydon observed that on the first Thanksgiving of the war, "shoulder straps" (a slightly derogatory term used by enlisted men for unpopular officers) in his regiment were quick to raise a glass and, apparently, drink and refill it, noting: "It is understood to be Thanksgiving in Mich. today and nearly all the officers in the 2nd, 3rd and 5th Regts. are drunk on the strength of it."

Christmas and New Year's, of course, brought on much revelry. Robert Sneden's Mozart Regiment was right in the thick of both snow *and* the chosen remedy for the cold conditions. His December 25, 1861, diary entry reads:

> Have had snow for past eight hours. It laid six to eight inches.... Could not have dress parade or drill today. All were eating and drinking all they could get. Rations of whiskey were served to the brigade and the 40th guardhouse was full of drunken soldiers before sundown.

But a Mississippi private, Jefferson J. Wilson, writing home from Virginia to his dad ("Father, Dear Sir"), could not help grumbling:

"It is a very dull Christmas up here. We cannot get any whiskey to make us an eggnog. Everything is very high up here. We have to pay three prices for anything we get…"

The Seventh Tennessee Infantry, however, had a different kind of eggnog problem—in essence, too much of it. The rebels of that particular regiment spent their first Christmas Eve of the war concocting eggnog, heavy on the whiskey. The stuff proved powerful enough that more than a few soldiers woke up on Christmas morning with pounding heads, rubbery legs, and—to make matters worse—orders to march. Captain John Fite confessed that there were some reveling Rebs not up to the task:

> The night before Christmas the boys got hold of eggs and whiskey and had a big time, and the next morning they were so drunk they had a hard time getting started. I have no idea how many of them were drunk; there were a great many of them so drunk that they couldn't walk. We put the drunkest ones in the wagon and hauled them along.

So these groggy men in gray trudged northward, first to camp at Winchester, Virginia, and by January 1, 1862, they found themselves attached to General Thomas "Stonewall" Jackson's command. Given Stonewall Jackson's track record in regards to punishing alcohol offenders, one presumes the Tennesseans showed up in a state of relative sobriety.

1862

"*There are three problems with our army and navy. The first is whiskey...the second is whiskey...and the third is whiskey.*"

—William Frederick Keeler

CHAPTER 3

APPLEJACK, IRONCLADS, AND SHILOH
1862

IN THE LAND OF APPLEJACK

John Sergeant Wise would one day become a United States congressman, but during the Civil War he was first a wide-eyed cadet attending the Virginia Military Institute and, eventually, a boy-lieutenant (not yet twenty years old) in General Robert E. Lee's army. His book *The End of an Era*, which chronicles the fall of Dixie, is an interesting collision of reality and humor, with generous splashes of colorful writing. (Describing concentrated enemy fire along a rural road that he needed to cross, for instance, Wise once wrote: "The bullets were singing up the road like bumble-bees..." Many authors, surely, wish that such vivid lines had bubbled up in *their* brains.)

Wise was by no means a stranger to the various and peculiar libations of his era and region. Reflecting back on his teenage years later in life, he recalled the fruit-rich valleys and hillsides of the Virginian countryside, observing:

Everybody in the country was engaged in converting his fruit into brandy. Wherever there was a clear stream and a neighboring orchard there was sure to be a still. Where all these stills and worms and kettles came from nobody could conjecture. It was a great fruit year…and it was apparent that liquor would be scarce and high. In July, 1862, I drove our horses and carriage from a point just above Richmond to an abode of the family in Franklin County, a distance of 200 miles or more, and I feel confident that there was not ten miles upon the route in which I did not pass one or more fruit distilleries.

While applejack's most infamous Civil War moment arguably would not arrive until near the end of 1864, it was already prevalent and causing some issues of note by 1862. For example, in early April General Stonewall Jackson ordered one of his officers, Captain Jedediah Hotchkiss, to destroy some bridges and hinder Yankee advances. Hotchkiss, primarily a mapmaker, was to have assistance from some local cavalry units. However, they soon ran into trouble:

We found the cavalry at the Shenandoah Iron Works, many of them under the influence from apple-jack…At the first fire they ran away and scattered and could not be stopped.

Dutch courage, apparently, did not *always* make soldiers brave in battle.

BAN THE CHAMPAGNE!

Months before young Wise's trip through applejack country, Lincoln—in January of 1862—named Edwin Stanton as his new secretary of war. Stanton immediately pushed to have the Union ratchet up its aggression and attacks on the enemy. He saw General George B. McClellan's sluggishness—and particularly the top officers' penchant for luxuries that Stanton felt out of place if not disgraceful on the frontlines—as in need of correction by whatever means necessary. He made this quite clear in a January 24 letter to *New York Tribune* journalist Charles Dana (soon to become part of Lincoln's staff):

> As soon as I get the machinery of the office working, the rats cleared out, the rat holes stopped, we shall *move*. This army has got to fight or run away; and while men are striving nobly in the West, the champagne and oysters on the Potomac must be stopped.

Stanton had his successes heading up the Department of War, but stopping the champagne, oysters, and accompanying revelry was not one of them.

CHAMPAGNE AND THE BLOCKADE

While Stanton failed to prevent "champagne and oysters" among his *own* forces, there were some signs that the Union blockade was preventing some imported delicacies from reaching Richmond, even as early as New Year's Day in 1862. One of those "casualties" appears to have been French champagne.

Although she was just sixteen years old, Sarah Ann "Sallie" Brock proved to be one of the most diligent observers of wartime Richmond—from the giddy days of secession to the fiery downfall in 1865. In her post-war book *Richmond During the War: Four Years of Personal Observation*, she writes that in 1862 Virginia Governor John Letcher held his traditional January 1 gathering for Richmond legislators and other Confederate notables, but did so *sans* champagne.

Minus champagne, through the rigid effects of the blockade, the giant punch-bowl was filled with the steaming beverage, the smell of roasted apples betrayed the characteristic toddy, and through the crystal cut-glass gleamed the golden hue of the egg-nog to regale the guests of the Governor.

Still, the hot apple toddy and thick liquor-laced eggnog filled in admirably, as Brock made clear:

As may be supposed, on this occasion Bacchus asserted his triumph over Mars, and the devotees at this convivial shrine were many of them oblivious, happily, to the sterner mandates of the God of War.

GENERAL SMITH'S WHISKEY

Stanton's letter to Dana had barely arrived when General Grant and his armies made Stanton's reference to Union troops "striving nobly in the West" look somewhat prophetic. Having captured Fort Henry on the Tennessee River on February 6, federal forces moved against the vital Confederate stronghold at Fort Donelson on the Cumberland River on February 12 and 13. The Federals had essentially surrounded Donelson and even repulsed a desperate breakout attempt by the rebels. From the river, U.S. Navy gunboats engaged artillery at the fort in heavy exchanges. Fearing the worst, the Confederate commander Simon Bolivar Buckner sent a message to Grant, apparently fishing for some favorable surrender terms.

Buckner's request brought Brigadier General Charles F. Smith to U. S. Grant's headquarters very early on the inhospitable morning of February 16. Smith—flinty on his best days—was chilled to the bone and not in the most charitable of moods. However, to add to the warmth of a small fire, a whiskey flask appeared during

this impromptu huddle. Grant's army surgeon John Brinton supplied the flask—though according to the good doctor, only Smith
hoisted it.

> Smith asked for something to drink. My flask, the only
> liquor on Staff, was handed to him, and he helped him-
> self in a soldier-like manner. I can almost see him now,
> erect, manly, every inch a soldier, standing in front of the
> fire, twisting his long white moustache and wiping his
> lips. "What answer shall I send to this, General Smith,"
> asked Grant. "No terms to the damned rebels," replied
> Smith. Those were his actual words. General Grant gave
> a short laugh, and drawing a piece of paper...began to
> write.

The result of this rather quick reply became quite renowned
and, of course, led to Grant's famous moniker, "Unconditional
Surrender Grant." His "unconditional surrender" letter finished
with a threat: "I propose to move immediately upon your works."

At any rate, Buckner accepted Grant's unbending terms rather
than further combat. The Confederates had lost the fort and Grant's
army bagged an incredible number of prisoners—more than 12,000
by some tallies.

THE CLASH OF THE IRONCLADS

As the armies out West were assessing their losses, the most
famous naval battle of the war was unfolding off Hampton Roads:
the USS *Monitor* versus the CSS *Virginia*. The *Virginia*, constructed from a section of a captured Federal ship once known as
the *Merrimack*, struck terror in the Union fleet—and some of that
terror reverberated in Washington, where authorities feared that
the ironclad might even shell the White House. On March 8, the

Virginia hammered the Union's wooden warships—but that was before the peculiar looking *Monitor* arrived on the scene.

Like most sailors, the combatants were familiar with alcohol. It was standard procedure, for example, for the crew of the *Virginia* to chase down breakfast with two jiggers (about three ounces) of whiskey—a ritual that they typically repeated again later in the day. And they did precisely that—knocked back two jiggers—before they steamed out to meet the Union ironclad *Monitor* on March 9.

Some of our best insights into life on the *Monitor* come from William Frederick Keeler's letters to his wife. Keeler was the ship's paymaster and also a firm temperance man. Keeler once wrote to his wife: "There are three problems with our army and navy. The first is whiskey...the second is whiskey...and the third is whiskey."

But so hot was the exchange of rattling shells between the *Virginia* and the so-called "cheese box on a raft" that even Keeler conceded whiskey might be a necessary "brace" to smooth out the sailors' nerves while under intense attack. The racket from the *Virginia*'s shells was so powerful that some Yankee sailors on the *Monitor* found they were bleeding from their ears and noses. When Captain John L. Worden ordered Keeler to open the ship's liquor cabinet and dispense a half jigger of whiskey to each man when the warship had to reload its own rapidly-firing turret guns, even Keeler conceded: "If liquor ever does any good to any one and is ever useful it must be on such occasion..." Having already endured three hours of battle, the men downed their meager ration, then steamed back out to prevent the *Virginia* from molesting the Union's vulnerable wooden ships.

Although wounded on the first day, and therefore recuperating on the day the ironclads jousted, Confederate commander Franklin Buchanan was an old salt who certainly embraced alcohol as part of the naval culture. Buchanan had served as an officer on Commodore Perry's historic voyage to Japan, when the Americans brought gallons of whiskey to the Japanese to help smooth the diplomatic process. But, thinking his native Maryland would side with the South, Buchanan became an admiral with the Confederacy. Buchanan is remembered by "alco-historians" because of a powerful concoction attributed to him and known as "Egyptian Punch." It purportedly was first made and sampled as Perry's fleet found itself near Egypt en route to Japan.

THE FATE OF THE GREAT IRONCLADS

Although forever commemorated in American history, both the USS *Monitor* and the CSA *Virginia* (a.k.a. *Merrimack*) met less than glorious fates.

The *Virginia* went first in early May, as the Confederate command realized that Norfolk and rebel ships harbored there might soon fall back under Yankee control. Her crew set the *Virginia* ablaze, but not before they gave the fighting ironclad a proper farewell: They toasted her ("splicing the main mast," as this ritual was known to Navy "tars") with a generous gill of whiskey as the flames took hold.

The *Monitor* met an arguably worse fate. As she was being towed down to North Carolina by another ship, the little *Monitor* went down in a violent storm off of Cape Hatteras. For more than fifty hours, the *Monitor* and crew fought to stay afloat, but—on New Year's Eve morning—it eventually sank and sixteen sailors lost their lives.

Controversy soon followed when John Ericsson, the Swedish-American inventor of the small-but-mighty *Monitor*, claimed in a military journal that the ship might have been saved had not many of the crew been intoxicated. Those charges of drunkenness were never proven and vigorously denied by the officers.

Photo showing crew members of the USS *Monitor. Courtesy of the Library of Congress.*

BLOODY SHILOH: GRANT STANDS ACCUSED

In early April of 1862, Ulysses S. Grant led his troops far down the Tennessee River, not far from the Mississippi state border, and approached a place called Pittsburg Landing. But just before dawn the Confederates—under General Albert Sidney Johnston—launched a surprise attack, hoping to turn the Yankees away from the river (and the support of U.S. Navy gunboats and supplies) and into swampy terrain to the west. The Confederates certainly carried the fight throughout the morning and afternoon, and at times it appeared the Union forces were in danger of suffering a major disaster, but they did manage to fall back to the east and the Tennessee River.

There are a few reasons why the rebels failed to press their attack—one certainly being that nightfall arrived. Torrential rainstorms, complete with wicked lightning and thunder, also arose that night, much to the misery of all, but particularly the wounded still on the field.

But perhaps another reason was that captured Union supplies also distracted some of the famished Confederates (many of whom were amazed by the vast stores), and chief among those lures were several barrels of "medicinal" whiskey. With the battle well in control, more than a few exhausted soldiers imbibed and none of their officers seemed enthused enough to stop them. The overall feeling was that the battle was over and the day had been won; General P. G. T. Beauregard assumed he had Grant trapped and it would simply be a question of mopping up the next morning.

In addition, the Confederates had lost their most aggressive commander on the field that day—Johnston suffered a mortal wound to his leg while directing an attack on his warhorse "Fire Eater." Despite the usual attempts of fellow officers to revive the popular Texan with alcoholic "stimulants," he was rapidly fading, if not already dead.

In fact, Johnston's unresponsiveness to the battlefield booze seemed to confirm the worst fears of those around him. General William Preston cradled Johnston's head in his lap and blurted out: "Johnston, don't you know me?" And when Major Dudley Haydon, the commander's aide-de-camp, tried to direct a few sips of medicinal whiskey down Johnston's throat, the amber elixir dribbled ineffectively off his lips. Albert Sidney Johnston was dead. His officers wrapped his body in a sheet to remove it from the field, so that the sight of it would not injure the morale of his soldiers. Prepping the general's body to send back to Texas for burial, an army doctor injected his corpse with brandy to preserve it for the long trip.

Unlike Johnston, Grant was alive and well, but his reputation suffered some bruising in the aftermath of the two-day battle. Accusations of Grant's drinking—something of a ghost from his pre–Civil War army days—had resurfaced. Even after his victory at Fort Donelson, when Grant's stock was on a dramatic rise,

General Henry Halleck (then Grant's superior) had dashed off a letter to McClellan in early March stating: "General Grant has resumed his former bad habits." McClellan, of course, would have translated this thinly veiled accusation as "Grant is drinking again."

Whether these charges had some validity to them or were simply lies conjured up by jealous enemies still seems to stir up debate. There is, however, no doubt that the *rumor* of Grant's drinking was persistent after Shiloh—and believed by some. Following the Battle of Iuka later in the year, Captain William Stewart in the Eleventh Missouri, for example, wrote: "Genl. Grant was dead drunk and couldn't bring up his army. I was so mad when I first learned the facts that I could have shot Grant if I would have hung for it the next minute."

But a high-ranking officer—who did not have any particular reason to laud Grant—was Colonel Jacob Ammen, an Indiana man on Buell's staff, and he did not seem to think that alcohol impaired Grant's leadership at Shiloh. If Grant was less than his best because of booze (and no hard evidence exists that he was), it must have been early on the first day, as Colonel Ammen stated: "I am satisfied Genl. Grant was not under the influence of liquor either of the times I saw him."

However, when the rebels paused for the night (and perhaps over-celebrated with captured Yankee spirits), General Don Carlos Buell's reinforcements arrived to support Grant's beleaguered troops. With Buell's relatively fresh soldiers leading the way, fortunes flipped the next day, and Shiloh eventually was recorded as a Union victory—albeit a bloody and costly one.

Grant himself dubbed Shiloh as the most "misunderstood" battle of the war, and so it is no surprise that historians debate the significance of Buell's arrival. Buell believed himself the savior of the day. Would Grant and Sherman (with some added support from Union gunboats) have held off rebel attacks anyway? In his memoirs, Grant maintained they had already repulsed the best the rebels could have mustered—though he admitted he was pleased to see Buell's troops arrive and, in fact, wished they had appeared sooner.

From Buell's point of view, there were many Union stragglers—perhaps thousands—in a confused jumble near the Tennessee River when he arrived on the scene. The mass disarray witnessed by General Buell was perhaps further complicated by the fact that some of these dispirited soldiers had managed to get pint cans of whiskey; they were disguised as canned peaches, but were, in fact, just a few slices of fruit awash in booze. But Grant's best men were still out on the perimeter and holding steadfast.

Before the rebels were able to resume an offensive the next morning, the Yankees—now in superior numbers—launched a ferocious counterattack at sunup. The now outmatched Butternuts were forced to "skedaddle" back to Cornith, Mississippi. The word eventually leaked out that some Johnny Rebs participated in an ill-timed whiskey break near the end of the first day, and it warranted a chiding entry in Mary Chesnut's diary, in which (peppered with her favorite spice of pessimism) she mentions:

> I read in a Western letter, "Not Beauregard, but the soldiers who stopped to drink the whisky they had captured from the enemy, lost us Shiloh." Cock Robin is dead as he ever will be now, what matters it who killed him?

THE COMBAT COCKTAIL

In the aftermath of Shiloh, a strange story arose that prior to battle some rebel troops mixed gunpowder and whiskey together in their canteens and drank this "combat cocktail" in order to reach a frenzied state just prior to a charge. These bizarre claims—which eventually appeared in an Ohio newspaper and spread from there—quite probably originated from the Fifteenth Illinois. Several days after the battle, men from the Fifteenth were saddled with burial detail, first interring their fellow Federals in a mass trench. As Private Lucius W. Barber of that regiment's Company "D" wrote in his memoirs:

> Now we turned our attention to the rebel dead. We noticed the faces of all of them had turned black. On examination, we found that their canteens contained whisky and gunpowder which was, no doubt, the cause of it. It seems that this had been given to them just before going into battle to make them fight. This was the cause of the rebels fighting so like demons the first day.

This strange story was scoffed at and dismissed as Yankee propaganda by Southerners. It did not escape comment from Mary Chesnut, for example, as she recorded (in reaction to accusatory remarks by U.S. Senator Henry Rice of Minnesota):

> I see from [Rice's] place in the Senate that he speaks of us as savages, who put powder and whisky into soldiers' canteens to make them mad with ferocity in the fight. No, never. We admire coolness here, because we lack it; we do not need to be fired by drink to be brave.

DREWRY'S BLUFF

Although there are dozens of examples in the Civil War when the use of alcohol arguably led to recklessness, there were some incidents when liquor may have mellowed officers and led them to opt for caution. One such incident occurred not long after Shiloh.

In mid-May 1862, five Federal warships—including two iron-clads—powered up the James River. Having been pre-warned of the Yankee advance, the rebels were well entrenched with cannon atop one-hundred-foot bluffs that overlooked a sharp bend in the river. The defenders included the crew from the recently scuttled *Virginia*, and the appearance of their arch nemesis *Monitor* on the river below must have had them salivating to provide a proper reception for their "guests."

The famous little *Monitor* was rendered all but useless due to its own design limitations; its guns could not rise sufficiently to deliver any rounds to rebel positions on the heights. The Confederates instead concentrated much fire on the iron-shingled *Galena*, which could raise her guns. In nearly four hours of exchange, that vessel suffered close to thirty hits and about as many killed or wounded among its crew.

The Yanks backed off and a number of officers gathered on the *Port Royal* where—according to a letter penned by Lieutenant Keeler—they broke out some liquor. Rather than warm them for a return to the fray, however, it may have produced some cold feet.

> As soon as they assembled...the second cause of failure manifested itself—*whiskey*. They got around the Ward Room table and drank until every shot fired by the sharp shooters sounded like a 32 pounder and the reports were multiplied indefinitely. Under these circumstances the expedition was given up and they returned on board their respective vessels with fearful stories of narrow escapes from the myriads of sharp shooters.

THE BEAST OF NEW ORLEANS

After Admiral David Farragut and the U.S. Navy steamed past some outer fortresses and quite handily won the Battle of New Orleans, the Yankee ground troops—commanded by General Benjamin Butler of Massachusetts—took possession of the bustling port in early May. The general soon earned the moniker "Beast" Butler from the conquered citizens of the sizeable city of more than 160,000 inhabitants. What made General Butler most notorious was his Order Twenty-Eight, issued on May 15, 1862, that read in part:

> When any female shall, by word, gesture, or movement, insult or show contempt for any officer or soldier of the United States, she shall be regarded and held liable to be treated as a woman of the town plying her vocation.

Though Butler was certainly an ironfisted, unbending military ruler, in his defense Order Twenty-Eight came about partly because the women of New Orleans were purposely antagonizing Federal officers. Some were fairly harmless snubs, such as immediately leaving a church if a Yankee officer came in for services, or crossing a street to avoid contact. But there also were women who would purposely dump the contents of a chamber pot off a balcony—coincidentally—when an officer in blue was walking past. Order Twenty-Eight was designed to abruptly halt such incidents.

General Butler—dumpy, bald, and small—was definitely no dashing prince of personality. Neither were his ethical bastions immune to the occasional breach. The suspicions on both sides of the Mason Dixon line were that the Beast—with crucial assistance from his brother Andrew Butler—worked a greedy scam that, by some accounts, left the general worth several million dollars by the war's end. Andrew Butler would buy huge amounts of commodities from desperate Southern citizens at rock-bottom prices—such as cotton and sugar—and then sell them for four times that amount up north.

Alcohol, however, was something to be manipulated more on the local level. As outlined in Chester Hearn's *The Devil Came Down to Dixie*: *Ben Butler in New Orleans*, it probably worked like this:

> What part collusion played is obscure, but it looked bad when the general issued orders forbidding the sales of

liquor because General Phelps could not keep his men from getting drunk after payday. Andrew went from store to store buying up all the intoxicants at reduced prices, and when he had the market cornered, the general lifted the ban. "The Colonel," who could be a tough negotiator when it came to money, sold every drop back at a huge profit.

During his stint in New Orleans, Butler also managed to anger the French by locking up a French citizen named Charles Heidsieck—also known as "Champagne Charlie" because he was the head of a large French champagne company. Butler said Heidsieck had disguised himself as a "bar-keeper" in an attempt to deliver treasonous messages. The general reluctantly had to release Champagne Charlie from jail when the French ambassador appealed directly to Secretary of State Seward in Washington.

Butler also executed a popular New Orleans gambler by the name of William Mumford after the man tore down and then burned a Union flag that had been hanging outside the U.S. Mint. Ignoring numerous pleas to spare Mumford's life, the general had Mumford hanged outside the U.S. Mint.

The pure hatred of General Butler was by no means confined to Louisiana. For his excesses in New Orleans, Confederate President Jefferson Davis declared Butler a war criminal and put up a $10,000 reward for his capture. It was understood that the "Beast" would face execution for his numerous abuses in New Orleans. Neither did the despised Yankee escape the "crosshairs" of diarist Mary Chesnut, who referred to him as a "hideous, cross-eyed beast" in her historic pages.

THE CONFEDERATE TOAST

Beast Butler's despicable reputation did not fade quickly. Two years later in the war, Yankee cavalrymen in a small town in

Georgia—while on Sherman's March to the Sea—were amused to find some young "Secesh" women willing to share a song or two, along with some accompanying piano. As Major James Connolly wrote in his memoirs:

> Then the [Yankee] Captain played "Dixie" in excellent style; this made the old man talkative and he brought in the daughter and some other young ladies, and we soon had them playing for us, while the Captain and I sat back and quietly enjoyed the discomfiture of the old man, and laughed at the efforts of the rebel damsels to appear composed. Finally…we induced these Southern ladies to sing us the "Confederate Toast" which they told us was their favorite song, and one verse of it I remember, viz:

> Here's to old Butler and his crew
> Drink it down!
> Here's to old Butler and his crew
> Drink it down!
> Here's to old Butler and his crew
> May the Devil get his due!
> Drink it down! Drink it down! Drink it down!

And then Major Connolly continued, somewhat cynically, musing: "We left them, though, notwithstanding their elegant and patriotic songs—they, no doubt, hoping we might be shot before night."

As for Beast Butler, he was replaced in New Orleans before the year's end and sent to Norfolk, Virginia. He was eventually removed from command altogether after the First Battle of Fort Fisher mission failed so spectacularly around Christmas in 1864.

GIN ON THE FLY: THE *ARKANSAS'S* LAST HURRAH

With the fall of New Orleans, the Union certainly held the upper hand on the Mississippi River. But in the summer of 1862, the ironclad CSS *Arkansas* caused some havoc for the U.S. fleet near Vicksburg. And when hostilities heated up around Baton Rouge in early August, Confederate ground commanders pleaded for the ironclad to come down and provide the boys in gray some support on the river.

The *Arkansas* tried, but ongoing mechanical difficulties did what Yankee warships had failed to do—knocked the ironclad out of commission. Faced with the vessel falling into Federal clutches, the crew purposely set fire to it, knowing that its ammunition stores would eventually explode and finish the job.

The crew, meanwhile, scrambled ashore. But as Baton Rouge came under increasing pressure from Union troops and warships, the crew of the *Arkansas* realized they had to evacuate the city, too. Sarah Morgan, a young woman living in Baton Rouge at the time, did not want to see those intrepid sailors go without something to bolster their spirits. As she recorded in her diary entry of August 6, 1862:

> Evening. I heard a while ago...the Arkansas's crew are about leaving...so Phillie, Lilly and I snatched up some five bottles of Gin, between us, and ran out to give it to them. A rough old sailor received mine with a flood of thanks, and the others gave theirs to those behind. An officer rode up saying, "Ladies, there is no help for it! The Yankee cavalry are after us, and we must fight them in the corn. Take care of yourselves!" We shouted "Yes!" told them to bring us the wounded and we would nurse them. Then the men cried "God bless you," and we cried "Hurrah for the Arkansas's crew!" and "Fight for us!"

CHAPTER 4

FRIENDS OF JOHN BARLEYCORN
1862

A GENERAL'S ODE TO THE MINT JULEP

Even in the middle of a horrific war, sometimes there arose a moment of respite—a temporary oasis in the swirling chaos or smothering boredom. When New Orleans fell to the Yankees in April of 1862, not only was it a serious blow to the Confederate cause, but it also proved to be deeply troubling for Confederate General Richard Taylor personally. Stuck in a muddy army camp in northern Virginia, Taylor found himself brooding and apprehensive as weeks went by without word as to the wellbeing of his family. In the middle of this funk, however, a local aristocrat of Southern loyalties sent word to General Taylor and implored him to come to breakfast at the plantation owner's nearby manor. According to his memoirs, Taylor accepted and was pleased to find that his host was serving one of the South's most famous libations. A servant stepped forward with a tray, upon which, rested a huge silver goblet filled with Virginia's nectar, mint julep. Quantities of cracked ice rattled refreshingly in the goblet; sprigs of mint peered above its rim; a mass of white sugar, too sweetly indolent to melt, rested on the mint; and like rose buds on a snow bank, luscious strawberries crowned the sugar. Ah! That julep! Mars ne'er received such a tipple from the hands of Ganymede. Breakfast was announced, and what a breakfast!

The sumptuous cocktail was a flashback to days of graceful living that perhaps General Taylor yearned to revisit.

"PERRY'S SAINTS" SLIP UP

While fancy indulgences like General Taylor's were rare, it took constant vigilance on the part of even the most temperate of commanders to keep their soldiers away from liquor. Most companies had at least a few men with an uncanny knack for finding alcohol if there was any to be had in a ten-mile radius. But sometimes John Barleycorn himself sought out the soldiers—and, in one case, not even a former man of the cloth could prevent it.

The former pastor in question was Colonel James H. Perry, a West Point graduate. He was in command of Union troops that helped capture Fort Pulaski on Tybee Island near rebel-held Savannah, Georgia, in 1862. Although Perry had resigned his ministry in Brooklyn when he formed his regiment, the Forty-Eighth New York became known as "Perry's Saints."

Although a modest amount of lager beer (purchased from the mostly German New York Forty-Fifth) occasionally made its way into Perry's camp, there were almost no alcohol incidents of any note—that is, until a schooner full of sutler supplies ran aground during "a fearful storm" on June 16 and 17. One of Perry's officers—James Moses Nichols—best related the strange chain of circumstances that then followed:

> With much difficulty the crew was rescued, but the vessel
> became a total wreck and the cargo…floated ashore.…
> Cases of claret and champagne and barrels of beer and
> wine were too strong an attraction to be resisted, and the
> result was that on the 17th the regiment was in a terrible
> state…

One can imagine Perry's so-called "Saints," their halos slightly tarnished, reasoning that such an obvious gift from Neptune should not be refused. They were, after all, thirsty soldiers confined to a remote island infested with mosquitos, snakes, and alligators.

It did not take long for Perry to discover those who had fallen particularly far from grace. The drunkest among them landed in the guardhouse or, worse, the dank dungeon inside Fort Pulaski. What remaining few bottles of alcohol could be rounded up were promptly secured in the fort's magazine. But worst of all, Colonel Perry suffered a deadly stroke at his desk the next afternoon. His admirers among the regiment (and he apparently had many, even among the boys nursing hangovers) saw it as more than just a cruel coincidence. As Lieutenant Nichols wrote: "It is probable, however, that the excitement and vexation so overcame the Colonel as to induce the attack the following day."

THE PENINSULA CAMPAIGN

One of the major Federal objectives during 1862 was to threaten the capital of the Confederacy in Richmond, Virginia. Confederate Colonel John "Prince John" Magruder stood opposite McClellan, who led the Yankee troops near the capital. Rumors that Magruder drank too much constantly swirled around the colonel. (Perhaps it did not help that he spoke with a lisp.) But even if he did overly imbibe, Magruder was successful in protecting Richmond with far less troops than his adversary. One of the ruses employed by Prince John was to march his men around and around, purposely kicking up great dust clouds to dupe the Yankees into thinking they were opposed by many more troops than the rebels actually had.

Nevertheless, Colonel Daniel Harvey Hill wrote home to his wife Isabella on May 30, 1862: "Col Magruder in command is always drunk and giving foolish and absurd orders. I think in a few days the men will refuse to obey any orders issued by him." Similarly, the "Fire-Eater" Edmund Ruffin vented in his diary in July:

> It is reported verbally, but not in the newspapers, that the inertness of Gen. [Benjamin] Huger and Gen. Magruder's being drunk, were the causes why these officers did not carry out Gen. Lee's orders and the consequent failure...by which McClellan's army would have been prevented from reaching the James river and the protection of the gunboats, without which his army must have been completely defeated...

When major defeats occurred—or when sure victories suddenly proved elusive—it was not uncommon for both sides to level charges of drunkenness against officers or even whole regiments.

WHISKEY TO THE RESCUE

Unfortunately for the Yankees, McClellan's attempts to move on Richmond (June 25 through July 1) got bogged down and might have ended in complete disaster if not for a strong stand by Union forces at Malvern Hill. During these multiple and savage clashes, Colonel John Cheves Haskell of South Carolina related the delicate balance of just how much alcoholic "relief" a wounded man might need. Haskell, who had been a college student when the war broke out, had an arm torn off at the shoulder from a close-range cannon ball blast and later recalled: "I fell and could not get up. I was lying there expecting to die when Gen. Whiting riding by, saw me. He at once dismounted and gave me some whiskey from his flask."

Whiting's whiskey helped address Haskell's immediate pain, but surgeons at the rear soon concluded that the brave officer was likely to die and their job was to make sure he passed on with minimal suffering.

> Then, telling me goodbye most affectedly, he put some bitter powder in my mouth. [The surgeon] told me afterward that it was morphine enough to kill several men, and that he gave it to me to allow me to die more easily. He often said that my recovery from him was more remarkable than my recovery from the wound.

REBEL BRASS AND THE SILVER FLASK

After the brutal Battle of Malvern Hill on July 1—with the Confederates getting the worst of it—the belligerents agreed to a brief truce to cart off their wounded and bury their dead. With more than 8,000 combined casualties, there was no shortage of either. To make matters worse, a steady rain hovered over Virginia in the grim aftermath and contributed to the misery.

Perhaps in an attempt to fortify the spirits of the Johnnies, Major Charles Marshall of General Lee's staff arrived at headquarters (where Jefferson Davis had arrived to meet with his top generals) with a surprise. As Henry Kyd Douglas related the story:

> [Marshall] came in with a silver flask, which had been presented him by General George A. McCall, United States Army, captured two days before, and which contained some excellent whiskey. Drawing off the cap, he handed it to the President, who touched it very lightly. General Lee declined, saying he would not deprive some

younger officer of a drink which he would better appreciate. General Longstreet took a good soldierly swig of it. General Jackson declined and also General Stuart, who said laughingly, he knew General McCall would not give away good whiskey unless he had drugged it and wanted to poison somebody. General Stuart's suggestion, however, did not deter the staff from trying it, and the flask was emptied in short order.

This apprehension about "poisoned" liquor was not an uncommon one throughout the war. In fact, a popular story (perhaps embellished) about General Philip Kearny on the Union side involved a similar storyline. Some of Kearny's staff found a decanter of spirits in a plantation parlor near Williamsburg, but suddenly got cold feet about actually trying it after one of the men pondered if retreating rebels would be dastardly enough to plant tainted liquor?

Never one to shy away from a dangerous mission, Kearny stepped up, hoisted the vessel, and took a significant pull of the stuff. Then he announced to his fainthearted sub-officers: "If I'm not dead in fifteen minutes, take all of the whisky you want!"

Liquor that was purposely poisoned and left with the bitter hope that some enemy soldier might drink it down seems to have been more talked about than actually encountered. However, certainly there were some crudely distilled "moonshine" experiments that were dangerous enough in their own natural state. Soldiers sometimes referred to the less refined intoxicants by colorful names such as "Bust Head" or "Dead at the Counter."

CHERRY BOUNCE

One of the more popular memoirs written about the Civil War originates from one Lieutenant William Nathaniel Wood of the Nineteenth Virginia. Wood's contribution to the era was titled

Reminiscences of Big I and is bound to bring a smile and a tear to readers. One of the more humorous entries involves the relatively naïve officer and a surprise attack from a fruit brandy that apparently packed a powerful punch.

In mid-August of 1862, Wood was travelling back to camp after "leave" when a friend from the Seventh Virginia Infantry "hailed" him and said: "Just got a box from home; so you must take dinner with me." Wood readily accepted and there was plenty of delightful food in the offering—fried chicken, Virginia ham, and apple pies—but before the lieutenant even had a bite, the requisite canteen suddenly appeared and his host insisted that he sample its magic elixir.

> "No, thank you, I never drink anything," was the reply, as a canteen was offered.
>
> "It is nothing but innocent cherry bounce—why it would not hurt a baby," with which assurance a good hearty pull was taken.... It was good—in fact, so very palatable was this cherry bounce that a second pull was taken before due attention was paid to the other contents of the box. Eating and talking consumed another thirty minutes and Big I arose to go—or rather he tried to, for somehow the trees seemed to be dancing, the men around the box wonderfully mixed up—the tongue was thick, the knees weak, the head whirling and the leafy shade inviting; all because cherry bounce was innocent. "All present or *accounted for*" at roll call that evening.

WHISKEY FEAR AT SECOND MANASSAS

In late August, Yankees under General John Pope clashed with rebels once again at Bull Run (or, as the Confederates preferred, Manassas). When General Thomas "Stonewall" Jackson slyly slipped around Pope's forces, he was joyfully surprised to find a massive Union supply depot at Manassas Junction defended by a mere 1,200 men who were soon overwhelmed by his superior numbers.

Numerous accounts in Confederate diaries and letters detail the grand haul of captured goods—everything from clothing and boots to some culinary delicacies that the majority of the gray-clad Southerners had never seen. It all added up to a bizarre scene, as one rebel noted that some of his "half-starved" comrades suddenly found themselves "eating lobster salad and drinking Rhine wine."

While a swig of white wine to wash down lobster probably caused little harm, Jackson was much more concerned about his soldiers guzzling hard liquor. Lots of whiskey fell into rebel clutches at Manassas, and Jackson—a strict temperance man—immediately issued strict orders to his officers to destroy John Barleycorn on the spot.

"Don't spare a drop, nor let any man taste it under any circumstances," Jackson declared. "I fear that liquor more than General Pope's army."

Whiskey barrels were bashed in and gallons upon gallons were dumped, but some of it inevitably found its way into a few empty canteens and parched throats.

STONEWALL JACKSON AND DEMON ALCOHOL

Thomas "Stonewall" Jackson was well known among his troops as a very religious man. In those early days after Sumter, Jackson—a Presbyterian of great zeal—even proposed to a clergyman that a day of prayer across the South might petition the Lord in such a way as to prevent the onslaught of war. Given his strict nineteenth-century Presbyterianism, it is perhaps not shocking that Jackson mostly saw alcohol as a potent evil.

It is well documented that General Jackson upon occasion admitted that he *enjoyed* liquor, but—knowing its powers of enslavement—avoided it almost always. Those few occasions when

Jackson did *not* avoid alcohol, therefore, were quite noteworthy. One incident mentioned by many of Jackson's biographers occurred in the spring of 1862. A Confederate congressman and colonel on Jackson's staff, Alexander Boteler, ordered two hot whiskey toddies to the Winchester, Virginia, hotel room that they were sharing. Predictably, General Jackson refused his tipple, reminding Boteler that he did not drink "intoxicating beverages."

Boteler countered by citing the supposed medicinal benefits of alcohol. Given the constant rigors of war, would not an occasional "stimulant" do them both good?

With some reluctance, Jackson took a sip of his toddy, but then said: "Colonel, do you know why I habitually abstain from intoxicating drinks? Why, sir, because I like the taste of them, and when I discovered that to be the case I made up my mind at once to do without them altogether."

"MOCKING BIRD" WHISKEY

But few soldiers were like Stonewall Jackson. Robert Knox Sneden, known for his watercolor sketches and maps that chronicle the Civil War, recorded this little gem on August 1, 1862:

> We had a fine serenade at headquarters…and whiskey punch flowed freely. General Kearny's favorite air is "The Mocking Bird," and the band leaders know that if this tune is played well they will be furnished whiskey "ad libitum." So we have this fine piece played over repeatedly, or as long as the musician can see his instrument. Sometimes the whiskey prevents his so doing…

Kearny—a wealthy man who appreciated the finer things in life—dispensed whiskey not only as a reward, but also for his own protection, as Sneden recorded in a July 20, 1862, diary entry:

Regimental bands were serenading at each general's headquarters after dark. That which serenaded General Kearny must have been the worst one in the army. It was a regular "sheet iron band." I did not learn of which regiment. General Kearny gave this band a gallon of whiskey "to go *away*!"

"OLD BALDY" AND THE MADEIRA CURE

General Richard "Dick" (a.k.a. "Old Baldy") Ewell performed quite well in the Shenandoah Valley campaigns in 1862—not an easy task in that his superior General Thomas "Stonewall" Jackson often kept the overall battle plans tight to the vest until the very last minute. On August 29, 1862, Ewell's luck went bust when he was severely wounded at the Battle of Groveton, near Manassas. In a field hospital the next day, while under the influence of chloroform, Ewell was still issuing "orders"—but he snapped out of it when Dr. Hunter McGuire began to remove his left leg, just below the knee, abruptly sitting up and bellowing: "Oh! My God!"

There was some initial doubt that the general would live, and even when he did, it was understood his recovery would be rather lengthy. For some reason, Ewell trusted in a certain fruit—both in fresh form and liquid—to rejuvenate him. He brought in fresh grapes and then, from an old friend, he gratefully received a dozen bottles of fine old Madeira. As his top aide, Major George Campbell Brown recorded: "This wine was the last relic of Mr. [Richard] Cunningham's very fine cellar—'Rain Water' of the vintage of 1837—and the pleasantest wine I have ever tasted."

Apparently the bottles Cunningham generously provided for General Ewell were the last survivors of his once formidable collection, as a disreputable overseer had colluded to sell off most of his fine cellar ("at a dollar, or less, per bottle") on the sly to none other than those rascally rebels, the Louisiana Tigers.

It was not *just* the splendid Madeira that brought Ewell around; he also was nursed by one Lizinka Campbell Brown, his first cousin, and, eventually his wife. They married the next year.

Even before Ewell called in the 1837 Madeira to assist in his recuperation, "Old Baldy" had a nose for top-shelf wine. Earlier in 1862, when the Confederates overran some Union lines, Ewell found that he had set up his new headquarters in a fine homestead that had only recently been abandoned by U.S. General Daniel Sickles. Ewell happily paid the homeowner a little bit of money for some excellent champagne that—in his hasty retreat—Devil Dan had been forced to leave behind.

Ewell rejoined the Confederate war effort in the spring of 1863. His missing left leg did not prevent him from participating in the Gettysburg campaign. Some historians have suggested that Ewell squandered a golden opportunity on July 1 when he did not push on and seize the high ground after driving the Yankees from Gettysburg proper to Cemetery Hill south of town. A more generous interpretation could be that General Lee's orders were somewhat open-ended, as they read: "...carry the hill occupied by the enemy, if practical...."

Perhaps a case or two of 1837 Madeira on top of Cemetery Hill would have provided "Old Baldy" an extra incentive to storm that lofty position.

MEAGHER'S "SPILL" AT ANTIETAM

The bloodiest one-day battle of the war took place in 1862 at Antietam near Sharpsville, Maryland, on September 17, 1862. On the Union side, the much-vaunted Irish Brigade launched an intrepid charge. It was the fourth Union assault of the day against rebel positions at the "Sunken Road," and they suffered more than 500 casualties.

But along with the waving of green flags, the charge is also known for a persistent rumor that General Thomas Francis Meagher's spill from his horse during the attack was due to the bottle, not bullets. Lieutenant Frederick Hitchcock of the 132nd Pennsylvania Volunteers—the unit relieved by the Irish Brigade—wrote:

> Meagher rode a beautiful white horse, but made a show of tumbling off just before he reached our lines. The boys said he was drunk, and he certainly looked and acted like a drunken man. He regained his feet and floundered about, swearing like a crazy man. The brigade, however, made a magnificent charge and swept everything before it.

In an attempt to explain his boisterous behavior, Meagher's supporters tried to claim that the general might have hit his head in the fall. But even the Irish Brigade priest—Father William Corby, the eventual two-time president of Notre Dame—admitted in his diary that the popular commander sometimes drank to excess.

THE BURNSIDE BRIDGE

While too much whiskey certainly was something that any wise commander sought to keep from his troops, an occasional controlled offering of "ardent spirits" could also serve as timely motivation. Usually whiskey was distributed to pacify soldiers asked to perform mundane or arduous tasks such as the digging of trenches or graves, or offered as a pick-me-up after standing guard in stormy weather.

Colonel Edward Ferrero, a man who had taught dancing in New York City before the war, knew all too well that whiskey was a seductive lure to soldiers. The colonel once insisted:

> Were my men to be cast on an island where whiskey was never known to have been, and they allowed to run at will, scarcely a man but what would come into camp

with his canteen full, even if they would have to rend rocks asunder searching for it.

The men of the Fifty-First Pennsylvania proved to be creative when it came to acquiring alcohol. During a coastal campaign in North Carolina earlier in the year, a new supply of medicinal whiskey arrived. When higher ups were not around, some inspired soldiers unscrewed their gun barrels and, inserting the shafts through the bung hole of the whiskey kegs, effectively used those barrels as large, metal straws to imbibe some sizeable drafts of hard spirits. Amazingly, they pulled off this stunt without getting caught.

But in mid-September the Fifty-First Pennsylvanians found themselves *sans* whiskey, apparently for punishment when they were snagged for infractions. And it took some dire circumstances and heroic efforts to reverse this situation.

In the waning hours at the Battle of Antietam, the Federals were determined to cross the Rohrbach Bridge (today known as "Burnside Bridge"), but well-entrenched rebels on the opposite bank and sharpshooters on a steep wooded bluff above it were sending forth some withering fire. Several attempts to take the bridge by other units had already failed.

Up galloped Ferrero, riding before the Fifty-First Pennsylvania and Fifty-First New York. He passionately addressed them: "It is General Burnside's special request that the two Fifty-Firsts take that bridge! Will you do it?"

A plucky Corporal Lewis Patterson of Company I promptly interjected: "Will you give us our whiskey, Colonel, if we take it?"

To which Ferrero responded:

> Yes, by God, you shall have as much as you want, if you take the bridge. I don't mean the whole brigade, but you two regiments shall have as much as you want, if it is in the commissary or I have to send to New York to get it

and pay for it out of my own private purse; that is, if I live to see you through it. Will you take it?

A resounding "Yes!" roared through the twin regiments. They took the bridge, though they suffered dozens of casualties in the process.

Colonel Ferrero made good on his liquid promise. The next day those brave men got their whiskey and, according to the regimental history, the liquor arrived "in no stinted quantities."

WATER INTO WHISKEY

Civil War era diaries often mention a few "pops" of whiskey on the eve of a battle, but some soldiers also used alcohol to take the edge off *after* the cannon smoke had cleared. In the aftermath of Antietam, while Lee engineered his retreat, John Edward Dooley of the First Virginia Infantry recalled:

We have to rest for about ten or fifteen minutes in Sharpsburg and while waiting, as usual, one of the men took about a dozen canteens of the more lazy fellows to fill them with water. This man, McCrossin, was fond of a practical joke.... Just as we were moving on he comes back and hastily delivered the canteens to their owners. I am very thirsty and take a good draught from my canteen immediately; it was nothing but strong raw whiskey. I went to several other canteens asking for water, and all I came to had whiskey in them. It appears McCrossin had filled the canteens from a whiskey barrel instead of from a spring; and he was the boy to know if there were any strong whiskey barrels about town, with no one particular to claim them. We easily obtained water for whiskey.

IRISH WHISKEY

Civil War diaries of American soldiers on both sides are rife with slurs—some humorous, some blatantly mean-spirited—concerning soldiers of Irish ethnicity and their drinking. One rather unique anecdote concerns the Irish-born General Patrick Cleburne after the Battle of Perryville in Kentucky. Cleburne's Confederate troops captured Union supplies that included several barrels of whiskey and, as one of his own officers later recorded, the situation soon went terribly awry:

> While in Kentucky some whiskey was captured, over which Cleburne ordered a guard to be placed. Inadvertently this was detailed to an Irish company. Passing a few hours later, the General found one of the barrels *empty* and the guard and most of their company *full*. Placing them under arrest, he turned, incensed, to his provost-marshal and said: "*Lieut-init*, I thought you had more *sinse* than to put an Irishman to guard whiskey!"

Ordinarily, Cleburne had very little of a "brogue," but it was very pronounced when he became excited or angry.

FREDERICKSBURG AND THE WHISKEY BET

From the Union perspective, the Battle of Fredericksburg in late 1862—with General Ambrose Burnside in charge of the Federals—proved to be one of the greatest disasters of the war. So foolhardy did the repeated assaults on entrenched positions at Marye's Heights appear that some rebels concluded that only men fired up on whiskey could have undertaken such a doomed task.

Without question, there was plenty of whiskey in Fredericksburg, along with other temptations. General Marsena R. Patrick, a provost marshal in the Union Army, perhaps best summed it up when he wrote: "This town is full of Brothels and Prostitutes and drinking saloons and all sorts of vile institutions…"

Since alcohol often functioned as a second currency among soldiers during the war, it sometimes became the center of various wagers. One such bet arose at the Battle of Fredericksburg between two rebel colonels, as Colonel Fite recalled:

> In every fight we'd ever been in, [Colonel Pete] Turney would always insist that he knew he was going to be killed. That day I bet him a gallon of whiskey that neither one of us was killed. He always insisted later that when I had seen him there at the field hospital wounded, I had said, "Pete, damn if I don't have to give you that gallon of whiskey. I think they got you this time, old

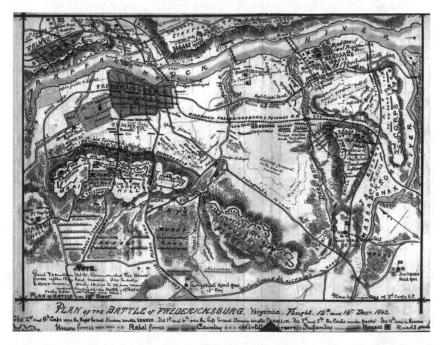

Map showing the plan of the Battle of Fredericksburg. *Courtesy of the Library of Congress.*

horse." But I know that I didn't say that, for I really did think that he was gone up.

"Gone up" was soldier-speak for "gone up to Heaven." But any wounded soldier awakening in a chaotic Civil War field hospital knew immediately that he was not on the peaceful side of the Pearly Gates.

A TOAST FOR FIGHTIN' JOE

With the Fredericksburg disaster falling squarely on General Burnside's record, President Lincoln and Secretary of War Stanton soon opted for General Joseph Hooker for top command of the Army of the Potomac. Hooker had a reputation as a man eager for battle, but he also brought some baggage: rumors of both heavy drinking and unbridled womanizing. Although the actual promotion did not become official until January of 1863, the African-American journalist George Stephens saw this likely change unfoding, writing:

> A grand Christmas dinner was given at the headquarters of Major Gen. Hooker. The arrangements were ample and sumptuous.... Toasts upon toasts were drank to the old hero, and so pressing were the attentions that he was compelled to make a few remarks...

Those "attentions" came with exaltations: "General Hooker, the future Commander of the Army of the Potomac!"

Hooker certainly drank at his Christmas bash, but not enough to deny the arduous task that he faced: "I don't know...whether you are my friends or not when you wish me to take command of the army; for this army is, so to speak, at the bottom of a well, while the enemy is at the top..."

When Hooker did ascend to the top rung, it was not without some trepidation from Lincoln and his inner circle. When the Secretary of the Navy Gideon Welles suggested Hooker as a replacement for Burnside, there were reservations about "Fighting Joe's" personal habits, as Welles noted in his diary:

> The President looked approvingly but said I think as much as you or any other man of Hooker but—I fear he gets excited. Looking around as he spoke. Blair who was present said he is too great a friend of John Barleycorn...I remarked at once if his habits are bad—if he permits himself to get intoxicated he ought not to be trusted with such a command, and withdrew my nomination. From what I have since heard, I fear he is both a drunkard and a gambler—at least he indulges in the free use of whiskey—gets excited and is fond of play. This is a result of my enquiries and with this reputation, I am surprised at his selection—though he doubtless has good points as an officer.

JOHN BARLEYCORN, GENERAL-IN-CHIEF

While Fighting Joe Hooker was toasting in the east, the western campaign did not lack for holiday "cheer" either. In his memoirs *Company Aytch: A Side Show of the Big Show*, the Confederate foot soldier Sam Watkins unflinchingly documented the festivity, just prior to the Battle of Stones River (or Murfreesboro, which began on New Year's Eve morning, paused for a January 1 truce to bury the dead, and then resumed with ferocity again on January 2, 1863). If we are to believe Watkins's observations, even allowing for some embellishment, the officers probably needed several days prior to the battle to get clear-headed:

It was Christmas. John Barleycorn was general-in-chief.
Our generals and colonels, and captains, had kissed John
a little too often. They couldn't see straight. It was said
to be buckeye whiskey.

One officer on the Confederate side who no doubt refrained
from "kissing John" was the temperate Braxton Bragg. General
Bragg complained loudly and often about drunken fellow officers
in his command, but had only limited success in either dismissing
or controlling them. Bragg's chief targets (and not without some
foundation) were General John C. Breckenridge, General Benjamin
Cheatham, and General George B. Crittenden, among others.

CHAMPAGNE AND SAVIORS

Contentions and rivalries among the Confederate command,
however, were far from uncommon, even between temperate men.
General Joseph E. Johnston, for instance, was never one of President Jefferson Davis's favorites. Davis believed Johnston was overly
hesitant in the field and Johnston felt Davis wrongly promoted
other generals above him. Near the end of 1862, Johnston was
transferred to the western theater of the war, while General Robert
E. Lee was promoted to direct CSA efforts in the East.

Still recovering from a wound incurred at the Battle of Seven
Pines, Johnston attended a breakfast in Richmond just prior to his
departure. The event was headed up by several anti-Davis politicians—chief among them Senators William Yancey of Alabama
and Henry Foote of Tennessee—who were fired up by numerous
bottles of champagne, perhaps supplied by some devil-may-care
blockade runner. As the festivities were drawing to a close, Yancey
appealed to the attendees that "This toast is to be drunk standing…" but instructed General Johnston to stay put. The Alabaman

enthused: "Gentlemen, let us drink to the health of the only man who can save the Confederacy—General Joseph E. Johnston!"

Johnston, a rare and careful imbiber, rose solemnly and answered: "Mr. Yancey, the man you describe is already in the field in the person of Robert E. Lee. I will drink to his health."

Yancey persisted: "Your modesty is only equaled by your valor!"

In the meantime, the bloodiest war in the nation's history—regardless of the valor and champagne on both sides—churned on.

1863

"He said then, and many times to me since the war, that the whiskey saved his life."

—Dr. William Graham

CHAPTER 5

MUD MARCHES AND SOAKS
1863

As the War of the Rebellion rolled into its third year with no end in sight, the Army of the Potomac—especially its officers—had by no means relinquished their raucous drinking stints. Secretary of War Stanton's year-old threat to squelch the "champagne and oysters" at the front had certainly had no serious effect on the celebratory culture of the Yankee brass.

A rare abstainer of high rank was General Robert McAllister of New Jersey, but his letters home prove that when it came to booze-guzzling officers, nothing had changed. Holidays, in particular, were considered prime time for "shoulder straps" to hoist a few and, unlike enlisted men, officers rarely had to fear any serious repercussions from drinking in camp.

McAllister was invited to General Daniel Sickles's New Year's "open house" reception, but wisely sent his regrets and stayed in his tent. McAllister—an organizer of regimental prayer groups—

probably suspected that the liquor-fueled event would become quite rambunctious. As he wrote to his wife:

> Col. Sewell of the 5th N.J. Vols. got so drunk at the reception today that he fell off his horse while passing our camp this evening and to the grate [sic] amusement of our boys. Of course he takes the ground that "officers ought to have a little." Brigadier Genl. Mott and others were with him; but our boys making so much fun of the drunken officer caused Genl. Mott to clear out. So Sewell's comrades tried to get him along. But he was rather a slow coach, and an ambulance was brought to take him home. No doubt he will be made a Brigadier General yet. Oh! When will our war powers awaken to a full sense of their duty and strike from our rolls all officers grate [sic] or small that will thus bring disgrace on the posts of honor that they hold and make brutes of themselves in the eyes of those who they command?

McAllister's account of Sickles's party was not merely a case of a smug teetotaler's exaggerated disapproval. Colonel Philippe Regis de Trobriand—the son of a French baron who was elected to officer rank in the New York Fifty-Fifth—also witnessed the bacchanalian scene:

> I wish I could add that they were used in moderation; but the truth is the subaltern officers, attracted by good cheer, partook of them so freely that it was not to the honor of the uniform nor to the profit of discipline.

HERE'S MUD IN YOUR EYE!

In an effort to redeem the crushing defeat at Fredericksburg, Burnside attempted a little winter campaign in late January. The idea was to make a feint or two, and then cross the Rappahannock with the Army of the Potomac and surprise Lee's forces.

But drenching downpours sabotaged the plan, as caissons, wagons, and large artillery pieces soon got stuck in axle-deep mud. Soldiers slogging through the muck were lashed by chilling rains for their ineffectual efforts. After three days (January 20 through 23) Burnside's dreams of revenge proved to be much ado about nothing. The hapless general resigned when he learned President Lincoln had taken the advice of others and ordered the ludicrous "Mud March" to cease—and he was soon replaced by the braggadocious Hooker.

Ordinarily, the soldiers might have been enraged about such a pointless ordeal. But they were placated somewhat by the officers dispensing commissary whiskey, presumably on the pretense of preventing soaking-wet men from falling ill. However, the whiskey also had its downside, as Private John Haley of the Seventeenth Maine noted in his diary—while taking the typical jabs aimed at Irish soldiers from nearby units:

> At night a generous dose of stimulant was served out all around and matters assumed a very lively hue. Some of the New Yorkers aired their eloquence at our expense, spoiling for a fight as the Irish always are when they have an "odd sup." As their chance of getting at the Rebels is as small as their desire to do so, they exercised their pugnacity on each other. Judging from the howling, I'd say a good number of them have been converted into sausage meat. Noise is an Irishman's special prerogative.

TRAIN "WRECKED"

Between the abject failure at Fredericksburg and the futility of the Mud March, General Ambrose Burnside was probably in need of a change. He got one in March when he was reassigned to the Army of the Cumberland, and so he and the Ninth Corps headed west.

The trip did not go smoothly, even from the start. They arrived by boat in Baltimore on March 27, but—as noted by George Hitchcock of the Twenty-First Massachusetts, "owing to the intoxicated state of many in the regiment, we are not allowed to land."

The next morning they were hustled onto trains for Pittsburgh and points further west. But in Pittsburgh—where the citizens treated the soldiers to a celebration—the situation went from bad to worse. Hitchcock's observation virtually drips with disgust:

> A more disgraceful sight could hardly be imagined as our regiment marched or staggered to the depot.… Fully nine tenths of the regiment were under the influence of liquor—officers and men—and the remaining sober ones were busy helping their drunken comrades into the cars.

Apparently many of the Union soldiers were still drunk (or drinking still) when the IX Corps reached Columbus, Ohio. In an effort to prevent the "tight" troops from causing trouble in the city, local militia actually fired into a crowd of boozed-up soldiers (killing one and wounding several others), nearly precipitating a full-blown riot. Somehow officers defused the potential donnybrook and got the infuriated soldiers back on board, and the troop trains steamed on toward Kentucky.

THE SIXTEENTH PENNSYLVANIA CAVALRY SIGNS ON

By 1863, one of the most well-known ways by which the Union eventually won the Civil War was already at work: the Federals simply formed more units and brought superior numbers into play. (The Confederacy never enjoyed such a luxury; rarely were they able to rapidly replenish men or materials lost in battle.) One of these newly formed Union regiments was the Sixteenth Pennsylvania Cavalry, recruited in the fall of 1862.

The men, most of whom were from central Pennsylvania, displayed typical soldier-like flaws en route to the war. Some of the most brazen had to be extracted from the bordellos of Harrisburg and, according to one cavalryman's diary, when the regiment reached Baltimore by train the next night, "Most of us slept in the cars—some officers got pretty boozy and men too."

By January of 1863, the horsemen of the Sixteenth found themselves—"green" and untested—down on the Virginia front. The Sixteenth drew particular interest from this author, because my great-grandfather John Kincaid Robison eventually became their colonel in 1863. Beyond battling the enemy, Colonel J. K. Robison also had to deal with "alcohol issues" among his troops; the primary evidence appears consistently in the letters and diary entries of Colonel Robison's aide-de-camp, Samuel Cormany.

In truth, most Civil War regiments indulged in an occasional waltz with the devil's temptations. When you might be killed in battle (or die of the half dozen or so prevalent diseases that flourished in most army camps) in the near future, the concept of "sin" seemingly weighed far less heavy than it did back home under the scrutiny of family, church, or county judge.

THE SIXTEENTH GETS PRANKED

A few months after the Sixteenth had settled in at the front, they became a target of their more experienced brothers-in-arms, the Pennsylvania Third Cavalry.

It seems some soldiers of the Sixteenth and some soldiers of the Third were to alternate guarding a camp supply station. The station contained various military items, but the Third was particularly interested in a barrel of "commissary whiskey." A simple but believable plan emerged; a few wags from the Third approached the greenhorns from the Sixteenth and told them to report immediately for "midnight scout" while the men of the Third would relieve them at their post. Off marched the newbies from the Sixteenth. And then, as related in the regimental history of the Third,

> In less time than it takes to write it, that barrel of whiskey was rolling over the hill toward the camp of the Third. Here the head was knocked in and the contents carried in mess kettles into the cook house on more than one company ground. By the time the guard of the Sixteenth had discovered the joke...the effect began to show itself among those who were in on the secret.

The officers became wise the next morning and an intensive search eventually found most of the whiskey (that which had not trickled down numerous throats) sitting in kettles in the various camp kitchens, attempting to pose as cold coffee.

The next step—aimed at exposing the most intoxicated culprits—involved all the men in a dismounted drill conducted on the "double-quick" under an interrogating sun. The over-imbibed soon melted down like butter in an iron camp skillet. Then came the punishment:

> By order of the Colonel, [the Sergeant] got all the drunken men in some way to the Potomac Creek, and there kept them in soak until they sobered up, which in the cold water did not take long. The Sergeant, who was a Methodist preacher and a total abstainer, took much grim pleasure in carrying out the order.

SAINT PATRICK'S DAY

Some units were overwhelmingly comprised of Irish-Americans or recent Irish immigrants, so it's no surprise that spirited St. Patrick's Day celebrations often had the blessing of the Army of the

Potomac's top brass. The one staged on March 17, 1863, certainly was a memorable one—including horseraces and footraces.

To make the event all the more "spirited," there was also some generous distribution of "commissary" whiskey as noted by Sergeant Peter Welsh of the Twenty-Eighth Massachusetts (part of the celebrated "Irish Brigade") in a letter home to his "Dear Wife":

> We had a great time here on St. Patricks [sic] day the whole event got up by General Meagher there was horse racing and foot raceing [sic] of all kinds nearly all the Generals in this army were present and some ladies from New York we all got two gills of whiskey each.

Samuel Cormany of the Sixteenth Pennsylvania Cavalry, however, recorded that this "sport" was not without casualties:

> Saw an awful specimen of the degradation incident to Army Life—Horse racing under the eyes of Genls Hooker, Humphry [sic], Pleasenton [sic], Sumner and any amount of other Commissioned Officers.—3 Men Killed and 4 Horses....

THE PLUCK OF THE IRISH

General Regis de Trobriand's regiment was comprised of various units that included Frenchmen, Germans, and the Irish, among a smattering of other European immigrants. Company K of the Fifty-Fifth New York Regiment, in particular, was almost entirely an Irish unit, and de Trobriand had some criticisms of the lads from the Emerald Isle. However, when the action was hot on the battlefield, de Trobriand also was quick to praise the Irish for their courage.

In his memoirs (*Four Years in the Army of the Potomac*), de Trobriand wrote:

The Irish have two prevailing faults, uncleanliness and a tendency to drunkenness. On inspection, their uniforms were seldom without spots or their bearing without fault. When whisky was introduced into the camp clandestinely, it was in the Irish quarter that the officer of the guard first found it. The most severe punishments availed nothing. But, on the other hand, they were fine fighters. When they were under fire, the spots on their uniforms disappeared under powder or blood;—good fellows after all, indefatigable, enthusiastic, and always ready for a fight.

Before the second day at Gettysburg, the lads were not only ready for the fight, but also anticipated its grim results. Father Corby—knowing that many would not survive—gave the Irish Brigade last rites en masse *before* they waded into the fray.

BRIDGE BUILDING

There were more than a few thankless jobs that soldiers endured during the Civil War, but building bridges (or "pontoons," as some of the makeshift spans were often called) ranked high on the list. There seemed to be a continuous need for such backbreaking labor, particularly since retreating armies would often wreck or burn pre-existing bridges in order to hinder attacks or pursuits from the enemy. In addition, bridges frequently were needed in swampy settings humming with mosquitoes and crawling with snakes.

Whiskey served as both enticement and remedy for those laboring in such adverse conditions. The army doctors also dispensed bitter-tasting quinine to fight malaria (often referred to as "ague"); but whiskey, obviously, was more popular with the soldiers. As Colonel Thomas Livermore recalled in his memoirs, even the "little drummer fifteen years old, marched up with a tin cup to get his grog."

As for the men actually building the bridges or pontoons, Livermore wrote:

> The work was done mainly in the water, sometimes waist deep, and amid mud and tangled underbrush. The men worked away with spirit, and did not let anything dismay them, and as we were composed largely of men who could wield the axe we got along finely. Details of the 64th and 69th New York were sent to aid us, and the colonel had a barrel of whiskey broached, at which the soaked soldiers could slack their thirst, and fan up their fires *ad libitum*, and such was the effect of this generosity that the Irishmen of the 69th cheered Colonel [Edward] Cross as the best of men.

According to Colonel Livermore, on this particular occasion the "spirited" New Yorkers produced a fine bridge across the Chickahominy River.

"TIGHT" AS A BRICK

Although whiskey in the Civil War was often called upon as a "stimulant" to keep a soldier charged up under rough conditions, too much of it, of course, could backfire. The artillery commander Charles Wainwright observed whiskey's downside firsthand in late April 1863, when Union troops were frantically fashioning pontoon bridges and placing them just prior to what would be their advance at Chancellorsville.

> Old General [Henry W.] Benham, who had charge of laying the bridges, came up now and was very loud in

his talk. He had been up all night and taken so much whiskey to keep himself awake that he was tight as a brick; had fallen off his horse once and scratched his face badly.

"Tight" and "brick" were both slang drinking terms in vogue during the Civil War, but apparently General Benham made such an impression on Wainwright that he felt compelled to use both terms in one sentence.

LOVE AND DEATH: VAN DORN'S DEMISE

Earl Van Dorn was one of the more experienced military figures from Jefferson Davis's home state of Mississippi. Although Van Dorn had graduated near the bottom of his West Point Class of 1842 (fifty-second out of fifty-six cadets), he later saw action in both the Mexican War and in subsequent campaigns against hostile Indians. In the early stages of the Civil War, the dashing Van Dorn was called to Virginia, but—needing a firm commander in the Western Theater—President Davis sent him back to the battlefields of Arkansas, Mississippi, and Tennessee. Van Dorn had some initial success at the Battle of Elkhorn Tavern, but by the end of the action at Pea Ridge in Arkansas, his troops got the worst of it. Later in 1862, Van Dorn's troops attacked a formidable position held by General William Rosecrans in the Second Battle of Corinth in Mississippi and got roughly repulsed. The general's star rapidly began to fade.

Beyond the battlefield, Van Dorn had a reputation as a relentless womanizer and a dedicated drinker. In fact, these allegations accumulated enough credence that the general was forced to dash off a letter of denial to President Davis, his fellow Mississippian, insisting that "I am not a seducer, nor a drunkard."

On May 7, 1863, Dr. James Peters arrived at Van Dorn's mansion headquarters in Spring Hill, Tennessee, and shot the general dead. Dr. Peters claimed that Van Dorn had been pursuing an illicit love affair with his wife Jessica and had "violated the sanctity" of his home. Van Dorn's death did not overshadow his tarnished reputation, and sympathy was hard to come by. The *Nashville Dispatch* bluntly stated:

> My informant tells me that [Van Dorn] had degraded the cause, and disgusted everyone by his inattention to his duties and his constant devotion to the ladies.... He was never at his post when he ought to be. He was either tied to a woman's apron strings or heated with wine.

CHAPTER 6

ON THE ROAD TO GETTYSBURG
1863

CHANCELLORSVILLE

In early May, Hooker came up against Lee and Stonewall Jackson—the result being a daring victory for the Confederates, with the Army of the Potomac just nearly avoiding a total disaster.

Hooker misinterpreted a large movement of troops to be a rebel retreat when, in fact, it was Jackson rapidly on the move to unleash a vicious surprise attack on the Federal flank. Hooker—who had at his disposal more than 130,000 soldiers—had hoped to trap Lee's smaller force, but found himself trapped instead.

Hooker had made the Chancellor House his headquarters and it was there that he was knocked nearly unconscious by an artillery shell. He was carried inside and dosed with brandy—the popular method of "stimulation" that battlefield doctors so often prescribed. Naturally, these occurrences led to rumors that Hooker (given his past reputation) was drunk at Chancellorsville. How else to explain such a debacle? But there is no evidence that Hooker consumed any major amounts of brandy dispensed to bring him around *after* he was nearly killed.

With his trademark cynical prose, Private Haley wrote:

> It has been asserted that Hooker was unconscious from a too generous patronage of the canteen. He doubtless is a close observer of canteens, as are most of the other generals, but no one could have been so overpowered by drink who only a few minutes before had shown such agility on the field. A man accustomed to his potations is not so easily overthrown.

Weirdly, another story soon circulated, the gist of which was that Hooker's passivity at Chancellorsville was, in fact, due to not drinking enough! The theory was that a body and brain so accustomed to the consumption of spirits could not function smoothly when the stimulants were abruptly withdrawn. Regardless, Hooker's collapse at Chancellorsville allowed his detractors in the Union army to attack both his abilities and his character flaws. In a letter to a friend, General Henry Slocum (whose Twelfth Corps suffered heavy casualties in the battle) wrote:

> It was a sad failure, a bitter disappointment to us all. Our movements up to the arrival at Chancellorsville were successful and unflawed. Everything after that went wrong, and fighting Joe sunk into a poor driveling cur. The fact is whisky, boasting, and vilification have been his stock and trade. Sickles and [General Dan] Butterfield are his boon companions, and everything is conducted as might be expected with such leaders.

The Army of the Potomac finally managed a desperate escape from Lee, crossing back across the Rappahannock in a driving rainstorm—the kind of weather that almost always warranted a gill or two of commissary whiskey. But in the depressing aftermath and the assessment of massive casualties (more than 17,000 in dead, wounded, or captured, though the CSA suffered similar losses), Hooker's days as Lincoln's top field general in the East were numbered.

THE FALL OF THE MIGHTY STONEWALL

Robert E. Lee was not a man prone to celebration, but even if he was, the dire news that General Jackson had been a victim of "friendly fire" would have done much to offset any rejoicing over his Chancellorsville victory. On the night of May 2, Jackson and his party were mistaken for the enemy and shots from the Eighteenth North Carolina Regiment whistled through the darkness and ripped into them.

Attempting to save Jackson, Dr. Hunter McGuire treated the religious with both whiskey and morphine. His left arm had to be amputated and McGuire utilized chloroform to help accomplish that gruesome task. For a few days it appeared that Jackson was rebounding. But by May 7 the general's prospects faltered again; he was struggling against the pneumonia that finally ended his life on May 10.

In some of Jackson's final hours, McGuire attempted to coax him into taking a few swallows of brandy to address his pain, but the general declined. Those by his deathbed said that Jackson's final words were: "Let us cross over the river, and rest under the shade of the trees."

THE ROCKY ROAD TO GETTYSBURG

It might come as a surprise to some history buffs that thousands and thousands of Civil War soldiers marching toward the pivotal three-day Battle of Gettysburg were quite drunk in the days just prior to it.

But the diaries, letters, and memoirs of the soldiers themselves bear witness (some in a humorous way) that this was certainly the case. In fact, many of the worst offenders might have been still shaking off the aftereffects of their "sore heads" and dry mouths—all of which were accentuated by severe heat smothering the countryside in early July—when the crucial battle began.

In his journal, Lieutenant Edmund DeWitt Patterson of the Ninth Alabama reflected the high spirits of most Confederate troops as they headed north to take the war onto Yankee soil. His regiment passed through Sharpsburg, Maryland and, per usual, had no trouble finding *liquid* spirits. From his June 26 entry he noted:

> Patronized the barber shop, hotel and saloon, and as it bade fair to rain all day we laid in a supply of the "needful." About 8 o'clock our command passed through Middleburg.
>
> Crossed the Pennsylvania and Maryland line at 11 o'clock precisely. Jim Crow, Van Whitehead and I persuaded an old gentleman to show us exactly where the line ran and then standing with one foot in Maryland and the other in Pennsylvania, we finished the contents of the canteen, drinking some pretty heavy toasts.

FOUR STATES IN TWENTY-FOUR HOURS

A rebel in the Fourth Texas Infantry wrote that some powerful whiskey ("It was chained lightning and knocked out many a valiant soldier...") was issued to his regiment—apparently with General John B. Hood's blessing—to fortify the men during a long march in stormy weather. In his June 26, 1863, entry Val Giles reflected on his four-state adventure:

A brilliant and eventful day in spite of the fact that it rained pitchforks.... We performed a feat never performed by any other troops during the war. We ate breakfast in the State of Virginia, dinner in the State of Maryland, supper in the State of Pennsylvania, and slept in the State of Intoxication—four states in 24 hours!

That this particular day got a tad out of hand also is reflected in the diary entry of Lieutenant J. Warren Jackson of the Eighth Louisiana Infantry (part of Colonel Harry Hays's brigade), who penned:

June 26—Recd order to march early... burned the Ironworks near Greenwood... went on to Gettysburg and captured between 3 and 400 "Melish" [militia]—camped in sight of town and drew rations of whiskey. The whole brigade got drunk. I never saw such a set in my life[.]

Not all of the jubilant Johnnies made it to Pennsylvania that night. For some, the Potomac River crossing—and the whiskey waiting for them afterwards—did them in. William Robert Houghton, a sergeant in the Second Georgia Infantry, recalled in his insightful account *Two Boys in the Civil War and After*:

On the way to Gettysburg we waded the cold and swollen Potomac at Williamsport. It was breast deep and over half a mile wide, and the winding road on either side down the long hills, afforded a view of near ten thousand men with their clothes hung on their guns, breasting the swift current. On the top of the hill in Maryland, were barrels of whisky with the heads out, from which each man was expected to take a gill [several ounces], but those who had them filled their quart cups. About one third of our command, including some officers, failed to get to camp on Pennsylvania soil that night, and the red mud on their uniforms attested the tangle leg quality of the liquor. Nothing was done about this breach of discipline, and some of the brave fellows were left under the rock bound heights of Gettysburg.

GRANNY LEE EXERCISES CAUTION

As was his wont, General Robert E. Lee—while camped near Chambersburg, Pennsylvania, with his army—displayed caution when he came up against John Barleycorn. Lee allowed his army medical staffs to replenish their supplies of alcohol, but then he sternly commanded his men to empty surplus liquor into the streets. As Lieutenant Colonel Arthur James Lyon Fremantle (a British officer, on leave from Her Majesty's Coldstream Guards, who was observing the war) recorded in his diary:

> Some Texan soldiers were sent this morning into Chambersburg to destroy a number of barrels of excellent whiskey, which could not be carried away. This was a pretty good trial for their discipline, and they did think it rather hard lines that the only time they had been allowed into the enemy's town was for the purpose of destroying their beloved whiskey. However, they did their duty like good soldiers.

KNOCKED FOR A LAGER LOOP AT CARLISLE

The advance regiments of Alabama's General Robert E. Rodes (part of General Richard Ewell's command) were among the first Confederates to cross into Pennsylvania in mid-June and, in the days just prior to Gettysburg, had established their base at Carlisle on June 27.

Their original plan was to capture Harrisburg—the Pennsylvania capital—and then perhaps sweep down on Philadelphia or Baltimore. But as the Union army rapidly moved north, those plans were scrapped. Pennsylvania militia units also astutely burned the Wrightsville bridge over the Susquehanna, which stymied Confederate designs to grab Harrisburg. Eventually the various rebel corps—totaling about 70,000 men—converged on Gettysburg, where they were confronted by Union forces of superior numbers.

But in the days just prior to the battle itself, rebel spirits were high. As they swept into these northern towns, the proud "Johnnies" often had their bands strike up "The Bonnie Blue Flag" or "Dixie" or some other rebel song, and the shabbily-dressed and dust-covered soldiers poured their voices into it. At Carlisle, where the rebels occupied the U.S. military barracks, they also decided to raise a ceremonial banner in honor of their cause.

It was here that the Confederate officers also took the opportunity to taste some captured German lager. But this wasn't any *ordinary* beer; this camouflaged foe had apparently been aged in a whiskey keg, or perhaps even had "ardent spirits" mixed directly into it.

Regardless of the specifics, the result was that Rodes (who by some accounts was normally a moderate drinker) and most of his staff got sloshed—something that would have been unlikely to happen had General Lee been with them at Carlisle.

Major Jedediah Hotchkiss did not need one of his well-drawn maps to see what direction this celebration was headed, remarking,

> Robert Rodes, Junius Daniel, and Isaac Trimble each took a turn speaking. The generals had shared a keg of strong lager beer before the ceremony and as the alcohol took effect, they became increasingly incoherent.

Most of their words lost their way, wandering away in side-street slurs or back-alley mumbles until the more sober among them mercifully removed the worst offenders from the limelight and put them to bed.

Not to be left behind, the enlisted men at Carlisle (approximately 8,000 strong—or slightly more than a tenth of Lee's full force) captured plenty of whiskey in town. There were some reports of soldiers mixing up mint juleps and drinking them from tin cans. The average Johnny Reb with Rodes—like a number of the superior officers—awoke with "sore heads." Then—just a few days later—they marched the better part of thirty miles, south toward Gettysburg. When the battle began on July 1, it seems unlikely that most of them could have felt at their best, given their consumption in the days just prior.

THE YANKEE SCRAMBLE

With Lee's army and its various offshoots already plowing into Pennsylvania, Hooker's army (soon to become General George Meade's army) began its pursuit. Lest one believe that only the Confederates were imbibing in the days just before Gettysburg, a quick glance through various Union journals or diaries proves otherwise; the Boys in Blue were drinking, too.

On June 22, Cormany of the Sixteenth Pennsylvania Cavalry admitted in his diary:

> The Boys found a barrel of whiskey—Got plenty to drink—Some rather too much—men filled their canteens—Strict orders caused the Command to be very cautious—and escape any drunkenness.

But just a week later (on June 29, just two days before Gettysburg), Cormany was lauding his regiment for showing some restraint:

Saw some artillery boys quite drunk, and some cavalry fellows acting like vandals.... We kept our 16th pretty well in line—our Colonel [J. K. Robison] being a good Presbyterian Farmer.

The observations of artillery officer Colonel Charles Wainwright—admitting that some of his cannon crews had too much of the local "tanglefoot"—supports Cormany's version.

We are cheered through all the villages by good wishes and pleasant smiles. Whiskey too is rather abundant; I caught several of my own men drunk, and had them tied by the hand to the rear of a gun so as to insure their keeping up. So soon as I found it out I rode ahead as we approached each village, and emptied all the liquor in the taverns and shops I could put my hands on. This was the provost-marshal's duty, but he contented himself with giving a warning not to sell, instead of removing the evil....

Union officers apparently were drinking, too. On June 28 (about the time Hooker was being replaced by Meade), Peter Vredenburgh Jr., a soldier in the Fourteenth New Jersey Volunteers, wrote home to his father, sharing: "Yesterday Hooker came here from Poolesville. I was introduced to him in General French's tent. Both he and French look as if they drank too much."

At least for French, that "look" apparently was quite standard. While allowing that French had performed "excellent service" during the Fredericksburg debacle, Private John Haley of the Seventeenth Maine nevertheless considered "Old Blinky" less than handsome, to put it kindly, and described him like this:

...so repulsive in appearance as to invite nausea at the sight of his bloated and discolored visage. He looks a perfect old soaker, a devotee of lust and appetite. One eye has a habit of blinking, which makes it seem drunker than the rest of him.

Private Haley would have gotten no argument about "Old Blinky" from Colonel de Trobriand who wrote that French had "a glass and a bottle of whiskey on the table *en permanence.*" Similarly, General David B. Birney, who may have been motivated by jealousy after French was promoted above him, charged that French was "drunk every afternoon, lately screeching drunk."

But drinking among officers was fairly common. Early in the war, a South Carolina newspaper wrote a story on what it was like inside a typical officer's tent. After the usual items one might expect, the writer noted: "[the flask] is an indispensable 'article of war' and go where you may you will find them as plentiful as prayer books on your family tables at home."

The officer's flask, indeed! That item had some of its finest moments during the Battle of Gettysburg, utilized in both the Peach Orchard and during the frenzied and ferocious circumstances surrounding Pickett's Charge.

THE PEACH ORCHARD

The second day of Gettysburg cannot be recounted without mention of the fierce fighting in both the Wheat Field and the Peach Orchard.

General Daniel Sickles, leading the Second Corps, was in the thick of it, and more than a few historians fault him for *causing* it with his impetuous advance away from Little Round Top. Sickles suffered a severe wound from a cannon ball that soon led to the loss of his right leg. But he was not caught unprepared; as he was waiting for assistance, a Yankee private saw him reach inside his officer's jacket and produce "the tiniest flask ever carried by a solider, and wet his lips with its brandy."

According to some accounts, Sickles also lit a big cigar so that his soldiers would get an impression of nonchalance and perhaps think that his wound was not a serious one. Of course, it was, and battlefield doctors soon administered more brandy to Sickles before they removed the general's leg. In contrast to Sickles, when the teetotaler McAllister got hit—blood gushing from his leg wound—he did all he could to *avoid* "stimulants." A doctor implored him to take a swig or two of whiskey to ease the pain, but the commander adamantly refused— perhaps not surprisingly, as General Regis de Trobriand once noted that "[McAllister] never touches liquor of any kind, not even beer." Famously, the battlefield surgeon then proceeded to outflank the general and secretly laced McAllister's milk with a wee bit of "the ardent." According to one New Jersey soldier from McAllister's regi- ment, the commander was sometimes "heard afterward speaking in terms of praise of the milk given by the Gettysburg cows."

LONGSTREET'S CONSOLATION

Such was the confusion as Pickett's Charge fell apart on the third day, that the British observer Colonel Fremantle—who arrived on the scene some minutes after the attack—did not initially com- prehend it. He approached General Longstreet (a.k.a. "Lee's War Horse" or "Old Pete"), who was following the ill-fated frontal assault—a strategy that Longstreet had argued against—from a fence line, and gushed: "I wouldn't have missed this for anything!"

"The devil you wouldn't!" Old Pete snorted. "We've attacked and been repulsed; look there!"

And as Pickett's shattered division—those not dead or cap- tured—limped back, Fremantle suddenly understood all too well, and looked to console Longstreet.

He asked for something to drink. I gave him some rum out of my silver flask, which I begged he would keep in remembrance of the occasion; he smiled, and, to my great satisfaction, accepted the memorial.

Longstreet was probably one of the more consistent imbibers among the CSA's elite generals, at least in between battles. Francis Dawson, an English-born officer on the general's staff, chronicled in his memoirs:

The great American game of poker was played nearly every night.... There was hard drinking as well as high playing; and it was reported after one debauch General Longstreet had played horse with one of the stronger officers of his staff, who on all-fours carried Longstreet around and around the tent until the pair of them rolled over on the ground together.

WILCOX, WHISKEY, AND WORDS OF WISDOM

A scene similar to the Fremantle-Longstreet flask offering took place when General Cadmus Wilcox spotted an apprehensive General George Pickett minutes after the latter's division began its advance across the soon-to-be-bloodied field. Having been Pickett's classmate years before at West Point, Wilcox rode up to his fellow officer and extended his whiskey flask, saying, "Pickett, take a drink with me—In an hour you'll be in hell or glory."

It took less time than an hour, and both men suffered from the sheer hell of that afternoon. When Pickett's initial wave was smashed up, Wilcox's men were sent in for support—whereupon they, too, incurred massive casualties. (Of the estimated 6,000 Johnny Rebs that participated in Pickett's Charge, about half were killed, wounded, or captured.) The British officer Fremantle

Print showing the Battle of Gettysburg. *Courtesy of the Library of Congress.*

reported that Wilcox was on the verge of tears after the attack—which had virtually no chance of success—had crumbled.

PICKETT AND THE WHISKEY WAGON

Years after General George Pickett had died, his wife LaSalle (she was just a teenager when Pickett wooed her) wrote a glowing and embellished book about her famous husband called *Pickett and His Men.* In that book she claimed that the general did not drink at Gettysburg because of a promise he had made to her. With that theme in mind, she described Pickett as refusing Wilcox's offer of a pop from his flask. But contemporaries of General George Pickett portray the Virginian and West Point graduate as at least a practiced imbiber. John Sergeant Wise once said of Pickett, "He was a free liver, and often declared that, to fight like a gentleman, a man must eat and drink like a gentleman."

But did Pickett—an aristocratic general with a lion-like mane featuring ringlets—do more drinking than fighting at Gettysburg? Pickett's detractors suggest that he might have and the controversy still swirls over those accusations concerning the infamous charge forever coupled with his name.

In a recent examination, author Phillip Tucker (in his book *Pickett's Charge: A New Look at Gettysburg's Final Attack*) writes that Pickett was "more of a lover than a fighter" and—although a divisional commander—should have considered leading his men during the historic (if wrongheaded) frontal assault on July 3.

Major Kirkwood Otey of the Eleventh Virginia, wounded in the attack, would write in a newspaper article years later that nobody who took part in the actual charge claims to have seen General Pickett in any forward position. Otey also said that, as he sought medical treatment at the whiskey wagon, he spied several of Pickett's aides there drinking, and concluded that Pickett himself would not have been far from them.

In short, was there any actual "Pickett" in "Pickett's Charge," or was he, in fact, in the vicinity of the whiskey wagon? (Pickett defenders claim that Otey's accusations may have been motivated by some bad blood between the two men.) Confederate Brigadier General Eppa Hunton, in his post-war autobiography, was one of Pickett's most inquisitive critics (though he does not mention the whiskey wagon), writing: "Did Pickett go with his division in the charge? The evidence is pretty strong.... No man who was in the charge has ever been found, within my knowledge, who saw Pickett during the charge." In addition, given the incredible toll on the other rebel officers in the thick of the assault, Hunton found it curious "that neither Pickett or [anyone on] his staff was killed or wounded, or his horse killed." Hunton's conclusion was that Pickett elected to stay back in a relatively safe spot, as did his staff.

Pickett most probably was directing the doomed attack from the back, still close to where the Confederate lines first assembled for the charge. Then the question seems to be, should a divisional commander have been exempt from the dangers (in deference to his higher rank) when—arguably—his presence at the front might have provided *esprit de corps* to his men?

There were other generals, such as Armistead, who could offer no opinion on the matter, as they died or were mortally wounded in the charge named for George Pickett.

ARMISTEAD'S FLASK

The iconic image of General Lewis Armistead (a.k.a. "Lo," for "Lothario") is of the North Carolinian courageously leading his men across an open field against a heavily fortified position on Cemetery Ridge. With his officer's hat stuck on the tip of his waving sword, Armistead appeared as the ultimate warrior to his troops as he led them through sweltering midafternoon heat and a field partially obscured by thick cannon smoke from the massive artillery barrages.

In an amusing contrast, Armistead once won the nickname "The Poplar General" for having allegedly taken refuge behind a tree (and drinking from his officer's flask while doing so) during combat. Whether there was truth behind that story, or whether it was simply a well-spun jest, is difficult to ascertain. But on the third day at Gettysburg, Armistead's courage was front and center— courage well documented by soldiers on both sides.

Along with that courage there was, most certainly, a flask of brandy. Just moments before Pickett's Charge, Armistead approached a Sergeant Blackwell and—according to Corporal James Carter's regimental history of the Fifty-Third Virginia—proclaimed:

> "Sergeant, I want you and your men to plant your colors
> on those works. Do you think you can do it?"
> "Yes, sir, if God is willing."

Then the General, taking out a small flask, told him to take some, which he did.

Fortunately, Armistead kept some of his flask's contents in reserve, for in a matter of minutes, he was going to need a brace of it himself.

Milton Harding, a private in the Ninth Virginia, was just one witness to Armistead's indisputable bravery at Gettysburg. He saw the wounded officer—struck in the arm and chest—plunge to the ground after reaching the enemy's cannons, the so-called "High Water Mark of the Confederacy." "I asked him if I could do anything for him. He requested me to get a small flask of brandy from the satchel he had carried…and from this he drank a swallow or two."

When the attack stalled and then disintegrated, Armistead was soon captured. Yankee privates stretchered the fallen general to the makeshift Union field hospital at Spangler's farm in Gettysburg. He died there on the morning of July 5, while Lee's army was limping back to Virginia—a wagon train of wounded stretching out behind him for miles.

CHAPTER 7

VICKSBURG, RUMORS, AND CHRISTMAS
1863

GRANT AT VICKSBURG

While Union troops were repulsing Lee's invasion at Gettysburg, the Confederates also surrendered the starved-out city of Vicksburg on July 4 to the forces of General U. S. Grant. Since Grant's victory was coupled with the success at Gettysburg, Lincoln (though frustrated with Meade's failure to follow-up against the retreating rebels) and his inner circle felt the war had taken a positive turn. Additionally, after a victory at Port Hudson, the U.S. Navy essentially had control of the Mississippi River.

But there were still persistent rumors about Grant's periodic bouts with the bottle. Lincoln and Stanton were apparently concerned enough to send down Charles Dana—a former journalist who became one of Lincoln's aides—under the pretense of reporting on troop strengths. But Grant probably discerned that Dana was really there to monitor his performance—and perhaps to investigate the rumors of his drinking. In a shrewd move, Grant welcomed Dana into his inner circle, and perhaps the former newspaper man downplayed the extent of the general's imbibing when reporting to his superiors back in Washington.

Not all of Grant's alleged indiscretions came to light during his lifetime. Sylvanus Cadwallader, a journalist from the *Chicago Times* during the war, claimed to have witnessed Grant on a two-day drinking spree during the Vicksburg campaign (including a drunken riverboat incident, followed by an intoxicated gallop along the Yazoo River on a horse dubbed "Kangaroo"). Cadwallader's book (*Three Years with Grant*) was not published until the late 1890s, and when it was, Grant's most devoted advocates blasted it as fabrication.

Grant had several rabid adversaries in the newspaper industry—a fact that seemed to have perplexed him. Foremost was Murat Halstead, an editor from Cincinnati who earlier in the war had sent a letter to Salmon P. Chase, the former Ohio governor and Lincoln's Treasury secretary. In his message, Halstead raged:

> You do once in a while, don't you, say a word to the President, or Stanton, or [General Henry] Halleck, about the conduct of the war? Well, now, for God's sake say that Genl Grant, entrusted with our greatest army is a jackass in the original package.... He is a poor stick sober, and he is most of the time more than half drunk, and much of the time idiotically drunk...

Chase (a temperance man) and others clearly expressed their concerns about Grant's attraction to alcohol. After Grant's victory at Vicksburg, however, Lincoln increasingly ignored the general's detractors. (There is even the probably apocryphal story that, when pestered with complaints of Grant's drinking, Lincoln quipped: "Find out Grant's brand of whiskey and send a barrel of it to my other generals.") In fact, by the next year, Lincoln brought Grant to the East and promoted him to commander of all the armies, answering only to the president, specifically with an aim to end the war.

SHERMAN TO THE DEFENSE

Strangely, Halstead's acrimonious letter did not come to public light until 1885. Grant had recently died, but his old comrade-in-arms General William Tecumseh Sherman was alive and bristling. "Uncle Billy" launched a spirited counterattack against Halstead's charges, which had been reprinted in the *New York Times*. The *Times* reporter remarked, "The [Halstead] letter states that Grant was drunk at [the Battle of Fort] Donelson and surprised and whipped at Shiloh."

Replying sharply, Sherman said:

> That is a pure lie. Gen. Grant never was drunk. At Donelson he won a great victory and at Shiloh we had two hard days' fighting; that doesn't look much like drunkenness, does it? Of course, Gen. Grant took a glass of wine or whisky occasionally. It was necessary. I took a glass of whisky myself once in a while. We could never had [sic] resisted the climate otherwise. Sometimes we worked knee-deep in water; at others we were exposed to unusual fatigues. But to assert that there was anything like drunkenness is a shameful untruth.

THE RAWLINS LETTER

Grant was never short of critics willing to nip at his reputation with wild tales of his drinking. But perhaps it was General John Rawlins—Grant's chief of staff and a longtime friend—who inadvertently provided history with the most damning evidence in a letter to his fiancée. With the exception of Grant's wife Julia (who was not often near the front), nobody took the task of keeping alcohol away from the general as seriously as Rawlins. But, as his letter to his fiancée reveals, he was not always successful. In late 1863, he wrote to her with obvious concern, admitting that,

> Matters have changed, and the necessity of my presence here made almost absolute, by the free use of intoxicating liquors at Head Quarters which last night's developments showed me had reached to the General commanding. I am the only one here (his wife not being with him) who can stay it in that direction and prevent evil consequences resulting from it. I had hoped but it appears vainly that his New Orleans experience would prevent him ever again indulging with his worst enemy.

Rawlins seemed perpetually on guard in Grant's behalf. W. W. Smith, a distant cousin of the general's, recalled in an 1897 interview with the St. Louis *Globe Democrat*:

> Rawlins was always fussing over Grant and was sometimes hasty and went to extremes. I remember once, taking a bottle of wine to the General from his mother. I turned it over to Rawlins and he said abruptly, "Who brought that?" I answered, "I did. The General's mother sent it." Rawlins became very angry and said, "The General's family are all damn fools."

GRANT'S SLIP-UP

Rawlins's reference to General Grant's "New Orleans experience" appears to confirm an incident involving the general's spill on a horse during a military review held in Grant's honor there in September 1863. The event was in New Orleans (firmly in Federal control since May 1862), held primarily to celebrate Grant's career-changing victory at Vicksburg.

When the general and steed crashed to the ground, Grant's leg was trapped underneath. Seriously injured, it took him several weeks to recover. Grant defenders claimed a train whistle spooked the horse and consequently caused the mishap. However, the general's enemies (and even some of Grant's most faithful followers, such as Rawlins) believed the accident occurred because he became intoxicated at a post-parade bash and then attempted to ride a skittish and unfamiliar horse. If Lincoln and his advisors were truly concerned about this incident, they opted to ignore it; Grant's victory at Vicksburg apparently trumped the occasional misstep.

None of this escaped the observant eye of Mary Chesnut, as she noted that even the recipients of Grant's relentless pursuit were forced to acknowledge that his successes were rapidly outstripping his flaws. "Now, since Vicksburg they have not a word to say about Grant's habits. He has the disagreeable habit of not retreating...."

And nobody understood that better than President Lincoln.

CHICKAMAUGA

On September 19–20, Confederate General Braxton Bragg provided the South with some good news when his army defeated General William Rosecrans in northern Georgia at Chickamauga and forced the Yankees back to Chattanooga.

Chickamauga was the war's bloodiest battle in the Western Theater (with more than 30,000 combined casualties), and surgeons were once again working long hours treating the wounded as best they could. Not surprisingly, whiskey was still a valuable tool for this onerous job. Dr. William Graham, a surgeon for the 101st Indiana, recalled treating a wounded soldier in unbearable pain, imploring the doctor for some kind of help.

I studied [him] a moment and thought nothing would do him much good, but decided to give him a drink of whiskey. I procured a half teacup full and held up his head and he swallowed it. I then dressed his wound and left him thinking he would be dead in the morning, but I found him better and he said then, and many times to me since the war, that the whiskey saved his life.

The whiskey treatment was, of course, quite common. But the results weren't always quite so successful.

THE ONE-MINUTE BRANDY FIX

The Battle of Bristoe Station in Virginia, fought in mid-October of 1863, was a Union victory, with General Gouverneur K. Warren smack in the middle of it. Warren devised a devious snare for approaching Confederate infantry from General Henry Heath's division, quickly concealing his men behind a railroad embankment that proved to be a perfect defensive position and gave them a deadly advantage over advancing rebels.

Although Warren's troops inflicted more casualties on the attacking rebels, they eventually had to withdraw when General Richard Ewell came up with even more Butternuts. Warren arrived back at headquarters between elation and fatigue. As Colonel Theodore Lyman wrote in his memoirs:

An hour before daylight came General Warren, exhausted with two nights' marching and a day's fighting, but springy and stout to the last. "We whipped the Rebs right out," he said. "I ran my men, on the double-quick, into the railroad cut and then just swept them with musketry." I got up and gave him a little brandy from my flask; he lay down and was fast asleep in about a minute.

Even when he wasn't battle-weary, General Warren—like U. S. Grant—may have suffered from low alcohol tolerance. Colonel Thomas Livermore describes Warren as getting the worst of a spirited joust with John Barleycorn one night in camp. Drawn by noise to a tent, Livermore walked in on Warren and two other officers apparently enjoying a whiskey punch with lemons.

> They were discussing punch and the exploits of the Second Corps in an enthusiastic way. Their lemons gave out and I went for more...
>
> When I came back, I saw Haskell and Bingham looking on at the struggles of the general, who had got his legs entangled among the tent ropes outside. Haskell proffered his aid, but the general gravely said, "No assistance is required," and extricating himself, started for the house. He met a little sapling with such force as to prostrate him, whereupon Haskell ran to help him up. He grasped Haskell and raised a great outcry to the effect that Haskell had knocked him down, and called for the guard and threatened to turn out the Second Corps, and no expostulations of Haskell convinced him of his error.

Colonel Livermore and other officers finally managed to lug the quarrelsome Warren to his sleeping quarters. But the next day, Warren asked Livermore to share dinner with him, and, somewhat sheepishly, asked about the details from the previous night. "I told him in as mild tones as I could invent," recalled Livermore, "and he vowed he would touch no more whiskey."

Warren—arguably one of the heroes of Gettysburg for recognizing that Little Round Top needed to be occupied and defended—had a somewhat checkered Civil War career. Just days before the end of hostilities in Virginia he was relieved of command (at the insistence of an irate General Phil Sheridan) for allegedly moving too slowly and not to the precise position requested at the Battle of Five Forks. Stunned, Warren challenged what he viewed as grossly unfair charges for the rest of his life. Eventually, during the administration of President Rutherford B. Hayes, the original charges were deemed to be unwarranted. Unfortunately, General Warren, who died in 1882, did not live long enough to revel in his official vindication.

A TOAST AT MISSIONARY RIDGE

Despite the defeats at both Gettysburg and Vicksburg, the war continued to grind on, both East and West. And drinking, whenever possible, continued to offer soldiers some temporary solace from the brutal realities. In the case of General Philip Sheridan, it also produced an amusing incident. During the Battle of Missionary Ridge on November 25, Sheridan (who would later achieve great notoriety as a cavalryman in the Shenandoah) glanced up at the heights. There he spied what appeared to be several rebel officers and he could not resist a mock toast to them with his silver whiskey flask.

But no sooner had Sheridan done so than an artillery shell landed close to him and splashed dirt on his boots and uniform. To which Little Phil—a diminutive Irishman with the disposition of a bantam fighting cock—allegedly blurted out: "That was damned ungenerous! I will take your guns for that!"

Coincidental or not, Union troops—apparently misinterpreting an order to merely take some enemy rifle pits at the base of the steep ridge—just kept going; they scaled the bluffs and seized control of the heights above Chattanooga, thereby lifting a siege of that key city on the Tennessee River.

SNEDEN GETS GOBBLED

"Gobbled" was a slang term that Civil War soldiers sometimes used to mean getting captured. In late November, the diligent diarist and artist Private Robert Knox Sneden became a prisoner of Mosby's Rangers and provided an intricate description of the notorious guerrilla horsemen. Sneden described Colonel John Mosby (the much-vaunted "Gray Ghost of the Confederacy") as "an undersized, thin visaged looking fellow, with a sickly looking yellow mustache."

Mosby himself was not a drinker, as he had been traumatized as a young lad when he witnessed his schoolmaster passed-out drunk by the roadside. Whether his sober state was a factor or not, the Gray Ghost was quite skilled at snagging Union officers—even generals—who were caught napping or sleeping off the aftermath of a bout with the bottle. Mosby's most famous exploit along that line occurred on March 9, 1863, when he captured a champagne-groggy U.S. Brig. Gen. Edwin Stoughton in his sleeping quarters at Fairfax Court House, Virginia.

But Mosby's men—a motley-looking crew of slouched hats, drab patchy attire (including some blue coats that made them resemble Yankees, when needed), and rough habits—were fond of drinking a regional concoction. Sneden (who would soon be delivered to Libby Prison in Richmond) described a major in the infamous unit thusly: "He swore like a dragoon all the time, and appeared to be drunk on the vile pine top whiskey made by the farmers in these parts."

The historian William C. Davis actually adds a recipe for pine top whiskey in his book *A Taste for War: The Culinary History of the Blue and the Gray*. Basically it involves boiling a half-pound of pine needles in a quart of water for thirty minutes, then straining the stuff into a large batch of pure grain alcohol.

Davis then concludes: "It does not taste very good."

MUSCOVITES MADE JOLLY

Europeans took a keen interest in the American Civil War and it was not uncommon for both sides to get occasional visits from foreigners—typically military observers or journalists and predominately men hailing from either England or France.

However, in early December of 1863, General George Gordon Meade wrote of a more curious visit from the eastern fringes of the European continent. This impromptu reception had its humorous moments, too, as Meade noted in a letter to his wife:

> I received yesterday your letter of the 13th...and would have answered it at once but around 2 p.m. we had a sudden invasion of Muscovites, some twenty-four officers of the fleet and I had to give them my full attention till after 10 p.m.... I had the Sixth Corps paraded and some artillery to show them. We had great fun with them in mounting them on horseback; which they all insisted on attempting; but we had not preceded far before one was thrown and half a dozen were run away with. After the review we gave them dinner, with plenty of brandy and whisky, and, making them jolly, sent them back highly delighted with their visit and reception. They appeared intelligent and gentlemanly, almost all speaking English quite well.

THE CHESNUTS: LEVITY AND REALITY

As the Christmas season of 1863 approached, Mary Chesnut was still in Richmond, where her husband Colonel James Chesnut Jr. served as a top aide to Jefferson Davis. A man who certainly grasped the seriousness of the war with the North, Chesnut sometimes chided his wife for her lavish splurges on the social scene. Both a party-thrower and partygoer, Mary continued to embrace her own curious wartime philosophy of "Eat, drink, and be merry—for tomorrow we may die!"

Despite his occasional reprimands, Mary secretively got together a holiday party, thinking her husband would be at Jefferson Davis's presidential home that evening. To her surprise,

He came straight home and found the party in full blast.

He did not know a word about it. How could he? It grew up after he left home. I trembled in my shoes.

He behaved beautifully, however.

If he had refused to dine at the president's because he wished to attend a party at my house, he could not have done better. He seemed to enjoy the whole thing amazingly. Played casino with Mrs. Lawson Clay, looked after [the wounded Gen. John B.] Hood, &c&c.

Today he spoke. I was very penitent, subdued, submissive, humble. And I promised not to do so anymore.

"No more parties," he said. "The country is in danger. There is too much levity here."

So he laid down the law.

But even after she was forced to flee south to the Carolinas in 1864, Mary Chesnut—though the best foods, wines, and brandies became more difficult to obtain—never fully relinquished the social scene. Her knack for bringing together a magnificent, civilized dinner party with bottles of equivalent merit brought generals, politicians, and friends to her table, even as Old Dixie crumbled around them.

CHRISTMAS IN PRISON

Soldiers captured in the Civil War still wanted—and sometimes even found a way to obtain—alcohol, particularly around the holidays.

Robert Sneden, snagged by Mosby and his guerrillas the month earlier, found himself enduring the degrading conditions at Libby Prison in Richmond. He rants in his diary that his Christmas dinner of cornbread, rice, and "goober bean soup" was "vile food" but that the Yankee prisoners were so famished that they wolfed it down nonetheless. Whiskey or even some German lager might have helped wash down the foul fare, but, sadly, Sneden had none.

Unfortunately for Sneden and his fellow prisoners, the rebel guards at Libby had *plenty* to drink. His 1863 Christmas diary entry read:

> All the guards and their officers were more or less drunk all day. Many fell down hopelessly drunk while on post, when another fellow was put in his place. Several fired their muskets right into the upper stories of Libby.

Apparently, whiskey only made the ordeal of imprisonment *slightly* more bearable. Virginian John Dooley, captured at Gettysburg when he was shot in both thighs during Pickett's Charge, found himself in a Union prison camp on an island in Lake Erie, several miles off shore from Sandusky, Ohio. Perhaps naïvely, Dooley had given a hospital staffer a few bottles of whiskey, hoping that the keeper would occasionally slip him some from the stash. But as Dooley's holiday entry reveals, his faith was fading:

> 25th. Christmas Day. Dismal Christmas! Alas, it is all the more gloomy because we can't help thinking of the loved ones at home, and the brighter the outer world, the denser grow our prison shadows. The hospital steward promised me another bottle of my whiskey, but he is a gay deceiver and so goodbye to any more whiskey. Pete and I are determined to have something extra for our Christmas dinner, so we make a bread pudding of the crusts of many a day's rations and the remnant of our sugar, and have moreover *sauce à la bourbon*. We drink the last of our whiskey at night.

Sauce à la bourbon indeed! Small consolation for Dooley perhaps, but a treat that the spiritless Sneden would have relished.

CHAPTER 8

MEANWHILE, BACK IN THE CAPITALS
1863

While the soldiers slugged it out on the various battlefields, life in Washington, D.C. (and, to some extent, Richmond before the very end), managed to maintain a vivacious social atmosphere. At the center of social life in Washington was the Willard Hotel, situated a few blocks from the White House. It had been the site of the failed peace conference in February of 1861, and guests at a dinner there in 1864 gave U. S. Grant a rousing ovation in response to the news that President Lincoln had promoted him to head all the Union armies.

The Willard was also the place to get a fancy cocktail or two *and* take in the latest gossip about the war against the secessionists. A grand description of the Willard's barroom during the war years flowed from the pen of celebrated author Nathaniel Hawthorne, who wrote in an *Atlantic Monthly* article:

> You adopt the universal habit of the place, and call for a mint julep, a whiskey skin, a gin cock-tail, a brandy smash or a glass of pure Old Rye, for the conviviality of Washington sets in at an early hour and, so far as I had an opportunity of observing, never terminates at any hour.

Journalists lurked at the Willard and other drinking establishments frequented by Union brass, hoping to glean a hot tip from loose-tongued officers. Sometimes a bought round or two did the trick. When *New-York Tribune* editor Horace Greeley complained about the bloated expense account of reporter Charles Page, his man glibly responded: "Early news is expensive news, Mister Greeley. If I have watermelons and whiskey ready when the officers come along from the fight, I get the news without asking questions."

Of course, for those not well-heeled enough to drink cocktails at the Willard or the Metropolitan Hotel, there were dozens and dozens of bawdy taverns, gambling dens, flophouses, and small liquor shops where the booze flowed freely and collided head-on with a variety of other vices.

ALCOHOL AT THE WHITE HOUSE

Although he had worked at a whiskey still as a young man, and sold whiskey at a "grocery" prior to his career in law and politics, Abraham Lincoln was *not* a drinking man. That did not, however, prevent well-wishing Americans from sending the commander in chief a virtual avalanche of alcohol as gifts. As William Osborn Stoddard, an assistant secretary under Lincoln, noted in his book *Inside the White House in War Times*, there was a room at the executive mansion set aside for these incoming liquid gifts.

> There are loads of champagne...red wines of several
> kinds, white wine from the Rhine, wines of Spain and
> Portugal and the islands; whiskey distilled from rye, and
> from wheat, and from potatoes; choice brandy; Jamaica
> rum, and Santa Cruz rum; and she [Mary Todd Lincoln]
> suspects one case containing gin.

When Mrs. Lincoln voiced concern over what to do with this
roomful of potent potables, Stoddard suggested giving it to the
military hospitals to treat the wounded soldiers. The Lincolns
apparently followed that advice.

LINCOLN'S SENSE OF (ALCOHOL) HUMOR

While Abe Lincoln lacked a real thirst for alcohol (there is some
meager evidence that he might have sampled "small beer" on rare
occasions), his wry sense of humor found John Barleycorn an easy
target. Lincoln was quite fond of storytelling, and alcohol sometimes came up in his homespun yarns.

Stoddard noted in his book what would happen when the
staff would pour the president a glass of wine at the dinner
hour.

> There is wine here, and a bottle of champagne has been
> opened! A glass of it has been put by the President's plate,
> and he seems to be taking more than a little interest in
> it. He takes it up and smells of it, and laughs merrily, but
> he does not drink. There is a story connected with that
> glass of wine, and after it is told he has more than one
> of his own to tell in return.

Years later, Robert T. Lincoln, the president's son, allowed:

I never saw him use spirituous liquors, and I do not think he ever did so—I have seen him take a taste of wine at his own dinner table in Washington, but only once or twice and I am sure it was no pleasure to him.

SEASICK ASHORE

Later in the war, President Lincoln arrived by steamer at General Grant's headquarters on the James River in Virginia. Grant was planning the Petersburg siege. Lincoln had his own challenges; recently renominated by his party, the president was preparing to face General George B. McClellan, the Democratic candidate, in November. Continued success of the Union war effort would, of course, help Lincoln's chances.

But the voyage had been over choppy waters, and Lincoln arrived with an upset stomach. As Lieutenant Colonel Horace Porter chronicled in his book *Campaigning with Grant*, the president admitted his discomfort to Grant and his staff when the officers inquired after the president's health.

> "Yes, I am in very good health," Mr. Lincoln replied; "but I don't feel very comfortable after my trip last night on the [Chesapeake] bay. It was rough, and I was considerably shaken up. My stomach has not yet recovered from the effects."
>
> An officer of the party now saw that an opportunity had arisen to make this scene the supreme moment of his life, in giving him a chance to soothe the digestive organs of the Chief Magistrate of the nation. He said: "Try a glass of champagne, Mr. President. That is always a certain cure for seasickness."
>
> Mr. Lincoln looked at him for a moment, his face lighting up with a smile, and then remarked: "No, my

friend; I have seen too many fellows seasick ashore from drinking that very stuff." This was knockdown for the officer, and in the laugh at his expense Mr. Lincoln and the general both joined heartily.

WARTIME RICHMOND

The Confederate counterpart to the Willard was the Spotswood Hotel in Richmond, where government higher-ups and prominent military officers were likely to be seen. In the early days of the war, President Jefferson Davis gave a rousing speech there, much to the delight of a crowd numbering in the thousands. During the war, if an officer of renown came to town—for example, the guerilla cavalry commanders William Quantrill and John Morgan—the newspapers would announce their appearances at the Spotswood or another noteworthy hotel. When most of Richmond burned in 1865, the Spotswood Hotel—by the mere whim of the wind—somehow avoided that fate. However, it was a temporary reprieve; the historic structure burned down on Christmas night in 1870.

Just like Washington, Richmond (which had grown rapidly to more than 120,000 inhabitants during the war years) also was awash in alcohol and its related sins of prostitution and gambling. The most depraved establishments—dozens of gambling dens and brothels—were located on Locust Alley, not far from the Exchange Hotel.

For those looking to avoid the scrutiny of the authorities, however, Drewry's Bluff—the heights overlooking the James River—was an attractive spot. However, in a July 17, 1863, article in the *Richmond Examiner*, the editor chronicled how the forces of morality were poised to crack down on the Bluff:

Visitors to Drewry's Bluff—We understand that no more passports will be issued to parties of pleasure seekers to visit the Bluff for the present. The commandant, Capt.

Lee, has been compelled to protect against these excursions, from the fact that among a great many respectable people who visited the Bluff, a few were found disreputable enough to introduce lewd women and whiskey, to the danger of dismoralization [sic] among the soldiers.

1864

"*The deep waters [are] closing over us. And we are—in this house—like the outsiders at the time of the Flood. We care for none of these things. We eat, drink, laugh, dance, in lightness of heart!!!*"

—Mary Chesnut

CHAPTER 9

DRINKS ON THE SINKING SHIP
1864

M ary Chesnut—the renowned diarist of the Confederacy—
began her New Year's Day in 1864 with an intriguing entry.
In recounting a dinner party conversation, Chesnut showed
how her aristocratic circle of friends were dealing with the sobering
reality of the Confederacy's precarious position in 1864:

> Jan. 1, 1864
> God help my country.
> Table talk.
> "After the battles around Richmond, hope was strong
> in me. All that has insensibly drifted away."
> "I am like David after the child was dead. Get up,
> wash my face, have my hair cut, &c &c"
> "That's too bad. I think we are more like sailors who
> break into the spirits closet when they find out the ship

must sink. There seems to be for the first time a resolute feeling to enjoy the brief hour and never look beyond the day."

"I now long, pine, pray—and—well, I have no hope. Have you any of old Mr. Chesnut's brandy here still?"

Mary then instructed the servant to get the key and bring back a decanter of her father-in-law's fine brandy for her somber guests. Her thought process seemed to be: If the Yankees are closing in, why not break out the very best brandy and savor whatever fading eloquence Old Dixie has to offer?

GENERAL HUMPHREYS ENTERTAINS

The Army of the Potomac may have gone through McClellan, Burnside, and Hooker at its head, but even with the rather dour General George Gordon Meade in command, the champagne was still flowing quite freely—despite Secretary of War Stanton's earlier insistence that the flagrant indulgence stop.

Champagne was the drink of choice when a number of "ladies" visited the Union front (an unusual occurrence) in late January, as Colonel Theodore Lyman documented. He was summoned to General Andrew Humphreys's tent from "whence came a sound of revelry and champagne corks." And, indeed, Lyman found a dozen or so women (one of whom had a badge of the Third Corps pinned "askew" to her hat) and perhaps twice as many officers hobnobbing in the tent. As Lyman noted:

> Such a set of feminine humans I have not seen often; it was Lowell factories broken loose and gone mad…And there was General Humphreys all red in the face and smiling like a basket of chips, and hopping round with a champagne bottle, with all the spring of a boy of sixteen. He spied me at once and introduced me to a Mrs. M, who

once married somebody who treated her very badly, and afterwards fortunately went up; so Mrs. M seemed determined to make up lost time and be jolly in her liberty. She was quite bright; also quite warm and red in the face, with hard riding and, probably, champagne.

Colonel Lyman said the party—with General Humphreys an exuberant participant—then proceeded to visit other generals in the Union camp, both riding and drinking. By the time Lyman got back to the relative calm of his own tent, it was dark.

GRANT GETS THE CALL

On the strength of Grant's victories in the West, particularly the capture of Vicksburg, President Lincoln promoted Grant to lieutenant general (the first commander since George Washington to achieve that rank) on March 9. However, rumors of his periodic collisions with Demon Alcohol continued to dog Grant. Though you will look in vain if you attempt to find any direct mention of it in the general's own memoirs, an avalanche of evidence from friends, foes, and neutral parties should leave very little doubt that Grant had a serious nemesis when it came to the bottle. Furthermore, Grant himself knew it and—occasional regressions aside—fought against his Achilles heel.

Take, for example, an entry from General John Schofield's *Forty-Six Years in the Army*:

> In St. Louis I met General Grant, who was then so soon to be assigned to the command of "all the armies of the United States," and for the first time really became acquainted with him. We were together much of the time for several days and nights. The citizens of St. Louis entertained the general in a most magnificent manner. At a grand banquet given in his honor, at which I sat on his right, he did not even

touch one of the many glasses of wine placed by the side of his plate. At length I ventured to remark that he had not tasted his wine. He replied: "I dare not touch it. Sometimes I drink freely without any unpleasant effect; at others I cannot take even a single glass of light wine." A strong man, indeed, who could thus know his own weakness! In reply to the toast in his honor, he merely arose and bowed without saying a word. Then turning to me, he said it was simply impossible for him to utter a word when on his feet. As is well known, the great general finally overcame his reserve.

But there were some not overly enthusiastic about Grant coming back East to be *the* commander. And Grant's drinking history had a bit to do with that feeling, as artillery officer Colonel Charles Wainwright admitted in his diary on March 10:

It is now certain that Grant is to have the new post of lieutenant-general, just created by act of Congress. This marks him officially as our major-general "most distinguished for courage, skill, and ability." I trust that he may prove himself so, and not only that, but equal in all respects to the greatest generals of history. But it is hard for those who knew him formerly in the army to believe that he is a great man; then he was only distinguished for the mediocrity of his mind, his great good nature and his insatiable love of whiskey...

Even very late in 1864, when it was quite clear that Lincoln was going to win or lose with Grant in command, Secretary of the Navy Gideon Welles admitted his guarded suspicions concerning the Union's top general and his periodic bouts with John Barleycorn, writing,

Fox [Gustavus Fox, assistant secretary of the Navy] says Grant occasionally gets drunk. I have never mentioned the fact to anyone—not even to my wife, who can be trusted with a secret. There are such rumors of him when [he was in the] west...

SNOWBALLS AND WHISKEY

After the setbacks at Chattanooga, the rebel forces reformed their defenses in northern Georgia, anticipating that the Yankees would eventually attempt to pressure the key city and rail hub of Atlanta. Approximately 40,000 Confederate soldiers under General Joe Johnston encamped just west of Dalton, Georgia, for the winter.

Imagine their surprise when on March 22—technically the second day of spring—the boys in gray opened their tent flaps and were greeted by five or six inches of freshly fallen snow! Since "boredom killing" took up much of the time between real battles, it was not long after breakfast before thousands of soldiers engaged in a gigantic series of snowball skirmishes.

General Patrick Cleburne, who gleefully led on his former Arkansas regiments in the snowball "charges" against similarly spirited units, was among the participants. The Irish-born commander was soon "captured" (but then "paroled"). Despite the rough play—faces washed in snow, a slew of bruises and black eyes, plus a busted nose or three—the donnybrook continued sporadically for several hours.

When fatigue finally set in, Cleburne only added to his popularity with his troops by granting a whiskey ration to be served all around. For the beleaguered Confederates—who had primarily been subsisting on cornbread, potatoes, and occasionally beef throughout the harsh winter—the jiggers of whiskey around crackling fires were no doubt a welcome respite from the horrors of a war they were losing.

Later in the year, Cleburne would meet his death in the Battle of Franklin—one of several Confederate generals to fall on the field that day.

THE FORT PILLOW MASSACRE: WHISKEY ON THE WALLS

Perhaps one of the most controversial incidents of the war involved CSA cavalry General Nathan Bedford Forrest and the so-called "Fort Pillow Massacre"—a dark day in American history in which whiskey most certainly played a role.

Forrest himself was *not* a drinker; in fact, one of his staff officers once stated that he only observed the general drink "liquor" (which is what Forrest apparently called it, whether it was brandy or whiskey or rum) on two occasions—both times when he was wounded and advised to take a few swallows by an army surgeon.

Forrest's troops had recently conducted a series of successful raids in both western Kentucky and Tennessee during the month of March. General Forrest—"The Wizard of the Saddle"—approached Fort Pillow (situated north of Memphis on the Mississippi River) primarily to replenish his cavalry with fresh horses and supplies. On April 12, greatly out-numbering the garrison of about 600 men, the Confederates, under a flag of truce, demanded an immediate surrender, and, by some accounts, said they would show "no quarter" to the defenders if they chose to fight. The surrender was refused. In the subsequent attack, Forrest's hardened veterans captured some outer positions around the fort (including some barrels of whiskey that some Johnnies certainly sampled).

Soon it was clear the Union defenders—comprised almost equally of black and white troops—were unlikely to hold. Most of the hapless Yankees abruptly fled the fort and headed for the river where they hoped Union gunboats might provide cover or escape. But according to the rebels, many of the defenders were intoxicated on barrels of alcohol that were situated on the very walls of the

Newspaper illustration showing the Fort Pillow Massacre. *Courtesy of the Library of Congress.*

fort. The insinuation seemed to be that these soldiers—emboldened by booze—were too fired up to surrender. As Forrest himself later told it:

> The citizens and Yankees had broken in the heads of whiskey and lager-beer barrels, and were all drunk. They kept up firing all the time as they went down the hill. Hundreds of them rushed to the river and tried to swim to the gunboats, and my men shot them down. The Mississippi was red with their blood for three hundred yards.

Forrest then claimed he rushed to cut down the flag inside the fort, to signal to his men that the bastion was in Confederate hands, and thereby "stopped the fight."

"Stopped the slaughter" was more in line with the Northern view on the battle. With more than 180 Union casualties (the Confederates had fourteen men killed in the attack and dozens wounded, by comparison), there were soon charges that the rebels ignored pleas of surrender, especially from black troops. A special U.S. Congressional subcommittee claimed that even women and young children were not spared in the bloody aftermath of the assault and that only the absence of "tomahawks and scalping knives" differentiated the incident at Fort Pillow from a massacre conducted by "savages." The Fort Pillow massacre became a rallying cry for Union troops later in the year, particularly (with even bloodier results) at the Battle of the Crater.

General Forrest (who eventually joined the Ku Klux Klan in post-war years, and purportedly may have served as a Grand Wizard) was darkly shadowed by the incident throughout the rest of his life, though he always maintained that he and his men acted within the parameters of warfare.

THE BRANDY BARRAGE AT LAUREL HILL

On May 8, Union forces (under General Warren and General John Sedgwick) moved toward Spotsylvania Court House, Virginia. But they were initially surprised and stopped by CSA forces under General Richard Anderson on the heights of Laurel Hill. The battle, in various forms, raged for nearly two weeks and—with neither side making any substantial headway—cost approximately 18,000 Union casualties and 12,000 Confederate casualties.

Amid the hellishness (including the infamous assault at the "Bloody Angle"), there occurred a strange incident at Laurel Hill, where the Thirty-Ninth Massachusetts was pinned down under a cannonading. As told in the regimental history:

> On the 10th of May at Laurel Hill, our men were lying flat upon the ground, under artillery fire…When a piece of shell ripped out the breast of his [Colonel Charles L. Peirson's] coat, smashed his field glasses in his case, and jammed the hilt of his sword. He doubled up, fell forward on his head, and then over sideways.

An officer a bit to the rear called up to a lieutenant and asked if the beloved Colonel Peirson was dead. The initial answer was "Yes," but that analysis proved premature. Colonel Peirson was certainly injured, but he came around blinking.

Peirson was described as "strictly a Temperance man," but he nonetheless carried a flask of brandy for emergencies and had told his officers to give him some in the event he was wounded in battle. However, the same shell fragment that crushed his field glasses and ruined his officer's jacket also cut his brandy flask in half, and it fell in front of a Private Richardson. Richardson promptly drained the last few ounces and announced: "They are throwing good brandy at us!"

THE THINGS THEY CARRIED

Like Colonel Peirson, Colonel James A. Beaver in the 148th Pennsylvania Regiment—a future governor of Pennsylvania—was a very temperate officer, which, in the Civil War, was an exception to the rule. In the same Spotsylvania campaign, Beaver found himself carrying a wounded officer across the Po River. He then crashed to the ground on the opposite bank, extremely exhausted from the ordeal. In an effort to stimulate the colonel, an attentive artilleryman rushed up and offered Beaver a flask of whiskey.

"I drank it down, and although strangled, felt immediately revived," Beaver later claimed. "It was the only drink of whiskey I took during the war."

JEB STUART'S DEMISE AND A RELUCTANT SIP OF WHISKEY

As part of the "Overland Campaign," General Phil Sheridan went around General Meade and directly to General U. S. Grant with a battle plan. Grant gave his blessing for a sizeable cavalry raid toward Richmond, with Sheridan's goal being to engage Jeb Stuart's cavalry troops head-on and also to worry Lee about defending the rebels' capital city.

About six miles north of Richmond, Sheridan's cavalry (estimates between 10,000 and 12,000 strong) clashed with Stuart's greatly outnumbered men (less than 5,000) near an abandoned inn at the Battle of Yellow Tavern on May 11. In an attempt to rally his men in a counterattack, Stuart was "gut shot" by a dismounted Michigan cavalryman named John Huff and barely managed to keep his saddle and get back to rebel lines. A Virginia trooper said he saw Stuart slump in his saddle, and his trademark plumed cavalry hat fall from his head.

Fearing (correctly) that the wound would be a fatal one, Stuart's staff tumbled the dashing cavalier into an ambulance and headed to the nearby capital, specifically the house on Green Street of his brother-in-law, one Dr. Charles Brewer. En route, the general's staff insisted that Stuart drink some whiskey. The weakened Stuart initially refused—the reason being that he had promised his mother that he would never let whiskey touch his lips—but apparently he did take a few swigs of spirits from a canteen to ease his pain.

President Jefferson Davis came to visit Stuart the next day, May 12. But the hero of Confederate cavalry glory would not live to see another sunrise. The Richmond *Examiner* wrote of his final hours:

> In moments of delirium the General's mind wandered, and like the immortal Jackson (whose spirit, we trust, he has joined) in the lapse of reason, his faculties were busy with the details of his command. He reviewed in broken sentences all his glorious campaigns...

Gettysburg was probably not one of them. Despite his many audacious raids and attacks, most historians fault Stuart's late arrival at Gettysburg as one of the reasons the Confederates failed in that pivotal battle.

GENERAL SIGEL'S LAMENT: "I VILL CATCH DOT DAM TIEF"

Warriors across the centuries have interpreted random incidents before battle as good or bad omens. On the Sunday morning of May 15, with dawn just washing over the Union camp in the Shenandoah Valley, perhaps General Franz Sigel's missing brandy flask should have been considered an omen.

Colonel David Hunter Strother of Sigel's staff captured the comic incident in his diary:

Rose early and tents were struck. While the troops were moving and everyone about packing up, General Sigel came out of the house at a full run towards the camp of teamsters and Negro servants. His high boots were hanging down and altogether he cut a very absurd figure as he ran, exclaiming at every jump, "By Got, I vill catch dot dam tief." It seems that in moving he had lost a favorite brandy flask and was accusing everyone he met of stealing it.

In a matter of hours, Sigel's problems soon loomed larger than a lost drinking flask, as the Battle of New Market commenced. Rebels under General John Breckinridge advanced rapidly on Union lines. A swig or two of brandy might have come in handy in terms of soothing Sigel's nerves, as Strother noted:

Sigel seemed in a state of excitement and rode here and there with Stahel and Moor, all jabbering in German. In his excitement, he seemed to forget his English entirely, and the purely American portion of his staff were totally useless to him. I followed him up and down until I got tired, and, finding a group of his staff officers together near a battery, I stopped and got a drink of whiskey and a cracker which an artillery man gave me.

The Confederates eventually carried the day and sent Sigel's troops scurrying north to Strasburg in a brisk retreat. A frustrated General Grant then replaced the German commander with General David "Black Dave" Hunter.

Among the victorious rebels were more than 200 young cadets from the Virginia Military Institute (all of whom Breckinridge called into the fray when necessity overrode his reluctance to put teenagers into real battle), including John Sergeant

Wise, a mere seventeen years old at the time. They suffered more than fifty casualties, but shared in the glory. The VMI cadets were honored in Richmond not long after, and as Wise described it they were "cheered by ten thousand throats, intoxicated with praise unstinted."

LAGER AND "THOSE DAMN DUTCH"

Like the Irish immigrants, who often are discussed disparagingly in Civil War diaries, the German immigrants absorbed a lot of ink-stained guff. As with the Irish, some of the barrages directed toward the Germans (often erroneously referred to as "Dutch"—a fumbled version of the word "Deutsch") are humorous and—when they are—typically make fun of both the Germans' accents *and* their consumption of alcohol.

The German love of lager beer, of course, was well established before they took up arms in the War of the Rebellion. But their insistence in having lager, whenever possible, as a necessary part of their daily nourishment, often invited comment. Indeed, Karl Heinzen—a publisher and editor of a communist journal titled *The Pioneer*—is alleged to have written: "The first theater of the Civil War for Germans was the beer hall."

There even was a song making fun of the Germans, called "I Goes to Fight Mit Sigel."

> Ven I comes from der Deutsche Countree,
> I vorks somedimes at baking;
> Den I keeps a lager beer saloon,
> Und den I goes shoe-making;
> But now I was a sojer been
> To save der Yankee Eagle,
> To schlauch dem tam secession volks,
> I goes to fight mit Sigel.

It is not to say that being German did not occasionally have an odd benefit, as some war histories claim that a soldier on leave in St. Louis might be treated to a free stein of lager simply by declaring that he fought "mit Sigel."

A POOR CHOICE OF PHRASE

German regiments were given a much freer hand when it came to alcohol consumption. Their camp beer gardens, with kegs of lager aplenty, reflected what most Germans—even the officers—viewed as a necessary part of their culture. But although the average German soldier was no stranger to a frothy stein, overindulgence could still lead to problems of insubordination. A classic case was documented in a letter from Carl Uterhard—a surgeon with the 119th New York Infantry Volunteers.

> My dear Mama,
>
> Here they have a special way of celebrating days of significance, they drink liquor. From the generals down to the common soldiers, they all drink liquor to celebrate happy events or to suppress miserable memories. They don't drink it out of glasses, but from the bottle, and get alarmingly intoxicated as a result. Every day, dozens of officers are dishonorably discharged without pay because they drank themselves into oblivion. A few days ago our regiment lost an officer this way, a Bavarian named Brunner, who was otherwise a good and decent officer, but then he got drunk and after he insulted our brigadier general Chrysanowsky [Kryzanowski], he went to our division general Carl Schurz and said the classic words: "Kiss my a—."

Officer Brunner sure knew how to pick them. General Schurz was only one of the most famous Germans in America and went on to become a U.S. senator and the U.S. Secretary of the Interior under President Hayes. There is no record of what became of Brunner.

"WHERE'S THAT DAMN JOHNNY REB?"

Rebel Colonel John Fite of Tennessee, captured at Gettysburg, spent some time in the Union prison at Fort Delaware (prior to a transfer to an Ohio prison on Johnson's Island). Extraordinarily energetic in his acquisition of alcohol, Fite managed to persuade Brigadier General Albin Schoepf (the prison commandant whom Fite erroneously identifies as "General Sheef" in his memoirs) to grant him a favor:

> [Gen. Sheef] talked might clever, saying he was sorry he wasn't allowed to do more for us than he was....
>
> About the time the General was getting ready to leave us, I said; "General, you are a German, and so am I, and you know a Dutchman can't live without his beer." He said: "That's so." He asked if we had any paper and pen and ink there. We got him out some.... He ordered this fellow that he had with him to write a permit for me to buy two gallons of beer a day and gave me that paper.

The ever-clever Fite, carrying a big bucket and some money pooled together by his fellow prisoners, proceeded to use Schoepf's note to get through several checkpoints and arrived at the lager tent outside the prison walls. Once inside the tent, Fite treated several Yankee soldiers there to a round of beers, then bought as much sausage, cheese, crackers, and sardines as his tattered pockets could hold. However, the resourceful rebel soon had his wings clipped.

> About that time a fellow came to the door, poked his head in, and said: "Where's that damn Johnny Reb?" I

Photograph showing the remains of soldiers killed in the Battle of Cold Harbor. *Courtesy of the Library of Congress.*

said: "Here I am." And he said, "The General never intended for you to come out here. He meant for you to send your bucket out." I said, "Well, I didn't know that. Come in and take a beer with me, and we'll then go back." He came in and took another beer. I had the fellow draw my bucket full and I went back to the fort and after that I had to send my bucket out.

COLD HARBOR: THE SOLDIER'S DISDAIN

On June 3, Grant's troops moved against Lee at Cold Harbor, Virginia—a small crossroads where there was an old tavern. Part of a series of battles known as the "Overland Campaign," Cold Harbor was far from Grant's best demonstration of generalship.

Years later, in fact, Grant admitted in his memoirs that he regretted sending a third wave of men against a heavily entrenched enemy.

In his diary, Private John Haley of the Seventeenth Maine explained the futility of it all in harsher terms, but—interestingly—makes no insinuation about Grant and the ever-circulating rumors of the general's drinking:

> It was reported that Hancock's corps lost 3000 men here in ten minutes…
>
> No further attempt to advance was indulged in. Not that Grant wouldn't have continued the work of slaughter, but the officers and men in the ranks refused to budge. We were tired of charging earthworks. Many soldiers expressed freely their scorn of Grant's alleged generalship, which consists of launching men against breastworks. It is well known that *one* man behind works is as good as *three* outside the works.

Never shy to tee off on those in high command (at least on the pages of his diary), Haley unleashed more colorful slurs against Colonel Thomas Egan (spelled "Eagan" in Haley's journal) of New York when he was sent out to establish a night picket line, just a few days after the major debacle at Cold Harbor. This time, drinking (and Haley's fairly typical prejudices against the Irish) was part of the private's rant:

> It was a miracle we weren't gobbled, wandering around in the dark with Johnny Reb all around us. I venture the assertion that old Tommy Eagan was at the bottom of this ridiculous order and that a large quantity of whiskey had recently disappeared down his Irish gullet. (This same Eagan is a firm believer in the doctrine that there is no sense in buying meat, since half of it is bone, when one can buy whiskey with *no* bones.)

CHAPTER 10

GENERAL WHISKEY
1864

THE BURNING OF VMI:
APPLEJACK AND FURNITURE

The war in the Shenandoah Valley had already taken an ugly turn long before General David "Black Dave" Hunter led 18,000 Union troops against little Lexington—where the late General Thomas "Stonewall" Jackson had lived and also taught at the Virginia Military Institute. General Hunter ordered the firing of VMI on June 12, 1864.

Given that the Institute cadets had taken part in the Battle of New Market, the Yankees certainly came to their threshold with a score to settle. A small force (less than 2,000 men) led by General John McCausland—who had once taught at the Institute—was forced to retreat against overwhelming odds. Then, as recorded by a sixteen-year-old girl from Lexington in a letter, "the wretches [the Yankees] galloped into town, yelling and whooping like so many savages."

By 10:00 a.m. on Sunday morning, the invaders had fired most of the buildings at the Institute. When Colonel David Strother arrived in the conquered town, various buildings at VMI were smoldering and looters were helping themselves to whatever they could find and cart or carry off. The Federals then began to fire other buildings, including Governor John Letcher's homestead.

And then a most peculiar scene occurred, as noted by Strother in his memoirs:

> The General stopped at the house of Major [William] Gilham, a professor of the Institute, and told the lady to get her furniture as he intended to burn the house in the morning. She was eminently ladylike and was troubled, yet firm. The house was a state building and it was fair to destroy it, yet it was her only home and it was hard to lose it, but she was a soldier's wife and a soldier's daughter, so she set us out some good applejack, apologizing she had nothing better, and then went to move out her furniture to the lawn.

A few days later, General Jubal Early's army defeated Hunter's troops at the Battle of Lynchburg and the Yankees retreated to West Virginia. They rested up in Charleston, and lots of alcohol apparently was part of their recovery plan (at least for the "shoulder straps"), as Colonel Strother penned in his diary entry of June 30:

> Ten miles to Charleston where we landed after dark. It was raining and we got into an ambulance crowded with officers and drove to a saloon. We here imbibed native wine and sherry cobblers until we all got on a spree. Re-embarked in the ambulance and drove around for an hour jabbering and singing in search of our quarters.

THE *ALABAMA* GETS SNAGGED

On June 19, 1864, one of the most famous naval engagements of the war took place off the coast of France (called the Battle of Cherbourg, and later immortalized in an Edouard Manet painting). The USS *Kearsarge* sank the CSS *Alabama*— a notorious rebel ship responsible for sinking more than sixty Yankee vessels, the vast majority being freighters. The *Alabama* outshot her foe but did little damage in a close-quarters duel that took about eighty minutes. The *Kearsarge* found the mark with some low shots that eventually caused the infamous raider to sink.

During their Civil War stints, both ships had typical sailor-like problems—which is to say, primarily drinking, fighting, and carousing, with the latter two issues often aggravated by the first.

The *Alabama* was built in 1862, near Liverpool, and much of her crew came from nearby there, too. In fact, British sailors on the rebel ship far outnumbered Johnnies. The crew was rough— "carved from the crooked timber of humanity." Proud that his crew had been whipped into shape, the ship's Captain Raphael Semmes once said:

> It has taken me three or four months to accomplish this, but when it is considered that my little kingdom consisted of 110 of the most reckless sailors from the groggeries and brothels of Liverpool, that is not much.

Although Semmes would allow his sailors some "grog" on special occasions or holidays (the ritual of "splitting the main brace"), he and his first mate John McIntosh Kell generally tried to keep their drinking under control. They were not always successful in this pursuit, particularly after the sailors captured another ship. Said Kell: "Carried away with victory, many of [the men] got gloriously drunk, and gave me a good deal of trouble to get them back and properly sobered."

And Semmes—after one of his crew's misadventures—complained: "It will take me at least a week to get the rum out of them, and to try the more vicious by court-martial."

Punishments could be severe. Once, after a sailor smuggled bottles of rum on board, twenty of the intoxicated seadogs were placed in irons. But then they were subjected to what sounds suspiciously like a forerunner of "waterboarding"—the drunken sailors were forced to stand on deck while muscular quartermasters tossed bucket after bucket of seawater, with great rapidity and force, directly into their faces. At first, some tried to smirk through it, but eventually all the captives began to swallow the seawater and then—in between gags—even the toughest old salts would beg for mercy.

A British yacht named the *Deerhound* rescued Captain Semmes, Kell, and most of the other ship's officers. Much to the chagrin of the Union sailors, the *Deerhound* then hustled them off to England and most of the *Alabama* brass therefore escaped capture.

JUBAL EARLY'S RAID ON WASHINGTON

With Grant continually pressuring Lee's forces outside both Richmond and Petersburg, the strategy of invading the North for a third time began to get some traction. General Jubal Early—General Lee's "Bad Old Man"—was a prime candidate to execute just such a gamble. Having briefly pushed General David Hunter and his troops into western Virginia after the Battle of Lynchburg, Early quickly calculated that a rather clear path toward Washington was spread out before him. On July 4, Early's army captured Yankee supplies near Harpers Ferry, and just days later began a slow-but-steady creep toward the Federal capital.

"Ol' Jube"—who by most accounts liked to occasionally tilt a bottle or two—would, in mid-July, bring more than 10,000

Johnnies (some Union estimates claimed as many as 40,000) to the outskirts of Washington and put a legitimate scare in a city guarded by unseasoned troops.

At the Battle of Monocacy on July 9, General Lew Wallace (better remembered as the author of *Ben-Hur* later in his life) provided some resistance—and perhaps gained some valuable time—before his men were slapped aside. By July 11, Early's troops were massed before Fort Stevens and could *see*—and even have some sharpshooters wing shots in the direction of—the Yankee capital.

In the process of Jubal Early's foray, a funny aside occurred—the rebel troops passed by "Falkland" (at Silver Spring, Maryland), the summer residence of Montgomery Blair who was the postmaster general on the Lincoln cabinet. Some stragglers were caught looting the fine manor and had to be chased out and a guard placed on the door. As CSA Major Henry Kyd Douglas then noted in his memoirs:

> Afterwards Early and Breckenridge took possession of it…and it was there the conference between Early, Breckenridge, Gordon and Ramseur was held that night and a determination to assault the works the next morning. However considerate these gentlemen and their staffs of private property were, I feel compelled to say that the wine cellar of Mr. Blair was much depleted before they got away.

Testimonial to drinking generals at "Falkland" also can be found in the letters of Elizabeth Blair Lee—Montgomery's sister. She was fortunately at the New Jersey seashore when Early's troops swept through, but the incident provided her correspondence with a lively topic for weeks to come. Mrs. Lee, in fact, described the scene as "a perfect saturnalia" and "a great frolic." She also testified that it wasn't just wine that quenched rebel thirsts:

Silver Springs was HdQts—and they left the demijohns of good Old Bourbon empty under the table and cleaned out the larder and poultry.

Whatever satisfaction Jubal and his fellow generals might have gotten from guzzling down Blair's booze may well have been offset the following morning. Realizing that General Grant had rushed up some veteran reinforcements from Virginia via rail, the Confederates wisely reconsidered attacking the firmly entrenched positions ringing the city.

Their fantasy of taking the Federal capital, looting the U.S. Treasury, and—just for kicks—seating Breckinridge (the former U.S. vice president under Buchanan) back in his chair in the U.S. Senate was over. The better part of valor demanded bolting for home before the Yankees blocked off the most likely crossing spots along the Potomac.

In his memoirs, General Gordon made some pretenses that an attack on Washington might have been successful had Ol' Jube not dallied at "Falkland"—but that opinion puts him in a distinct minority. Early's raid was daring, but, when all was said and done, it was more "show" than "go." By July 14, Early's Butternuts had successfully crossed the Potomac back into Virginia—with at least one victory notched and some good tales to tell. Considering the war would end in less than ten months, Early's raid on Washington was arguably one of the last few pieces of good news for "the Cause" that summer.

"Major, we haven't taken Washington, but we've scared Abraham Lincoln like hell!" Jubal Early reportedly enthused to Henry Kyd Douglas. That may have been somewhat true. One report has it that a curious President Lincoln, sauntering about Fort Stevens, had a relatively close buzz from a rebel sharpshooter's bullet.

The "Falkland" homestead was put to the torch—although General Early, Major Douglas, and others swore there were never orders issued to do so. As Douglas reported in his remembrances, the flames were immediately observed by the Federals at Fort Stevens and served as a virtual announcement that the Confederates were retreating—not a situation that the adventuresome Johnnies would have wished to advertise. The riled-up Yanks, of course, were only too willing to pursue them.

A BOOZE BREAK WITH BURNSIDE

About the same time Jubal Early and his Johnnies were putting a good scare into Washington, D.C., the largest concentration of Union troops were about a month into the siege of Petersburg. There were, of course, days when nothing of significance was going on, as both armies dug trenches, kept watch, and hunkered down for the long haul.

During one such stint, artillery officer Colonel Charles Wainwright visited troops under the command of General Ambrose Burnside—still a high-ranking officer, but never again in a position of supreme command since his debacle at Fredericksburg and his exercise in stupidity aptly dubbed "The Mud March."

As reputation would have it, the bewhiskered general was never far away from a potent potable. Wainwright recorded in his diary entry of July 7:

> Speaking of drinks, General Burnside would appear to like them as well as his staff. I was over there one day to call on some of them, when happening near the General's tent, I found him sitting in his shirt sleeves, alongside of a great pile of boxes labeled ale, cider, and whiskey. The General insisted on taking some, so I drank a pint of cider with ice, which was most excellent. Indeed, I found Burnside himself so hearty and agreeable that I made a very short call on his staff.

THE BURNING OF CHAMBERSBURG

Early's troops had barely returned to the relatively safe haven of Virginia when he sent some of his men north to Pennsylvania on another mission—one that he hoped would either prove to be lucrative or punitive in its result. The destination was Chambersburg; the same bustling town—one that pre-dated the Revolution—that, ironically, had glimpsed the well-behaved Army of Northern Virginia under General Lee en route to its fateful rendezvous at Gettysburg.

On July 29, two brigades under the command of General Bradley T. Johnson and General McCausland slipped across the Potomac and then pushed rapidly north to reach Chambersburg at first light. Roused by the sudden appearance of the grim-faced "Graybacks"—for the rebels knew they were on a potentially less-than-pleasant mission—the town fathers were informed to either produce a hefty ransom of $100,000 in gold or $500,000 in U.S. currency or watch their homes and businesses be put to the invader's torch.

The rebels also made clear to the denizens of Chambersburg that, if the town were to be torched, it would be justifiable revenge for burnings in the Shenandoah Valley conducted by General David Hunter earlier in the summer. Those burnings included the Virginia Military Institute in Lexington and also some private homes of prominent Confederates—such as the homestead of Governor Letcher.

After a few hours, the citizens failed or stubbornly refused to raise the required "contribution" and—on the strength of Early's written orders, and McCausland's spoken ones—the Confederates began to fire the town. So repugnant was this order that one officer, Colonel W. E. Peters of the Twenty-First Virginia, refused to enact it. But then the Maryland guerrilla cavalryman Harry Gilmor was called upon to start the blaze—an order that one observer said he carried out "with promptness and zeal." McCausland briefly imprisoned Peters for his plague of conscience.

Whiskey was already in play in this situation, or soon came into play—which should not be a startling revelation. Some of the rebels were drunk, a fact well documented in the letters and memoirs of a number of Confederates. In fact, some of the most impaired either refused to leave or were unable to leave town, and soon fell victim to either revenge-minded citizens or Yankee soldiers that arrived hours after the deed.

Confederate officer George W. Booth presented the atrocity at Chambersburg in his memoirs, recollecting:

> The burning was systematically done; door after door was opened and fires kindled, and in a little while the heart of this thriving town was in flames. The distress of the citizens, especially the women and children, was heartrending and exemplified the hellish nature of war.

Apparently *some* of the soldiers (according to Booth) were moved enough to stop their destruction and help some of the hapless burghers rescue their personal items from the flames. The most intoxicated, however, only added to the chaos. As Booth wrote:

> I remained among the very last in the effort to clear the town of those who were under the influence of liquor. Some several, however, remained and fell victims to the enraged populace when our troops had retired. The horrible story of the punishment inflicted upon these unfortunate wretches who, through their own vices, became prey to the revengeful passions of the people I will not recall. It is enough to say the whole episode is one of regretful experience and unutterable sadness.

Writing home to his wife several weeks later, Captain Jedediah Hotchkiss confirmed Booth's observations, stating: "Henry K. Cochran was drunk and remained behind at Chambersburg to ransom houses for 'greenbacks' and was killed by some of the Yankees or citizens, no one knows which—Some of our boys behaved badly... "

PETERSBURG: WILL DIG FOR WHISKEY

In July, as Grant vowed to stick to the task ("I propose to fight it out on this line, if it takes all summer... "), a seemingly clever plan occurred to General Ambrose Burnside and was approved by his superiors; the Yankees would engage Pennsylvania coal miners to dig under the Confederate lines. Then, as the plan was designed, a powerful charge would be detonated directly under the rebel breastworks and, hopefully for the boys in blue, open up a big gap through which—in the anticipated chaos—Union troops would rush.

The secretive digging of this underground tunnel—which at its completion would stretch nearly 200 yards in length—proved to be hot and dirty work. The diggers took on the task in rotating three-hour shifts and, in recognition of their labors, a miner emerging from his stint was rewarded with a generous dram of whiskey.

In addition to this spirit-lifting ration of John Barleycorn, the miners occasionally got visits from Union big shots—including General Burnside himself and some Yankee politicians. The higher-ups, in fact, even kidded the laborers that they shrugged off the harsh, tedious work all for the enjoyment of the approved whiskey offering.

THE CRATER

On July 30, the Union forces put their grand scheme to the test. The result was a battle as terrible as any fought in the war; one that left thousands of dead or wounded out on the field, bloating or suffering in excruciating summer heat.

The volcano-like explosion occurred before 5:00 a.m.; approximately four tons of lit powder blew a crater some 170 feet long, eighty feet wide, and roughly ten yards deep. Confederates located directly about the blast suffered around 300 casualties. But when Union troops poured in, the rebels rallied and a so-called "turkey shoot" transpired. Yankee casualties hovered around 4,000 and the Confederates—after the initial casualties endured in the surprise explosion—suffered significantly less than that.

A controversy swirled around the use of "Negro" troops in the battle—as, by some accounts, the sight of armed black men in blue uniforms further incensed the rebel defenders. Some Confederates claimed that the black troops attacked with cries of "Remember Fort Pillow!" and "No quarter!" and so the Confederates responded with heightened force. Interestingly, the Richmond *Times* claimed that the black soldiers were "stimulated by whiskey." How else to explain why they rushed into battle? The Southern press was not about to admit that black soldiers might be sober and brave.

But the battle rapidly became a rebel triumph, as General William Mahone directed his troops to rim the crater and most avenues of escape were cut off. Desperate hand-to-hand combat made this battle one of the most brutal engagements of the war.

As was fairly typical in battlefield disasters, there was plenty of blame to be distributed in the aftermath. Much of it was directed toward General Edward Ferrero—the Spanish-born former dance instructor from New York—and General James Ledlie, an engineer by profession. According to the testimony from a Michigan army surgeon, the two generals were all but cowering in a bombproof shelter (safely away from the fray) and sharing a bottle of medicinal rum as their troops endured the hell of the crater. Their "generalship" apparently consisted of sending couriers back and forth with messages, without actually observing the battle themselves.

FLAG OF TRUCE—AND A FEW BOTTLES HOISTED

Although 1864 and 1865 were certainly years of bitter fighting and occasional incidents that can only be called atrocities, there were still occasional glimmers of remorse, empathy, and chivalry. Recognizing the terrible tumult that had been unleashed in the crater, both sides agreed to a truce the next morning, scheduled to take place between the hours of 5:00 a.m. and 9:00 a.m. It would have taken some grizzled veterans not to be shaken by the gruesomeness of that morning—smothering heat rising with the sun, bloating bodies turning black, a wafting stench, and pathetic pleas from some wounded still on the battlefield. Buckets of lemonade sloshed their way out to combat a hovering humidity that was oppressive even in the early morning hours. Water and whiskey were delivered to the wounded. Meanwhile, the lucky officers still among the living—those meeting on the field under the temporary magic of the white flag—seemed to take it in stride. But that was not without a little help from a flask or a bottle.

As one Southern journalist documented the scene:

> On the Yankee side there was a number of nice young men, dressed jauntily, carelessly smoking cigars and proffering whiskey, wine, and brandy of the best labels, and of sufficient age to warrant its flavor. More than one Confederate took a smile. Some took two, and one told me that finding the liquor of the "peace" order went it seven times.

GENERAL WHISKEY

Be it hastily distilled "tanglefoot" or well-aged bourbon, soldiers sometimes personified whiskey in their letters or diaries. When this occurred, the soldiers gave a respectful nod toward whiskey's "spirited" and influential power by referring to it as an officer of very high rank.

During the siege of Petersburg (a month after the gamble at the crater failed), Jacob Haas—a Pennsylvanian infantryman from Easton—chronicled on September 1 that: "A few boys became somewhat noisy in camp last night.... The noise was caused by General Whisky. The names of the party I shall not insert. All this day there are a few who remain drunk..."

CEDAR CREEK AND FISHER'S HILL

Despite his heady advance to the very gates of Washington, by the fall of 1864 Ol' Jube was in trouble in the Shenandoah Valley. The sheer numbers were against Early—essentially 10,000 men versus Sheridan's forces nearly four times that size. With victories at Cedar Creek (a.k.a. "The Third Battle of Winchester") and then Fisher's Hill, Sheridan had obviously gained the upper hand.

It was not uncommon during the Civil War for newspapers to accuse losing generals of suspect behavior, especially after bitter defeats were incurred on the battlefield. In the aftermath of Cedar Creek and Fisher's Hill, the Charleston *Mercury* seemed to take steady aim at Early and his rumored love of spirits when it claimed: "We have two enemies to contend with in the Valley...one of whom has never been beaten since Noah drank too much wine and lay in his tent..."

However, sympathy and support can be found for Early in Jedediah Hotchkiss's letter to his brother Nelson on October 3:

> There is a tale in circulation that Gen. Early was drunk
> at Winchester and also at Fisher's Hill. There is not one
> word of truth in it. A baser slander was never circu-
> lated. It is true Gen. Early is a drinker of spirits, is too
> fond of it, but I have never seen him under the influence

of liquor since we started on this campaign. He is sober enough to know his duty and attend to it at all times, and it is much to be regretted that such stories should be circulated.

DAMN THE TORPEDOES!
(BUT GOD BLESS THE COFFEE!)

When the U.S. Navy decided to curtail its allowances of grog rations (usually rum or whiskey) on its warships in the fall of 1862, this sudden reverse of course came as a bit of a shock—and not just to the average "Jack Tar." Some naval officers turned a blind eye and let their sailors continue to imbibe, at least in moderate amounts. In fact, Secretary of the Navy Welles had already reprimanded Admiral Dahlgren for allowing some of his sailors to stay just a little "groggy" during a sea battle; the old school of thought being that sailors in a heated duel at sea would be stimulated by a bit of booze.

At the Battle of Mobile Bay (August 5), Admiral David Glasgow Farragut went in a different direction. When an under officer hinted that the sailors might perk up for battle if they were only supplied with a little good Navy grog, Farragut reportedly replied that *he* had never needed rum to get ready for battle—and he had seen "a battle or two" in his day. However, Farragut added: "I will order two cups of good coffee to each man…"

And the admiral did just that. Perhaps jacked up on caffeine, the sailors were able to endure the rigors of the subsequent, and ultimately successful, attack. Most of the Union ships survived the guns of Fort Morgan and the harbor's minefield—even if Farragut's alleged declaration of "Damn the torpedoes! Full speed ahead!" was very likely created *after* the fact and, therefore, most likely apocryphal.

CASSANDRA'S DINNER FOR JEFF DAVIS

In early October, Mary Chesnut (having left Richmond for the comparatively safer South Carolina) got word that President Jefferson Davis would be coming to "be with us here in Columbia next Tuesday…" Despite her building belief that Old Dixie was unraveling toward its inevitable doom, Mrs. Chesnut (described by an acquaintance around this very time as "a regular Cassandra") apparently pulled out all the stops to extend a grand hospitality befitting the president of the Confederacy.

When word leaked out that President Davis was in the Chesnut home, a large crowd gathered and Davis consented to give an impromptu speech from the front piazza. That the war—and perhaps the effort to appear resolute in the face of a tightening Union noose—had exacted its toll on Davis might be inferred from Mrs. Chesnut's line: "He was thoroughly exhausted [after his speech], but we had a mint julep ready for him as he finished."

Mrs. Chesnut then said, "my head was intent on the dinner to be prepared" and lauded her Columbian circle for chipping in with various dishes to put together a modest feast. And that, of course, included top-shelf—in this case, almost historically aged—wine.

> So the patriotic public had come to the rescue. I had been gathering what I could of eatables for a month, and now I found everybody in Columbia nearly was sending me whatever they had that they thought nice enough for the president's dinner. We had the sixty-year-old Madeira from Mulberry [the Chesnut's family plantation in South Carolina] and the beautiful old china…. Mrs. Preston sent a boned turkey stuffed with truffles, stuffed tomatoes, and stuffed peppers. Each made a dish as pretty as it was appetizing.

WHISKEY AND TORCHES—ATLANTA IN FLAMES

While Mary Chesnut was entertaining President Jefferson Davis in Columbia, General Sherman already had been in possession of Atlanta for weeks.

During the siege of Atlanta, Sherman sent a proclamation urging that the women and children of the city should be evacuated before the warfare escalated. When the leading authorities attempted to protest Sherman's decree, he dismissed their arguments in a letter that included the phrase: "War is cruelty, and you cannot refine it."

When the city finally did fall in September and the Yankees prepared to abandon it in mid-November (to kick off Sherman's "March to the Sea"), the remaining citizens must have expected the worst. Sherman had predetermined to burn anything remotely helpful to the rebels, as is documented in a telegraph message he wired to Union General George Thomas in Tennessee: "Last night we burned Rome (Georgia), and in two or more days will burn Atlanta."

Between November 13 and 16, fires arose in the city and converted it into a raging inferno that witnesses inevitably compared to scenes from hell. Citizens of Rome, Georgia, had already experienced Sherman's scorched earth policy, and—early in the next year—citizens of Columbia, South Carolina, would understand such a terrorizing scene all too well.

Burning cities was a gruesome task, but one somewhat easier to conduct once the troops got ahold of alcohol.

One witness was Major James Austin Connolly, an officer from Illinois. Connolly was quick to note the contribution of whiskey swilling to the burning of Atlanta:

> The soldiers found many barrels of whisky and of course they drank of it until they were drunk; then new fires began to spring up…drunken soldiers on foot and on horseback raced up and down the streets while the buildings on either

side were solid sheets of flame, they gathered in crowds before the finest structures and sang "Rally around the Flag" while the flames enwrapped these costly edifices, and shouted and danced and sang again while the pillar and roof and dome sank into one common ruin.

Years later in his memoirs, Connolly envisioned his commander as most likely nonplussed by the city's fate, noting:

> The night, for miles around, was bright as mid-day; the city of Atlanta was one mass of flame...Well, the soldiers fought for it, now let the soldiers enjoy it; and so I suppose General Sherman thinks, for he is somewhere close by, now, looking on at all this, and saying not a word to prevent it. All the pictures of hell I have ever seen never gave me half a vivid an idea of it, as did this flame wrapped city tonight. Gate City of the South, farewell!

As for alcohol, it would continue to play a supporting role as Sherman's army slashed across Georgia on its infamous March to the Sea.

GIVING THANKS—TO THE STUFFING

It arrived two days *after* the actual holiday, but a massive Thanksgiving feast was shipped from New York City to the Army of the Potomac to bolster the soldiering spirits on the Virginia front. However, some spirits were boosted higher than others, when they found special surprises stuffed inside their turkeys. As one officer wrote:

> Now I must tell you who were the lucky ones that got them, and it was all by chance, for when they were all

given out, no one dreamt of any such thing as liquor being in them. So last night Lieut. Smith, our adjutant, went to cut up his turkey into halves, but his knife would not go straight through, on account of some hard obstacle. He began to investigate the cause by removing the stuffing, when the first thing that greeted his eyes was a bottle of brandy stuck in. So this morning I looked at mine, and there was one sure enough. I called the colonel in and I treated him, and he said he must look after his, and sure enough there was one in his, and one in Capt. Bolton's, the Capt. Brooke thought it was time for him to look, and he also found one. It afforded considerable amusement for a time…

AN OMINOUS SIGN

The rank-and-file soldier normally welcomed the distribution of whiskey rations. For many, it made the drudgery of tasks such as constructing fortifications, laying pontoons, or battlefield burials more bearable. However, since whiskey was sometimes dished out just prior to an attack, or when officers suspected the men were about to receive an onslaught from the foe, veterans learned that freely distributed whiskey might be a sign the situation was about to "get hot."

Such was the case with a U.S. Lieutenant William Mohrmann (part of General Thomas Ruger's division) as already exhausted Union troops began to brace for General John B. Hood's desperate bid at Franklin, Tennessee, on November 30. As Mohrmann recorded:

Arrived about 8 in the morning, hungry and tired out, half dead with want of sleep. We drew rations, made coffee, were given an allowance of whisky—ominous sign—and then set to fortify. I showed my men where to dig a line of small pits and when the bright sun warmed up the side of a small stump I made my headquarters right there and fell asleep at once.

Too much whiskey may have contributed to poor generalship at Franklin, as Union General George Day Wagner refused to withdraw two extremely vulnerable brigades about to be ava-lanched by the full blunt force of Hood's aggressive advance. Years later, General David Stanley remarked in a letter to a friend that "Wagner was, to say the least, 'full of whisky' if not drunk...He was in vainglorious condition, though it was not known at the time by General Scofield or myself."

Alcohol, of course, was a well-trotted explanation when it came to blatantly bad decisions on the battlefield—an explanation seen frequently on both sides during the four years of war. Its validity typically needs to be weighed against possible motives of those making the accusations. In this case, would Stanley—decades after the Battle of Franklin—still have an axe in need of sharpening? And, if so, why understate those accusations in a private letter, as opposed to sending them along to a newspaper as a letter to the editor, as some war veterans did?

Stanley, a West Point graduate and veteran soldier, himself had been accused of over-imbibing in the field. The most damning obser-vations came from former journalist Charles Dana, who essentially tarred Stanley as drunk, lazy, and careless during the fall of 1863.

Defenders of Stanley, however, point out that for much of late 1863 the general suffered greatly from dysentery (which could explain his overall ineffectiveness and lethargy) and, in fact, was forced to return to Ohio for several weeks for total rest and recovery from it.

Regardless of his drinking habits (and his primary biographer does not deny that Stanley was familiar with John Barleycorn), the

Ohio-born officer won the Medal of Honor at the Battle of Franklin, when he courageously launched a vigorous counterattack after Hood's troops overran Wagner's embarrassingly exposed brigades.

CHAPTER 11

MIGHTY APPLEJACK
1864

Applejack could certainly trace its roots back to colonial days, but it perhaps basked in its greatest notoriety during the Civil War. It was there from the beginning, of course, but as Union troops plunged deeper into rebeldom in 1864 and 1865, it seemed increasingly prevalent. The rural swathes of Dixie were strongholds of distilling.

In November of 1864, for example, Colonel Charles Wainwright remarked:

> If money, real money, and eatables are scarce in this part
> of Rebeldom, there is one drinkable called "Apple Jack"
> which seems to be more than abundant enough. [Cavalry
> commander David] Gregg says that he has had over 50
> barrels of it stove today; yet notwithstanding every pre-
> caution he could take, very many of his men have got

beastly drunk on it. One man I saw who had got so drunk that he could not stand; his joints were entirely powerless, and after every attempt to get him along his comrades left him by the roadside.

THE APPLEJACK RAID

In December of 1864, General Gouverneur K. Warren embarked on a mission to tear up the Weldon Railroad near Hicksford, Virginia—the idea being to inflict more suffering on the Confederates defending Petersburg by constricting their already stressed supply lines.

This five-day campaign (December 7–12) accumulated a few nicknames ("The Hicksford Raid" and "The Weldon Railroad Raid"), but one of the most popular among the soldiers themselves was "The Applejack Raid"—a respectful nod to the powerful liquor that, unfortunately, played a role in the darker aspects of the mission.

Although the idea of a "raid" typically conjures up a vision of a relatively small force moving quickly, this mission was definitely *not* that. Warren moved with 25,000 men—mostly infantry—but also shielded by cavalry units. The Yankees marched down and ripped up the rails well enough—more than fifteen miles worth of track, in fact—but the troubles started on the way back. The raiders found applejack along the way—probably while plundering, as was their wont—and local guerrillas found these stragglers, especially intoxicated ones, easy prey. When some Yankee stragglers were found bushwhacked and, in some cases, stripped nearly naked for their boots and clothing, the Federals (again with the help of alcohol, most likely) retaliated with their own harsh measures.

As Colonel Theodore Lyman of General Meade's staff wrote:

The troops were so enraged by such cases, that they fired every house on their march, and what made them worse, they found a great deal of apple-brandy in the country, a liquor that really intoxicates. The superior officers destroyed a great deal of it, but the men got some and many were drunk. The people make this brandy on account of its great price...

In the history of the Thirty-Ninth Regiment of the Massachusetts Volunteers, the enticing power of applejack during the raid on the Weldon Railroad is well chronicled:

No mention is made in the official report to the quantity of applejack, which the curiously inclined Yankees sought and found and, to their own harm, imbibed. The section had not been overrun before and consequently better stored farm houses were found than the men had been seeing of late and, not withstanding the rigors of the campaign, possibly on account of them, [the men] made merry with the seductive liquids made from innocent cider.

To make matters worse, the tired (and a great many intoxicated) troopers ran into cold and sleeting conditions on the return trip; all the more reason to guzzle down some applejack.

The Thirty-Ninth regimental history also mentions a story of one trooper—who had just knocked back "three fingers" of applejack—feeling cocky enough to approach General Warren, slap him on the back, and pronounce him to be "the little corporal"—a moniker typically attached to none other than the great Napoleon Bonaparte.

But there were also reported incidents that were far from lighthearted ones. Never one to dodge even mild abuses by high-ranking officers, the cynical Private John Haley from Maine, who was on the "Applejack Raid," chronicled this disturbing scene:

> During the night, Colonel Byles [actually Edwin Biles], of the 99th Pennsylvania, and his adjutant were perpetrating one of the foulest outrages upon two defenseless women whose house was within our lines. These women were compelled to submit to their infamous proposals or have their house burned down and themselves turned out into the bleak December. Had this been the work of privates, said privates would have suffered death. The nearest tree would have been requisitioned, and it would have been just punishment. But old Byles is an officer, and was drunk, as is his custom.

Atrocities aside, the mission (with very few Union casualties) was deemed a success. The Yankees had managed—despite terrible weather conditions on their return—to tear up more than fifteen miles of railroad track, destroy three railroad bridges, and force the Confederate forces to scramble out against them.

Applejack even warranted a mention in General Warren's official report, as he recorded:

> It is not believed the enemy picked up prisoners from straggling, except for a few who became drunk to complete prostration, on applejack found on the way, which to our surprise, was in almost every house in appreciable quantities.

AMAZONS AND APPLEJACK: LITTLE PHIL GETS A SHOCK

One of the strangest anecdotes of the war pops up in General Philip "Little Phil" Sheridan's recollections, in a memoir that more typically busies itself with the details of battles and tactics. The incident involved two women (one working as an army teamster, the other posing as a cavalry trooper), until an overdose of apple-jack caused both of the imposters to tumble into an icy river. As Sheridan wrote it:

> Colonel Conrad, of the Fifteenth Missouri...informed me that in returning he had been mortified greatly by the conduct of two females belonging to the detachment and division train at my headquarters. These women, he said, had given much annoyance by getting drunk, and to some extent demoralizing his men.
>
> To say that I was astonished by his statement would be a mild way of putting it.... I was informed that there certainly were in the command two females, that in some mysterious way had attached themselves to the service as soldiers....
>
> While out on a foraging expedition these Amazons had secured a supply of "apple-jack"....got very drunk, and on the return had fallen into Stone River and been nearly drowned. After they had been fished from the water, in the process of resuscitation their sex was disclosed, though up to this time it appeared to be known only to each other.

General Sheridan eventually had the "Applejack Amazons" brought before him, terminated from the Union service, and unceremoniously dispatched to civilian life.

THE FUTURE PRESIDENTS IMBIBE

Grant was not the only Union officer of high rank who would eventually become president of the United States. Future presidents Rutherford B. Hayes, James Garfield, William McKinley, and

Benjamin Harrison all served in the Union army and were all subject to the dangers and discomforts of that service.

Although the Hayes White House (primarily motivated by First
Lady Lucy Hayes and her embrace of the temperance movement)
was with a very few exceptions alcohol-free, Rutherford B. Hayes
the soldier definitely drank alcohol, including whiskey. As he relates
in his own diary, at a snow-drifted camp in remote Virginia:

> December 10, 1864.—A cold day; deep snow (eight
> inches) on the ground. [I] am the centre of congratula-
> tions [on promotion to generalship] in the camp. Gen-
> eral Duval and staff, Colonel Comly, etc. drink poor
> whiskey with me! A rational way of doing the joyful,
> but all we have!

Benjamin Harrison, who would one day become the twenty-third
president of the United States, was a religious man with temperance
leanings. He held prayer meetings in his tent during the war. However, in his letters home to his wife Caroline, General Harrison of the
Seventieth Indiana Regiment occasionally showed both a practical
application of alcohol in the war and also a sense of humor about it.

As to his practicality, Harrison wrote of the dismal weather
and road conditions the Union forces—pushing out of Tennessee
toward Georgia—encountered in the late winter of 1864:

> Some of the wagons did not get in until noon the next
> day and the rear guard was forced to stand all night in
> a swamp and without a fire to do any good. I went out
> four miles the next day and took a ration of whiskey
> to them.
>
> Last night when we and all our bed clothes were wet
> it turned cold and froze quite hard this morning. We got
> up stiff all over.

While the future president's letters from the field suggest that he drank a bit more than when he'd been a young lawyer back in Indiana, his letters also reflect that his consumption was quite moderate. One letter to Carrie about an officers' get-together (aided by generous amounts of bourbon) reads: "Some of the officers got quite mellow and I laughed more than I did for a year before at the antics of some of them, particularly Col Dustin..."And then Harrison admitted to his wife that he perhaps he might have "touched it lightly myself."

Harrison's letters, however, do not disguise his disgust with fellow officers who succumbed to hard boozing; he vented particular venom toward General William Thomas Ward of Kentucky, accusing Ward of being "beastly drunk" and "a lazy sot." Proof that General Joseph Hooker's reputation (warranted or not) preceded Hooker to the Western Theater in 1864 is also reflected in Harrison's correspondences: "whiskey...would be the ascendant now, if the stories about Hooker are well founded."

THE TWO MCKINLEYS

William McKinley was a promising young officer from Ohio (and the future twenty-fourth president) who served with General Hayes. But there was also a Sergeant John McKinley—a hard drinker—about whom Hayes had major reservations. When the sergeant was on leave back in Ohio, Hayes apparently sent him to his (Hayes's) home to deliver a letter.

> Heard from home. Sergeant [John] McKinley, with letter and watch—tight, drunk, the old heathen, and insisting on seeing the madame! I didn't dream of that. He must be a nuisance, a dangerous one too, when drunk. A neat, disciplined, well-drilled soldier under rule, but what a savage when in liquor! Must be careful whom I send home.

However, Hayes had nothing but glowing reports about Major *William* McKinley, describing him in a letter home to Lucy as "an exceeding bright, intelligent, and gentlemanly young officer. He promises to be one of our best..."

Not that William McKinley did not occasionally kick up his heels. Though certainly not a chronic boozer, Major McKinley apparently once drank to excess at a social reception hosted by General George Crook in Cumberland, Maryland. The incident came to light in a letter from Colonel James Comly to Hayes, who had been back in Ohio on leave at the time. Comly recorded:

> ...a grand party. The belle of the evening was Chf. Quartermaster Farnsworth, who parts his hair in the middle. Gardner was the best dancer...and from what Kennedy tells me of the latter end of thing, McKinley must have been the drunkest. I guess they had a little difficulty about it.

William McKinley—long before he climbed in the ranks—achieved a measure of fame at the battle of Antietam when he delivered coffee (not whiskey) and food to exhausted troops fighting near the Burnside Bridge. On his own initiative, McKinley grabbed a wagon of supplies, coaxed a few soldiers around him to help, and brought in the much-desired nourishment, despite Confederate fire.

James Garfield (yet another Ohioan and the twentieth president of the United States) also served in the Civil War. Garfield—an academic before the war—was a moderate imbiber. He complained about losing the commanding perch in his volunteer unit because of "brandy-and-bargain" underhandedness committed by another officer. Though it might well have been a case of sour grapes in Garfield's situation, there was indeed a culture of "treating" (i.e., bribing with free alcohol) when men campaigned or jockeyed for various ranks in volunteer units where officers were often elected by the soldiers.

CHAPTER 12

SHERMAN'S MARCH TO THE SEA
1864

FORAGING AND HORS DE COMBAT

With the fall of Atlanta, General Sherman began his infamous "March to the Sea"—often described as a "scorched earth" campaign, as "Uncle Billy" sought to supply his troops and deny the same to the enemy around him. For the rank-and-file soldier, this also meant capturing whiskey and applejack and wine whenever possible and in whatever amounts available.

A typical diary entry from Colonel Oscar L. Jackson, who was sometimes in charge of "foraging" details in the surrounding towns and countryside, points out the downside of this ongoing soldierly affair.

Dec 6 1864
Our division remains in camp, our brigade tearing up the railroad. I am detailed Field Forage Officer and I have

Print showing Sherman's March to the Sea. *Courtesy of the Library of Congress.*

charge of all parties from the brigade.... Get plenty of hogs and see some rebel soldiers who appeared more anxious to get away than fight us. Found large quantities of books, pictures, furniture and so forth, secreted in a swamp on Brewer's farm. I afterwards saw a Miss Brewer who was rather good looking. Just as I was ready to return, the men found a barrel of spirits which put the devil in them, and gave me some annoyance, as for awhile I could have offered no resistance to the enemy had we been attacked, and we were at any moment liable to be. The drunken spree gave me no serious trouble, but I could see how an army could be put *"hors de combat"* by a few barrels of spirits.

BRANDY IN THE STATE HOUSE

Brigadier General Hugh Judson Kilpatrick (nicknamed "Kilcavalry" by some for his alleged willingness to place his men in harm's way) led a wing of Sherman's march to the sea into the city of Milledgeville, Georgia, on November 21. They met with token resistance, and soon dozens of officers found themselves celebrating—with some powerful peach brandy—in the Georgia State House, where in January of 1861 the Georgian legislature had voted to secede from the Union. Wrote Colonel Henry Hitchcock in his diary: "This P.M. a number of our officers went to the State House and held a mock legislature. I was named to draw up resolutions, etc., but was luckily busy..."

What the Yankee officers did was "vote" themselves in as legislatures and then conducted various shenanigans, such as imitating Southern politicians supposedly writhing beneath their desks with delirium tremors, or voting themselves generous drinks of brandy. Kilpatrick hoisted a bottle in a mock toast to the famous hospitality of Georgia.

General Sherman, who had set up headquarters in the governor's mansion, also acknowledged the incident in his memoirs, writing: "I was not present at those frolics, but heard of them at the time and enjoyed the joke."

CHESNUT'S DILEMMA: DENIAL AND DESPAIR

With Sherman's troops resolutely trudging toward Savannah, Mary Chesnut's diary near the year's end was quite similar to how she opened 1864 on January 1—a strange mixture of despair and denial. On December 19, the aristocratic wife penned:

The deep waters [are] closing over us. And we are—in this house—like the outsiders at the time of the Flood.

We care for none of these things. We eat, drink, laugh, dance, in lightness of heart!!!

The drinking must have been a welcome buffer to reality, as two days later Savannah surrendered without a fight to the relentless Sherman.

SHERMAN'S CHRISTMAS

With more than 60,000 hardened veterans (opposed by approximately 10,000 rebels), General Sherman completed his march to the sea with the capitulation of Savannah, Georgia, just a few days before Christmas. The mayor of the city negotiated the surrender with the hope that the offer of no resistance might spare the city the fate Atlanta had already suffered.

After some deliberation, Sherman set up his headquarters in the neo-Gothic mansion owned by an Englishman named Charles Green—its owner having shrewdly offered his homestead perhaps with the idea that his generosity might insure that the lavish estate (and its large stores of cotton) would be spared the torch. It was at this mansion that Sherman penned his famous message to President Lincoln on December 22: "I beg to present you as a Christmas gift the city of Savannah with 150 heavy guns and plenty of ammunition, and also about twenty-five thousand bales of cotton." Lincoln was overjoyed at the news and the *New York Times* followed up with a story on the message the day after Christmas headlined: "Savannah Ours…Sherman's Christmas Present."

Given the joyous achievement, one might suspect that Yankee officers opened some bottles and hoisted some glasses—and that certainly happened, but in a reserved way. On Christmas evening, after church services and a serenade by some military bands, Sherman hosted a dinner for his top officers. As Major Henry Hitchcock, one of Sherman's staff, chronicled in a letter home:

Capt. Nichols—our mess caterer—having secured three or four lovely turkeys and sundry other good things—Col. Barnum contributing some very good wine.... We had about twenty at table, Gen. Sherman presiding and a very pleasant dinner it was. Gen. Sherman's health being drunk first, he made a little speech, patriotic, modest and pointed.... I withdrew quietly soon after the toasts began, fearing a little, I confess, that they might become too lively, but in that I was mistaken. It was as quiet and pleasant a Christmas dinner as one could wish—away from home.

CHRISTMAS WHISKEY AND "A WEE BIT BOOZY" AT PETERSBURG

Back on the Petersburg siege front in Virginia, Jacob Haas—the foot soldier from Easton, Pennsylvania—noted that the holiday was also celebrated in festive fashion, though obviously lacking the luxury of Sherman's grand dinner in Savannah. Haas's December 25 entry reads:

Whiskey has been the program of Christmas Eve, and all this day. Some have their roasted turkey, while some have hard tac [sic] and coffee...The troops are on a spree. The day has been quite lively with cannonading and music by the band at headquarters...

Meanwhile, the men of the Sixteenth Pennsylvania Cavalry were sent to collect lumber on Christmas Eve Day. Lieutenant Cormany, however, managed to find some side interests—twin temptations might be more accurate—as he penned:

...got all the lumber we could haul—While the men were loading I was in the house awhile. Made the acquaintance of Miss Rosa Roder, an inveterate little Rebel—and bewitchingly beautiful—but withall [sic] exceedingly interesting socially…Also found some fine "Apple Jack"—We got back to camp at 8 p.m.—I certainly became a wee bit boozy on Applejack—the deceiving thing! Went to bed at once—and had a fine nights sleep on the exciting day— Exceedingly cold Christmas Eve.

"FOUND ALIVE": SNEDEN GOES HOME

While General Sherman was graciously offering Savannah to President Lincoln as a Christmas gift, Robert Sneden—the sketch artist and mapmaker captured by Mosby's guerillas in 1863—was simply trying to get back home. He had been shipped around Dixie to various prison camps, including the notorious hellhole of Andersonville down in Georgia.

But in early December of 1864, Sneden managed to get on the prisoner exchange list and was swapped out under a flag of truce in Charleston Harbor in the middle of the month. A friend arranged it so Sneden would not have to make the voyage north (by steamer) without provisions, including the liquid variety: "I was given a pillow case half full of cake and fruit, and one bottle of whiskey and two of brandy for use on the home voyage."

When Sneden finally got to Washington (en route to New York City), he visited the Eutaw Hotel barroom (presumably his supply of alcohol had run low, or out) and then he inquired about his back pay. After leafing through pages and pages of paymasters' records, he finally found his name, next to which was written: "Missing or Killed." Sneden—perhaps with some defiant flourish—quickly added his own correction in pencil: "Found alive."

1865

"We are drunk and reckless, and if you want to fight come over!"

—Confederate soldiers of the Eleventh Texas

CHAPTER 13

THE END IN SIGHT
1865

With Sherman serving up Savannah as a Christmas present to Lincoln, and General John Bell Hood's army smashed to smithereens at Nashville in mid-December, only the most die-hard rebels held out hope as the new year of 1865 dawned on an imperiled Confederacy. But the common soldier on both sides mostly felt frustration—mixed with justifiable fear—at the state of his world. Yes, the end of the war seemed tantalizingly near, but fate still held considerable sway when it came to day-to-day survival. Lewis Carroll's words from *Alice's Adventures in Wonderland* (published that year in England) nearly applied: "Down, down, down. Would the fall never come to an end?"

One infantryman acutely aware of his own mortality—and that his life was in the hands of officers he considered less than geniuses—was the embittered Private John Haley from the Seventeenth Maine. On the first of the New Year, he scrawled:

Hope and fear mingle—hope the war will soon end; fear that however soon it ends, I might not live to see it. These fears are reduced to an absolute certainty as I consider that the confounded Rebels are as defiant as ever. Though I know that much of this is bluster, I also know that the battles still to be fought will be like worrying a wounded tiger in his death struggles, determined to injure many of us before the finale.

Alcohol proved to be a convenient remedy for soldiers looking to numb such depressing thoughts, even if the relief provided by booze was temporary and sometimes came with head-pounding consequences.

BUSY WORK AND BOOZE

Late in the war, some veteran soldiers were increasingly resistant to being put through mundane and repetitive drills that were simply designed to keep the men busy and, presumably, out of trouble. In his usual cynical tone, Haley took aim at the "shoulder straps" on these issues in the winter of 1864–1865, writing:

Commenced to drill three hours per day. Our officers have made a discovery of immense importance: "Inactivity is destructive to good morals."

One consoling thought looms up out of the dreariness. If we have to drill, some officers must drill us. This falls to the lower officers, yet they are not the instigators of this folly. Our higher-grade officers play cards, swill whiskey, and generally raise the devil.

Always one to point out the glaring differences (access to alcohol being a major one) between the relatively cushy life of officers and the drudgery endured by the common foot soldier, Haley's diary entry of January 10, 1865, reads: "It is raining hard, as it has done all night. This is a rather alarming state of things, as there can be no drill. The officers, having plenty of tanglefoot, are all right, of course. With us the rain has a different effect."

Although Haley's most prejudiced swipes were typically aimed at the Irish (particularly Colonel Thomas Eagan), the French also could not escape his critical eye. As with the Irish, he worked in an alcohol-related jab against the French on January 24 when he mused:

> More firing and pounding, cause and effect unknown to us. At 10 a.m. had company drill, ending at noon. At 4 p.m. had dress parade by General de Trobriand. This conduct on the part of Old Froggy must have been the result of intoxication, for he hasn't been guilty of such silliness heretofore.

THE FALL OF FORT FISHER

With Farragut's victory at Mobile Bay the previous year and the fall of Savannah in late December, the options for imported goods via blockade-runners were all but drying up in Rebeldom. And precious wines and liquors were always prime and profitable cargo.

Wilmington, North Carolina, however, remained defiantly open, chiefly due to the strength of Fort Fisher, a well-constructed military bastion with numerous batteries that guarded the entrance to the Cape Fear River. In 1865, Wilmington was the last lifeline port of any major significance on the Atlantic coast between the Confederacy and Europe. Wilmington attracted serious attention from Union brass looking to choke off all supplies to the South and end the war. Near the end of 1864, in fact, the garrison had held off an attack on Christmas Eve—but Colonel William Lamb, the fortress's commander, was sure the Yankees would try again.

With the exception of the Christmas Eve attack, the Butternuts at Fort Fisher were mostly untested when it came to combat. However, they were well acquainted with "ardent spirits" and how to get some on leave—or pilfer it from medical stores when the opportunity presented itself. In addition, like other troops stationed in coastal areas, they sometimes were the lucky beneficiaries of shipwrecked booze. Barrels of powerful brandies and top-shelf wines, mostly from Europe, occasionally washed up on the beaches or could be pried from nautical wrecks. Regardless of how they got it, if there was a surplus of it around, both rank-and-file soldiers and officers might be in various stages of intoxication for several days at a stretch.

The top CSA officers also needed no introduction to John Barleycorn. Captains of the sleek ships that ran the blockade would automatically dish out gifts of potent potables (and precious food items, such as high quality coffee or exotic fresh fruits) to high-ranking officers. It was a small price to pay in the risky—but potentially lucrative—career of a blockade-runner.

Colonel Lamb accumulated and sold substantial amounts of drinkables and once made more than a thousand dollars on one deal—a sizeable sum, even if the currency was Confederate dollars. The commander's wife Daisy once gushed about a virtual embarrassment of liquid riches, detailing in a homeward-bound letter that a sea captain had graced her with "four bottles of rum...half a doz. bottles of claret, 1 doz. bottles of sherry and 1 doz. of port, two bottles of brandy and two of Madeira" and adding, for good measure: "Isn't that doing well?"

On January 15, the Union once again attacked the so-called "Southern Gibraltar" at Wilmington. With 9,000 troops, plus a heavy barrage produced by dozens of warships from the blockade, the outnumbered rebels (less than 2,000 defenders) eventually yielded after hours of fierce fighting. Colonel Lamb and General William Whiting had hoped in vain that General Braxton Bragg might bring his troops (perhaps 6,000 in total and within twenty miles) to aid Fort Fisher, but messages were ignored. The wounded Whiting died (more from the effects of dysentery than from his battle wounds) in a Union prison several months later, but not before he got out word that he fully blamed Bragg's inaction for the crucial defeat.

On the night the fort fell, numerous Federals—soldiers, sailors, and marines—became intoxicated while celebrating their victory. But not all the drinking was rooted in their triumph; dozens of men recorded horrific carnage inside the fort. The naval bombardment had yielded grim results, as rebel defenders were found with limbs and heads separated from their bodies. In addition to the usual increased jiggers of whiskey for those assigned to burial details, some reported they needed a brace of ardent spirits simply to cope with what their eyes were forced to see. As one sailor wrote home:

> I never saw such a sight in my life. There was soldiers and sailors laying around me dead, some with arms and legs and heads off. I [found] a demijohn of whiskey. I filled a quart bottle with the whiskey, took a drink of it and I tell you it did not come amiss. I never wanted it more than I did then.

Shortly after sunrise on January 16, an unnecessary tragedy occurred when the Fort Fisher powder magazine blew up and killed around 200 men—mostly Federals, but also some captured Confederates in the same vicinity. Union authorities initially suspected rebel sabotage, but a Court of Inquiry soon deduced that the disaster was probably accidental—with Demon Alcohol playing its role. The official report noted:

> —That soldiers, sailors, and marines were running about with lights, intoxicated and discharging firearms.

—That personas were seen with lights searching for plunder in the main magazine some ten or fifteen minutes previous to the explosion.

The "personas" were believed by some to have been two drunken Union sailors that wandered into the main magazine and inadvertently ignited the contents there while sniffing about for booty.

The fall of Fort Fisher was yet another spike in the heart of "the Cause." Wilmington was effectively shut down as a port, applying even more pressure to the shortage of supplies in the constricted Confederacy.

A BID FOR PEACE AND A PARTING GIFT

Within days after the surrender of Fort Fisher, rumors of a peace conference between the North and South were circulating and—unlike most rumors during wartime—these had some validity. Francis Preston Blair was carrying correspondences back and forth between President Lincoln and President Davis on the very subject. Strangely, the French presence in Mexico gave the Southerners the idea that Lincoln might agree to postpone hostilities and form a joint CSA-Union campaign to remove the armies of Napoleon III from North America.

On February 3, 1865, three Southern peace commissioners— CSA Vice President Alexander Stephens, Assistant Secretary of War John Campbell, and Senator Robert Hunter—met with Lincoln and Secretary of State William Seward on the *River Queen* near Hampton, Virginia, not far from where the *Monitor* and the *Virginia* had pounded out their epic draw in 1862.

The peace conference achieved very little (other than an agreement to resume exchanges of prisoners) because the Southern representatives were still demanding separation from the Union—an

issue that Lincoln would not even consider—and refused to enter-
tain the idea of emancipation.

Seward was fond of top-shelf alcohol, especially champagne,
as was well known. The New Yorker would not have endured
a conference without some close at hand. When the Southerners
left empty-handed, Seward—as an afterthought—must have felt
compelled to send them off with a consolation prize. So he sent
a basket of champagne out to them on a boat rowed by a free
black man. The Confederate peace commissioners were back
on the deck of a steamer that would take them back to Richmond when their basket arrived. They cheerfully flapped their
handkerchiefs back at Seward to acknowledge his generous gift
of bubbly.

Perhaps Seward could not resist a parting jab on the slavery
issue, however, for (with the assistance of a boatswain's trumpet)
he then bellowed across the water: "Keep the champagne, but
return the Negro!"

The peace ambassadors from Dixie were no doubt more pleased
with the wine than the words.

BUCKETS OF WHISKEY AND
THE TORCHING OF COLUMBIA

One of the great tragedies of the Civil War took place on February 17–18 when General Sherman's armies captured Columbia, the
capital city of South Carolina. There is still some debate about how
the city of approximately 25,000 people caught fire. Retreating
rebels had set bales of cotton ablaze so the commodity would not
fall into the hands of the enemy, but most accounts concur that
those initial fires had been put out. Plenty of eyewitness testimo-
nies—some of the most damning of which came from Union men—
indicate that drunken Yankee soldiers were primarily to blame for
the disaster.

In his diary entry of February 17, the U.S. artillery officer Thomas Ward Osborn wrote:

> This morning Columbia was a beautiful little city, tonight it is a "sea of fire"...The scene is both terrible and grand.
>
> ...all went on well, but when the brigade occupied the town the citizens and Negroes brought out whisky in buckets, bottles, and in every conceivable manner treated the men to all they could drink. The men were very much worn and tired and drank freely of it, and the entire brigade became drunk.

So chaotic was the situation that some soldiers sent in to quell the fires and looting became drunk—truly becoming part of the problem and not the solution. Commanders were forced to find whatever sober troops could be scrounged up and send in yet another wave. As U.S. soldier Theodore Upson of an Indiana regiment recalled:

> Some of our boys got some whiskey as we came through the City. The Negroes were running around with pails of the stuff...About 8 o'clock [after Upson's unit had already settled into camp] we were ordered down into the city but told to leave any drunken men or those likely to get drunk in camp.

In fact, dozens of Yankee soldiers refused to be subdued and had to be shot by their own troops. Several thousand men were arrested for drunkenness or looting. Major Henry Hitchcock of Sherman's staff similarly was overwhelmed by the riotous and shameful situation, as he chronicled in a March letter to his wife:

One word about Columbia. It was not burned by orders, but expressly against orders and in spite of the utmost effort on our part to save it. Everything seemed to conspire for its destruction. The streets were full of loose cotton, brought out and set on fire *by the rebels* before they left,—I saw it when we rode into town. A gale of wind was blowing all that day and night, and the branches of the trees were white with cotton tufts blown about everywhere. The citizens themselves—like idiots, madmen,—brought out large quantities of liquor as soon as our troops entered and distributed it freely among them, even to the guards which Gen. [Oliver Otis] Howard had immediately placed all over the city as soon as we came in. This fact is unquestionable, and was one chief cause of what followed. Here in Fayetteville a lady has told Gen. Sherman that Gen. Joe Johnson [Johnston] told her yesterday morning that the burning of Columbia was caused by liquor which the people gave our soldiers. Besides there were 200 or 300 of "our prisoners" who had escaped from rebel hands before, and when we reached Columbia burning to revenge themselves for the cruel treatment they had received, and our men were fully aware of the claims of Columbia to eminence as "the cradle of secession."

On February 18, Colonel Oscar L. Jackson, an officer in the Ohio Infantry, observed:

I went over to the city this morning and found it mostly in ruins...It is not an exaggeration to say that the city is burned...It is generally understood that at dark our drunken soldiery fired it in numerous places. Perhaps the brigade on duty in the city made some efforts to put out

the fires, but I do not think you could get enough men
in the army disposed to stop to have affected anything.
A few soldiers were so drunk that they were burnt. There
were no residences of noted rebels left unburned except
a few occupied by our Generals for headquarters.

The burning of Columbia remained a controversial issue years
after the war ended, partly due to British lawsuits that were filed
in hopes of claiming damages for shipments of cotton that were
lost in the flames.

Sherman, interestingly, did not mention the role of whiskey and
drunkenness in the burning of the city in his famous memoirs
(blaming it more on the windy conditions). But General Oliver Otis
Howard, on the witness stand in 1872 in Washington, was quite
open and truthful about drunken boys in blue, stating—for start-
ers—that when "Uncle Billy" himself entered Columbia "[he] was
met with much enthusiasm by a company of soldiers; observing
them closely, I saw that some of them were under the influence of
drink." General Howard also testified that—after "investigating
thoroughly"—he discovered "citizens carried pails of whiskey
along the ranks, and that the men of the leading brigade of Colonel
Stone drank with dippers out of pails."

And, as history has recorded, from there the situation unfolded
in ways most disastrous, and any efforts to remedy the burning of
Columbia proved futile.

CHUGGING IN CHERAW

By March, Sherman's army headed north, in pursuit of General
Joe Johnston's army. What little rebel resistance could be mustered
was mostly in the form of hit-and-run cavalry raids and rearguard
actions of retreating troops. Bridges were often torched or blown
up in an effort to hinder Sherman's advance.

Cheraw, South Carolina—a small town less than twenty miles from the North Carolina border—was one of many swarmed under by Sherman's invaders. But the soldiers were delighted to find the town was loaded with a certain kind of plunder that was always high on their list, as Colonel Oscar Jackson's diary of March 3, 1865, revealed:

> Among other things found in the town were immense quantities of liquors, much of it in the original cases in which it had run the blockade. Our division occupies the town and there is scarce a squad of soldiers but can treat you this evening to a bottle of fine wine and brandy. I went out among the boys and like to have got intoxicated. A gay time this.

UNCLE BILLY'S FINE WINE

If there is one comparative constant when it comes to alcohol and the Civil War, it is that *both* sides enjoyed "liberating" bottles and barrels from the other. Horses and cattle were considered prime thefts, too, but there was nothing quite like popping the cork on some top-shelf bottle that perhaps only hours before had been in some enemy general's pantry.

Advanced regiments of Sherman's army were already established in Cheraw when the general himself arrived on March 3—the day dampened by a bone-chilling Carolina drizzle. Sherman was only too happy to find General Francis Preston Blair Jr. in possession of a splendid house—once owned by a blockade runner—serving as his headquarters.

When Blair invited his commanding general to lunch with him, Sherman soon discovered that Blair was in possession of more than just the blockade runner's homestead. As Sherman fondly reminisced in his memoirs:

We passed down into the basement dining-room, where the regular family table was spread with an excellent meal; and during its progress I was asked to take some wine, which stood upon the table in venerable bottles. It was so very good that I inquired where it came from. General Blair simply asked, "Do you like it?" but I insisted upon knowing where he got it; he only replied by asking if I liked it, and wanted some.

Soon after, General Blair sent his superior a case of this wine, and, as Sherman chronicled, it turned out to be "the finest madeira I have ever tasted." The Madeira had once belonged to an old aristocratic Charleston family and had, ironically, been sent to Cheraw for "safe keeping"—where, in fact, *eight wagons full* of the much-vaunted wine fell into the possession of General Blair. Apparently "Uncle Billy" was not the only lucky recipient of Blair's windfall, as Sherman noted his general "distributed [the wine] to the army generally, in very fair proportions."

CHAPTER 14

BURNING CITIES AND SURRENDER
1865

THE DRUNKEN TAILOR

Not all the scandals involving alcohol occurred on the front lines or in the field, as became obvious at President Abraham Lincoln's second inauguration on March 4. Lincoln's vice presidential candidate—Andrew Johnson of Tennessee—tried to beg off on the grounds that he had been feeling ill. But Lincoln insisted that Johnson travel from Nashville to Washington and participate in the ceremony, and Johnson reluctantly agreed to come.

It is likely a toss-up whether Lincoln or Johnson regretted this decision more. Once the Tennessean arrived in Washington, he attended a party hosted by John Forney—an editor, writer, and political operative, but also a hard drinker. Whiskey certainly would have been offered Johnson, perhaps to salute his pending office or even under the guise of medical treatment. And Johnson apparently did not refuse.

Dreary wet weather hovered over the capital on Inauguration Day, and some degree of intoxication apparently hovered over Andrew Johnson. But in a desperate move to feel better, Johnson—on one of the most important days of his political career—opted for the "hair of the dog" strategy and decided to drink more. While there is some debate about whether Johnson drank brandy or whiskey that morning, there is *no* debate about its effect on him.

In short, Johnson slurred words that made little sense and weirdly seemed accusatory toward the audience; about what exactly was difficult to decipher. The huffy little man was supposed to speak for about five minutes, but rambled on long after his allotted time. The former tailor by trade finally had to be given the equivalent of the "Vaudeville Hook" and was essentially steered off the stage.

Secretary of the Navy Gideon Welles recapped Johnson's incredible smashup in his diary:

> The Vice-President elect made a rambling and strange harangue, which was listened to with pain and mortification by all his friends. My impressions were that he was under the influence of stimulants.

General Rutherford B. Hayes (the future president) was on leave in the capital and witnessed Johnson's bombastic bumbling. He wrote home to his wife Lucy (who would one day earn the moniker "Lemonade Lucy" for her staunch temperance stance against booze in the White House), bluntly stating: "It was lucky you did not come to the inauguration. The bad weather and Andy Johnson's disgraceful drunkenness spoiled it."

With the war still dragging on, bad publicity on the home political front was hardly something Lincoln wanted to deal with.

Johnson was hustled off to Francis P. Blair's home as the Lincoln forces waited for the tempests kicked up in various newspapers to die down. Lincoln saw Johnson's actions as an unfortunate occurrence, but not reflective of the man's typical behavior. According to Hugh McCullough, his treasury secretary, Lincoln assured him: "I have known Andy Johnson for many years; he made a bad slip the other day, but you need not be scared. Andy ain't a drunkard."

WADE HAMPTON'S CLOSE CALL

Confederate cavalry General Wade Hampton, an aristocratic plantation owner and one of the most famous men in South Carolina, nearly lost his life to drunken troopers who were—at least presumably—on his own side. The story, which appears in Mary Chesnut's diary entry of March 30, 1865, underscores just how rapidly the "cause" was unraveling into chaos and mob mentality. Whiskey, of course, was almost always in the mix in such incidents, greasing the skids of Dixie's downward spiral. As Mary wrote:

> General Chesnut [her husband James] told a story of [General Joseph] Wheeler's men in Columbia. Either they did not know Hampton or were *drunk* and angry at his being put over Wheeler's men. He called out, "Chesnut, these fellows have drawn their pistols on me." He is a cool hand, our Wade. General Chesnut galloped up— "Fall in there, fall in"—and by instinct the half-drunken creatures obeyed. Then Chesnut saw a squad of infantry and brought them up swiftly. The drunken cavalry rode off. Wade was quite tranquil about it all. He insisted that they did not know him, and besides they were too much intoxicated to know anything. He did not order any arrests or any notice whatever to be taken of this insubordination.

SHAD À *LA* WATERLOO

If Gettysburg and Vicksburg are often billed as "the turning points" of the Civil War, then the Battle of Five Forks—fought on April Fools' Day, a few miles southwest of Petersburg—might best be described as "the breaking point." A few historians, in fact, have referred to the 1865 rout as "The Waterloo of the Confederacy."

With a decisive defeat at Five Forks—a position of such importance that General Robert E. Lee had instructed General George Pickett to hold "at all hazards"—the already stressed Confederate supply lines were severely compromised. The fall of Petersburg and Richmond inevitably followed, as Lee's army was forced to flee west to Appomattox. Lee hoped to re-supply there and perhaps, eventually, hook up with General Joe Johnston's army (then in North Carolina) to create a more formidable force.

As the war dragged into 1865, the Confederates were lacking in many necessary items to fight against an enemy that far outnumbered them and comparatively was much better supplied. But on April 1, 1865, they were also severely lacking in leadership—as three of their highest-ranking officers were more than a mile behind the front lines, indulging in a shad bake along the banks of Hatcher's Run. General Pickett, General Fitzhugh Lee, and General Thomas Rosser (the host of the ill-fated picnic) were the prime culprits.

The trio of generals enjoyed drinking, and consuming so much shad during the long luncheon would have very likely required some accompanying spirits. As author David M. Jordan envisioned this scene in his Civil War biography of General G. K. Warren:

> Unfortunately the Confederate officers left in command
> at the front had no idea where Pickett and [Fitz] Lee had
> gone. With bottles of bourbon and brandy on the table
> before them and a confident feeling that there would be
> no real fighting that day, the rebel commanders sat under

a tent, enjoyed the succulent shad, washed it down with a libation of choice, and passed several lazy hours of the early spring afternoon.

Whether the scene was *exactly* like that is hard to say. But what is certain is this: the next rung of officers (chiefly General W. H. F. "Rooney" Lee and Colonel Thomas Munford) were not sure where Pickett and Fitz Lee had gone. As they observed the Federal activity indicative of an attack, they sent out messengers in a vain attempt to find their superiors.

Strangely, the three generals apparently did not hear the battle commence. By some accounts, in fact, Pickett, Rosser, and Fitz Lee narrowly escaped capture by roaming Yankees that stumbled upon their riverside outing.

One officer who was not feasting on shad or indulging in refreshments on a quiet riverbank was the Englishman Francis Dawson. Fortunately, when Dawson took a bullet, a fellow soldier came to his assistance with a full flask of battlefield booze. As he wrote in his memoirs:

> Towards evening a desperate charge was made by W. H. F. Lee's division, in which we lost heavily. I flattered myself that my usual good luck would attend me, for, as I rode abreast of the line and bowed my head in passing under a tree, the bough which I had stooped to escape was struck sharply by a rifle ball.
>
> But only two or three minutes afterward I was shot squarely in the arm, near the shoulder, and put *hors de combat*. Archie Randolph was by me in a minute, and poured an indefinite quantity of apple brandy down my throat. This revived me, and, with my arm in a sling, I rode back to where General Fitz Lee was.

If Fitz Lee (or Pickett and Rosser, for that matter) was indeed back on the scene in the late hours of the day, his presence was certainly a case of too little, too late. The Yankees, commanded by General Philip "Little Phil" Sheridan, had already carried the day.

RICHMOND BURNING AND WHISKEY FLOWING

On April 2, realizing how the situation was rapidly collapsing following the debacle at Five Forks, Lee sent a short but clear message to General J. C. Breckinridge. Lee allowed that he saw "no prospect of doing more than holding our position here till night" and admitted that he was "not certain" even that was possible. After holding out for the better part of nine months on the Petersburg-Richmond front, Lee knew that—with his lines stretched thin and ready to snap—defense of the capital was no longer possible. "Our only chance, then," he wrote Breckinridge, "of concentrating our forces, is to do so near Danville railroad, which I shall endeavor to do at once. I advise that all preparations be made for leaving Richmond to-night..."

As Sunday morning broke in the capital, most of the average citizens suspected nothing out of the ordinary. Churchgoers headed to worship, including President Jefferson Davis, who was in his usual pew for the Episcopal service at St. Paul's. But before the service was over, Davis was handed a telegram and he left the congregation to read it outside the church. It was from General Lee and, in clear English, laid out the same emphatic orders that Lee had already sent to Breckenridge.

Word soon leaked out across the city, first gradually and then in earnest. The city council held an emergency meeting at 4:00 p.m. and, among other orders issued, ordered that all liquor stores be destroyed in case Richmond was abandoned.

John Barleycorn, as per usual, proved impossible to destroy in totality. By late afternoon, drunken riffraff were already skulking about for plunder—a situation that only threatened to get worse when nightfall came. As Colonel John C. Haskell reported:

> ...the low characters of the town had broken into every-thing, gotten a lot of whiskey and were looting the town, being aided to a considerable extent by the soldiers who had broken through all discipline.

But far more disturbing were scenes of barrels of whiskey with the heads bashed in, hundreds in some cases, sending a virtual river of booze into the city streets and gutters. This putrid flow did nothing to deter the most intoxicated—or the most determined—from attempting to gather as much as they could in canteens, bottles, jugs, even pots and pans. And, failing that, the worst cases reduced themselves to lapping up the streams of alcohol from the ground like wild animals.

The pandemonium (and John Barleycorn's predictable role in it) was readily captured in Myrta Lockett Avary's *A Virginia Girl in the Civil War, 1861–1865: Being a Record of the Actual Experiences of the Wife of a Confederate Officer*:

> As darkness came upon the city confusion and disorder increased. People were running about everywhere with plunder and provisions.... Barrels of liquor were broken open and the gutters ran with whisky.... There were plenty of straggling soldiers about who had too much whisky, rough women had it plentifully, and many Negros were drunk. The air was filled with yells, curses, cries of distress, and horrid songs.

Richmond was on fire in several places by the time the first Union troops arrived—including tobacco warehouses and city bridges. Confederate ships were purposely scuttled or blown up in

BURNING AND EVACUATION OF RICHMOND APRIL 3ʳᵈ 1865.

Print showing the Burning and Evacuation of Richmond. *Courtesy of the Library of Congress.*

the James River. Unlike the scene in Columbia, however, most witnesses (and most historians) gave the Federal occupiers high marks when it came to their behavior and their ability to keep the city under reasonable control.

As much of Richmond's citizenry was attempting to flee the flaming capital and its crescendo of chaos, the body of General Ambrose Powell Hill, recently killed in action, was being hauled *in* by ambulance—against the panicky tide—in search of a coffin and a burial befitting a hero. The South had lost another general.

PISTOLS AND PETTICOATS

On the edge of Richmond, Chimborazo Hospital stood perched on a high hill of the same name. Throughout the war, Phoebe Yates Pember served as a matron of the facility and—according to her memoirs and letters—was constantly on her guard to prevent the theft of alcohol meant for treatment of the Confederate wounded.

But with the Yankees already in Richmond by the evening of April 3, some desperate characters (apparently already under the influence) made one last play for something Pember had. "Thirty gallons of whiskey had been sent to me the day before the evacuation and they wanted it," the hospital matron noted.

> "We have come for the whiskey!"
> "You cannot, and shall not have it."
> "It does not belong to you."
> "It is in my charge, and I intend to keep it. Get out of
> my pantry; you are all drunk."

The ringleader tried one bold and wrongheaded move more. In his intoxicated state he perhaps made his adversary all the more determined when he called her a name "that a decent woman seldom hears and even a wicked one resents."

When the would-be whiskey thief advanced toward a barrel of spirits, the telltale click of Ms. Pember's pistol soon sent him scurrying in the opposite direction. She then barricaded the pantry door and slept with the whiskey supply until the next morning, when Federal authorities arrived at the hospital and posted their own guards on the sizeable stash.

MINT JULEPS, TEARS, AND RETREATS

On the heels of the crushing rout at Five Forks, abandoning Petersburg and Richmond was now a grim necessity. As Lee's Army of Northern Virginia trudged west, slowed by supply wagons and sleep-deprived troops, the situation behind them was unraveling with great rapidity.

About a dozen miles west of Petersburg, the remnants of Lee's proud forces—veterans who had twice invaded the North—passed near an English-styled country manor called Clover Hill, the home of Judge James Henry Cox. Cox invited General Lee and General James Longstreet, plus their staff officers, to what was a rather lavish luncheon, considering the ravages of war.

In *My Confederate Girlhood: The Memoirs of Kate Virginia Cox Logan*, the Judge's daughter describes meeting a melancholy General Robert E. Lee at her family's homestead. The young woman attempted to buck up Lee by suggesting that perhaps the glorious "cause" could still be salvaged, especially if the general could join forces with General Joseph Johnston's forces in North Carolina:

> As we were talking, the butler brought in a large tray of mint juleps, the beverage so prized in old Virginia. General Lee took his glass and, according to the universal custom, asked me to taste it. He scarcely touched it himself, but took a goblet of ice water, saying, as he looked around at the men enjoying the juleps:
>
> "Do you know that this glass of cold water, I believe, is far more refreshing than the drinks they are enjoying so much?"

Since Clover Hill had managed to stay supplied with quality cuisine and a well-stocked wine cellar, a scrumptious dinner followed. Kate Cox somberly recorded that "Old Pete" Longstreet—his wounded arm essentially unusable—needed to have his food cut up for him before he could dine.

When General Lee left on his horse Traveler—his "grey cape lined with red" thrown back over his shoulders—Cox admitted that her eyes were "tear-dimmed." It was the last elegant supper of significance, under a real roof, that the Confederate officers would enjoy together prior to the bitter surrender at Appomattox.

Meanwhile, the battered Confederate soldiers, camped along the roads while their highest officers sipped mint juleps before a small feast, were subsisting on parched corn. The urgent hope that something more substantial and rejuvenating might be waiting for them further west would prove elusive.

THE DRINKS ARE ON JEFF

Mere days after Union forces marched into burning Richmond, President Lincoln arrived with a modest entourage in the city. The contingent arrived at Jefferson Davis's home—the so-called White House of the Confederacy—though Davis had already fled the chaotic and flame-engulfed city. There was, however, still a house servant on the premises who managed to conjure up a bottle, much to the lip-smacking delight of Lincoln's thirsty bodyguard, William H. Crook. As Crook recalled, the servant told him:

> "Yes, indeed, boss, there is some fine old whiskey in the cellar."
>
> In a few minutes, he produced a long, black bottle. The bottle was passed around. When it came back it was empty. Every one had taken a pull except the President, who never touched anything of the sort.

Jefferson Davis did not limit himself just to whiskey, however. Union naval commander David Dixon Porter found this out first hand (and later related it in his 1885 book titled *Incidents and Anecdotes of the Civil War*) upon capturing a British blockade runner in early 1865 and sorting through its precious cargo. Wrote Porter:

> It looked queer to me to see boxes labeled "His Excellency, Jefferson Davis, President of the Confederate States of America." The packages so labeled contained Bass ale or Cognac brandy, which cost "His Excellency" less than we Yankees had to pay for it. Think of the President

drinking imported liquors while his soldiers were living on pop-corn and water.

SAILOR'S CREEK: WHISKEY PUNCH FOR THE VANQUISHED

On April 6, Lee's retreating army incurred another serious hit at Little Sailor's Creek. Cavalry units—some under the command of the brash twenty-six-year-old George Armstrong Custer—cut off General Richard Ewell's men from Lee's main body of troops. In what was actually a series of three little battles (typically grouped together as the more convenient "Battle of Sailor's Creek"), Ewell's rebels were eventually forced to surrender against superior odds.

Nearly 8,000 CSA soldiers either were captured or surrendered—approximately one fourth of Lee's remaining troop strength in the Army of Northern Virginia prior to the latest setback—and that included the capture of eight rebel generals, among them Ewell and George Washington Custis Lee, Robert E. Lee's oldest son. The captured generals spent a "miserable snowy night" under guard near the battlefield. But on April 7, they were moved to U. S. Grant's headquarters. One can hardly imagine how disheartened and exhausted this lot of gray-clad officers must have been when they arrived at Nottoway Junction.

Perhaps it was of small consolation, but one of this hapless bunch—General Eppa Hunton of Virginia—would years later in his autobiography reflect on the unexpected hospitality of their Yankee captors, remarking:

> We were conducted to a big log fire at General Grant's headquarters. Grant was at the front, but quite a few of his officers were present. We had not been there long before hot whiskey punch was handed around.

Warmed by both the fire and the "firewater," the rebel officers perhaps felt a bit more comfortable. They even got a warm bed indoors that night, as Yankee guards put them up in a house in the village. Soon after, they were sent north to wait for exchanges—which fortunately were not so long in coming.

Sailor's Creek proved to be such a decisive blow to the reeling rebels that General Phil Sheridan sent an exhilarating message to Grant, imploring: "If the thing is pressed, I believe Lee will surrender." When Grant passed along Sheridan's opinion to Lincoln, the president responded: "Let the thing be pressed."

FARMVILLE: COLONEL ROBISON GETS HIT

Though it is tempting to view Sailor's Creek as the last major battle of the war in Virginia, this author's great-grandfather, J. K. Robison—if he were here to defend his position—would surely beg to differ. It was at Farmville, on April 7, that he suffered his third serious wound of the war. Colonel Robison was leading a saber charge against a Confederate supply train, robustly defended by stubborn infantry guards—when Samuel Cormany (riding next to him) heard him exclaim: "Go on in, Adjutant—I'm hit." Despite his strong Presbyterian faith, Robison undoubtedly would have been treated with alcohol or laudanum. With a battlefield surgeon digging a bullet out of his thigh, perhaps he even welcomed such substances—at least for their practical applications.

APPOMATTOX: BRANDY, ACCEPTED AND REFUSED

As Lee's army limped west to Appomattox in an attempt to gain desperately needed supplies, engagements with the enemy occurred sporadically. But on the evening of April 7, bright moonshine flooding the lines, the Union brought forth a flag of truce, in order that Grant could send a letter to Lee. The letter essentially pointed out what Lee already knew; that the Army of Northern Virginia was on the verge of collapse from lack of food and basic supplies such as boots. General Seth Williams, a native of Maine and by most reports a gregarious man around camp, strode forth to meet Colonel Herman Perry of Georgia and brought with him what Perry called "the first demand of surrender of [Lee's] devoted army."

Williams also brought something painfully enticing, as Perry related years later:

> After I introduced myself he felt in his side pocket for documents, I thought, but the document was a very nice-looking silver flask, as far as I could distinguish. He remarked that he hoped I would not think it unsoldierly courtesy if he offered me some very fine brandy. I will own up now that I wanted that drink awfully. Worn down, hungry, and dispirited, it would have been a gracious God-send if some old Confederate and I could have emptied that flask between us in that dreadful hour of misfortune. But I raised myself about an inch higher, if possible, bowed, and refused politely, trying to produce the ridiculous appearance of having feasted on champagne and pound-cake not ten minutes before, and that I had not the slightest use for as plebian a drink as "fine brandy."

General Williams may well have sensed his adversary's unenviable situation, but he did not push Perry to accept the offer, nor did he use his liquid wealth to tease his counterpart. As Perry noted:

> He was a true gentleman, begged pardon, and placed the flask in his pocket again without touching the contents in my presence. If he had taken a drink, and my Confederate

olfactories had obtained a whiff of the odor of it, it is possible that I should have "caved." The truth is, I had not eaten two ounces in two days, and I had my coat-tail then full of corn, waiting to parch it as soon as an opportunity might present itself. I did not leave it behind me, because I had nobody I could trust it with.

PEACH BRANDY AND BEES

The day of April 9 brought yet another curious meeting that involved brandy. Colonel Thomas Munford's Confederate cavalrymen were fighting it out with Yankee horsemen, when, during a brief pause in the shooting, blue-clad officers emerged with a flag of truce. Their main purpose was to alert Munford that Lee had agreed to surrender the Army of Northern Virginia to Grant—and to suggest that Munford follow suit.

Munford had received a large canteen full of excellent peach brandy just that morning. The gift was from his quartermaster, who lived in the Appomattox vicinity and feared the splendid liquor would only fall into the hands of the hated Yankees if left on the premises. Ironically, this grand brandy suffered that exact fate, but in a roundabout way. As Munford explained in his memoirs:

> It was a big canteen, but I do not think I had yet tasted it when I rode into the Federal lines. As we stood talking together, one of the bluecoated officers with an exceedingly delicate nose must have detected its presence. He looked at me rather meaningly, smiled thirstily, and asked me if I knew where there was a good spring about. I took the hint and told him, no. But, I added, "Here's some old peach brandy that a friend of mine gave me this morning—if you could make that do?"

The light in his eye was a lovely thing to see. "Well," said he, "it is not often soldiers meet under such circumstances. I believe I could."

I handed the canteen to him and said to them all, "Gentlemen, you are welcome!" and sent it around the circle of officers.

When Munford finally got his canteen back, he was somewhat chagrined (but slightly amused, too) to find that "all the aroma was there, but the fluid was gone." One of the more jovial Yankees wisecracked to him: "Look out, General, that the bees don't attack you. It smells good enough. You see we are your friends now."

To which Munford could only shrug and later write: "They were in the best of spirits and the best of spirits was in them."

The peach brandy may have been "captured," but Munford and his men were not. Honoring the flag of truce, the Yankee officers allowed him to ride back to his own lines (albeit with an empty canteen). But when Lee was surrendering at Appomattox, Munford and the last remnants of his cavalry regiments rode on to Lynchburg, which was still in rebel hands, intending to join Joe Johnston in North Carolina. That last slim hope also evaporated before the end of the month when Sherman accepted Johnston's surrender on April 26.

On April 29, a despondent Munford gave himself up to Federal authorities at Lynchburg and officially emerged as a parolee. Not unlike other Confederate officers, Munford became involved in some post-war squabbles over what *really* happened at certain pivotal times during the war. Specifically, Munford—who had been involved in the worst fighting at Five Forks—held a grudge against his superiors who had attended a shad bake (most likely, not one washed down with cold water) instead of the battle on that grim day.

For example, Munford once stated that Fitz Lee could not write an account about a battle that he did not actually take part in. He also had some acrimonious exchanges—mostly through newspapers—with the pugnacious General Rosser, who even sent him a challenge to a duel through an intermediary. Munford found the challenge rather ridiculous and did not accept, but neither did he retreat into silence. "I believe I have worked out a truthful story of the battle of Five Forks," he once wrote, "It will make every true Confederate soldier who served in the Army of Northern Virginia realize that someone failed in duty."

THE "INTOXICATION OF TRIUMPH"

Boxed in and facing inevitable defeat after a morning breakout attempt (led by General John B. Gordon) failed to gain any real or lasting advantage, General Robert E. Lee met General U. S. Grant at the McLean house and signed what most historians view as very generous surrender terms. The defeated Confederates could keep their sidearms and horses. It was around 3:00 p.m.—Palm Sunday. The Federal officers on hand, whether by instinct or order, displayed no inclination to gloat. Lee admitted to Grant that his men had mostly been subsisting on "parched corn" for several days. Grant arranged to send over massive amounts of food for Lee's famished fighters, including much of what Sheridan's cavalry had captured from the tattered and retreating Butternuts over the previous few days.

No doubt there were bottles broken out and canteens passed about by both officers and common soldiers when the official news finally came, but—for once and perhaps the only time in the terrible war—John Barleycorn was *not* the most potent spirit abounding. As General Regis de Trobriand (the same officer who was the target of Private Haley's acerbic "Froggy" barbs) penned in his memoirs:

All at once a tempest of hurrahs shook the air along the front of our line.... Mad hurrahs fill the air like the rolling of thunder, in the fields, in the woods, along the roads, and are prolonged in echo.... All the hopes of four years at last realized; all the fears dissipated...all the sufferings, all the misery ended; the intoxication of triumph; the joy at the near return to the domestic hearth...

This "intoxication of triumph," however, was soon to be blunted when, less than a week later, the stunning and horrific news of Lincoln's murder would come out of Washington.

CHAPTER 15

THE HANGOVER
1865

LINCOLN'S ASSASSINATION AND ALCOHOL

Abraham Lincoln may have been an extremely temperate drinker (if not a complete abstainer) himself, but men drinking alcohol played a major role in his assassination on April 14. The evening of Lincoln's murder at Ford's Theatre, Lincoln's substitute bodyguard John Parker allegedly ducked over to Peter Taltavull's Star Saloon to sip a tankard of ale, just prior to the third act of *Our American Cousin*. While Parker imbibed his ale, John Wilkes Booth entered the bar. As Taltavull testified in the post-assassination trials:

> [Booth] just walked into the bar and asked for some whiskey. I gave him the whiskey; put the bottle on the counter…he called for some water and I gave him some. He put money on the counter and went right out. I saw

him go out of the bar alone, as near as I could judge, from eight to ten minutes before I heard the cry that the President was assassinated.

The president's regular bodyguard, William H. Crook (off duty on the night of the assassination), insisted that whiskey played a role in Lincoln's murder. That—and what Crook saw as Parker's inexcusable abandonment of his post outside Lincoln's theater box—certainly sealed Abe's fate. As Crook chronicled:

> Booth had found it necessary to stimulate himself with whiskey in order to reach the proper pitch of fanaticism. Had he found a man at the door of the President's box with a Colt's revolver, his alcohol courage might have evaporated.

In addition, Secretary of State William Seward narrowly survived a knife attack in his bedroom from one of Booth's accomplices—an Alabama native known as Lewis Payne (a.k.a. "Paine"). Vice President Andrew Johnson also was on the conspirators' hit list, but he most likely escaped because George Atzerodt—a German immigrant in Booth's band—could not work up the necessary nerve for it. Instead of carrying out his assignment, Atzerodt brooded in a tavern and got drunk.

REACTIONS TO LINCOLN'S MURDER

Word of Lincoln's assassination and subsequent death caused a variety of reactions around America—with most of the North, of course, in shock, and then mourning. However, reaction to President Lincoln's murder by the "crazy actor" was more complicated for the Confederates. As John S. Wise admitted in his *End of an Era*:

In blood and flame and torture the temples of our lives
were tumbling about our heads. We were desperate and
vindictive, and whosoever denies it forgets or is false.…
To us, Lincoln was an inhuman monster, Grant a butcher,
and Sherman a fiend.

Years later, Wise and other deep-thinking men of the South
would be much more forgiving toward Lincoln, but days after Lee's
capitulation—and with Johnston's surrender all but inevitable—
there was only room for bitterness.

And for many rebels, hard drinking seemed like a logical chaser
to that bitterness. News reached the forces in North Carolina several days after the act—first as a rumor, and finally as fact. While
Sherman and Johnston hammered out a feasible surrender agreement, Pierre Beauregard was forced to deal with drunken soldiers
singing and celebrating Lincoln's death outside his tent. According
to one of his staff officers, the normally reserved Creole lost control
of his temper: "Shut those men up," demanded the hero of Fort
Sumter and Bull Run. "If they won't shut up, have them arrested.
Those are my orders."

As Lieutenant R. M. Collins of the Fifteenth Texas Infantry
recalled in his memoirs, "the boys" got staggeringly drunk on
applejack while Johnston and Sherman pondered the exact and
final surrender terms near Greensboro. But their soaking was
admittedly half out of sorrow for the doomed "cause" and half out
of jubilation for what most of them could only view as just retribu-
tion for a tyrant:

The next morning we were a hard looking set, and for
the boys we plead as an excuse for this spree the peculiar surroundings. We were just at the threshold of the
dying days of the Confederacy, and we had received
that morning the news of the assassination of President

Lincoln.... Referring to the last named incident it was
very natural for a large majority of the boys to rejoice
at the news, while a few wagged their heads and said
they feared it portended bad luck and hard times for
the South, and history has demonstrated that they were
right...

The stunning revelation of Lincoln's death took longer to reach
the more remote places around the continent. Somewhere in rural
Kentucky, for instance, the news reached the guerrillas still serving
under the notorious Captain William Quantrill. The hardened
hit-and-run raiders of "Bloody Kansas" infamy also saw Lincoln's
assassination as a reason to celebrate. As John McCorkle recalled
in his memoirs *Three Years with Quantrill*:

> Just before we reached Salt River, a man met us and
> handed Colonel Quantrill a paper, telling him to read
> it to us. It was an account of the assassination of
> Abraham Lincoln. Before the Colonel had finished
> reading it, we all began to cheer and, breaking ranks,
> we all started at a gallop and never stopped until we
> reached Jim Dawn's still house, where we stayed for
> a day or two.

Perhaps seeking a slightly more refined place to imbibe, Quantrill and several of his officers later showed up at a pro-slavery
judge's homestead. They confessed to those within that they already
were "a little in our cups" over the grand news. Glasses emerged
and Kentucky whiskey gurgled into them. One of the guerrillas
proposed a bold toast, brimming with pure hate: "Here's to the
death of Abraham Lincoln, hoping that his bones may serve in hell
as a gridiron to fry Yankees on."

ONE FOR THE ROAD

Rebels hoping to make their way south to join Johnston's army in North Carolina, or recently paroled men merely trying to head back home, were still on the lookout for some spirits—be it whiskey, wine, or applejack—to make that journey more tolerable. One of those recent parolees was the Virginian John Dooley, who found himself near Danville with a travelling friend, as he recalled in his memoirs:

> By and by young Jackson points out a house by the road side where he thinks we can get some apple brandy. We enter and a nice and gentle woman with a sad expression...consents to sell us a pint (for accommodation sake), but is far more concerned for her absent husband whom she fears has been killed in the recent battles...
>
> We divide the brandy, but I think young Jackson gets the largest share for he very soon after as we resume our journey shows unmistakable signs of elevation; doffing his hat and twirling it high in the air he puts his nag to redoubled speed and bids us follow him.

With the dissolving of Lee's Army of Northern Virginia, scenes quite similar were no doubt unfolding throughout Dixie, as wounded, dog-tired soldiers continued to limp back to their farms and villages. A bottle, flask, or canteen—particularly if filled with some of "the ardent"—was considered a precious accessory for these Butternuts, whether downtrodden or defiant in their defeat.

AN APPLEJACK BREAKFAST

As the end game played out—even as Johnston and Sherman were arranging for final surrender discussions—there were ongoing skirmishes. One of the last (perhaps even *the* last of significance) occurred near Chapel Hill, North Carolina, and—as fate would have it—the rebels had just stumbled upon "some gallons of applejack" that they had divided between a water bucket and a washtub.

However, Yankees soon rudely infringed upon their planned morning refreshments, according to a rebel trooper named David Sadler who was part of Wheeler's cavalry. Sadler, as quoted in a 1902 article for *Southern Heritage*, remembered:

> ...before the cups had gone around the outer pickets fired. Of course, we could not pour the jack out; it was too rich for the Yanks. So we drank it in a hurry, and mounted our horses. The enemy was on us, and the scrap began.

After a series of small but spirited engagements, there was a pause in the vigorous action some hours later, and the Federals tried to make contact with their "lubricated" adversaries.

> "Hello, Johnny; don't shoot! We want to make peace with you." We hallooed back: "All right." Then he rode out in the fence corner in plain view and hallooed:
>
> "Johnny, what command is that?"
>
> "The Eleventh Texas."
>
> He hallooed back: "What is the matter with you boys this morning?"
>
> "We are drunk and reckless, and if you want to fight come over!"
>
> "I thought there was something the matter, for we never saw you boys so lively before; go into camp, the war is over for to-day."
>
> He turned and went away.

TIGHT TEXANS

These bonanza finds of applejack rippled through various Texas regiments under General Johnston's command in the final days of the war, as is strongly evident in various journals and diaries of other Lone Star State soldiers. As Captain Samuel T. Foster of the Fifteenth Texas Infantry noted:

> Soon after we arrive[d] at our new camp today some of our men found two barrels of Old Apple brandy buried under the root of an old pine tree that had blown down. One barrel of it was brought to our brigade and tapped— Everyone helped themselves and of course some get funny, some get tight, some get gentlemanly drunk and some get dog drunk, of this latter class are all the officers from our Major up. Kept up a noise nearly all night but no one gets mad—all in good humor.

Lieutenant R. M. Collins of the same unit described a similar scenario—although admitting he could not remember all the intricate details because he himself had over-indulged:

> All hands got drunk. Even our chaplain, the Reverend Hayes, a very excellent man, got drunk as an "English lord." The effect of the fluid extract of apples on the mental and physical outfit of the writer [Lieutenant Collins] was such that he cannot keep in the middle of the road in an effort at describing what the boys said and done during the remainder of the day and night.

BRECKINRIDGE: THIRSTY AND HOG-TIED

When General Johnston arranged to meet Sherman for surrender discussions, he asked if Breckinridge—the former U.S. vice president, though a rebel general for the most recent four years—could attend. After some initial reluctance, Sherman allowed it. John S. Wise related some comic relief in this particular episode, claiming that General Johnston told him the story. But Wise, out of deference to his confidant, declined to share it until after "Uncle Joe's" death.

Johnston claimed that Breckinridge—in addition to all the other hardships during the final days of Dixie—had to endure an extended period of unplanned abstinence from alcohol. The Kentuckian had, however, managed to secure some fine tobacco and chewed upon these brownish plugs in lieu of ardent spirits. But without his usual liquid stimulant, Johnston told Wise that Breckinridge seemed "rather dull and heavy" on the day they powwowed with Sherman at James Bennett's farmhouse in Durham County.

"Uncle Billy" arrived late, but with saddlebags, which he settled carefully upon a chair. There was a suggestion that the parties should start hammering out terms. Then, according to Johnston (as Wise reported):

> "Yes," said Sherman, "but, gentlemen, it occurred to me that perhaps you were not overstocked with liquor, and I procured some medical stores on my way over. Will you join me before we begin work?"
>
> General Johnston said he watched the expression of Breckinridge at this announcement and it was beatific. Tossing the quid into the fire, he rinsed his mouth, and when the bottle and glass were passed to him, he poured out a tremendous drink, which he swallowed with great satisfaction. With an air of content, he stroked his mustache and took a fresh chew of tobacco.

What transpired next, according to Johnston, was that Breckinridge—perhaps on the strength of his recent refreshment—lobbied most eloquently for terms. Sherman supposedly groused that he wondered just which side was surrendering and that his downtrodden adversaries would soon have him writing a "letter of apology to Jeff Davis" if they had their way. But Breckinridge's eloquence soon dried up when Sherman gurgled out a *second* drink for himself—but then placed the bottle back in his saddlebags without offering refills for his gray-clad visitors.

As they were leaving the Yankee headquarters, Breckinridge admitted to Johnston (who had known Sherman from years prior to the Civil War) that Sherman was a "bright man" and a "man of great force." However, "raising his voice and with a look of great intensity" Breckinridge added: "General Johnston, General Sherman is a hog. Yes, sir, a *hog*. Did you see him take that drink by himself?"

The surrender terms may have been quite reasonable. But Breckinridge—the same jolly Johnny who had helped decimate the Blair wine cellar during Jubal Early's Washington raid the previous year—obviously thought a second pour should have been forthcoming. Johnston tried to assure Breckinridge that Sherman was simply absentminded, but Breckinridge claimed that "no Kentucky gentleman" would have denied them the rest of that bottle when it should have been quite obvious to Sherman that they were in such need of it.

REVVED UP REBELS

Wise also documented the discontent—some of it alcohol-fueled—among the Confederate ranks; first, as they waited for official word, and then again when that official word finally came (on April 26). Johnston, like Lee, had surrendered. But not all the Johnnies were ready to graciously accept defeat and reconcile with the Northern invaders. According to Wise:

> They were defiant and more than ready to try conclusions with Sherman in a pitched battle. Many expressed

disgust and indignation when the surrender of the army was announced. An epidemic of drunkenness, gambling, and fighting prevailed while we waited for our final orders. Whatever difficulty General Breckenridge may have experienced in procuring liquor, the soldiers seemed to have an abundance of colorless corn-whiskey and applejack, and the roadsides were lined with "chuck-a-luck" games. The amount of Confederate money displayed was marvelous. Men had it by the haversackful, and bet it recklessly upon anything. The ill-temper begotten by drinking and gambling manifested itself almost hourly in free fights.

DECEPTIVE JACK

The shooting had stopped, but the boys in blue did not go home, at least not immediately. What they *did* do—with danger less likely and camp boredom back with a vengeance—was drink more.

The Sixteenth Pennsylvania Cavalry was a fairly typical example of this behavior, as Samuel Cormany's diary clearly shows. The boys may have been a bit off the leash, in fact, due to the absence of Colonel Robison, who was still recovering at the U.S. Cavalry Corps hospital from the bullet that ripped into his thigh at Farmville. On April 15, 1865, still in camp in Virginia, not far from the vanquished city of Petersburg, Cormany wrote:

> Saturday. Rainy day—Capt Snyder and Lieut Barnes took out a foraging party—captured a wagon—also apple Jack—got some trophies—Is a general time of drunkenness amongst the Officers—Capt Snyder goes on awfully—were our dear Col Robison here there would be some putting under arrest—...[W]ould be happy, but for the drinking of the Officers.

By May, the regiment was ordered to Lynchburg, Virginia, and there was still an abundance of applejack about, as reflected in Cormany's journal. In fact, despite his previous complaints about his fellow officers, Cormany admitted that he, too, had a joust with "Jack" and did not fare so well. On May 26, he penned:

> Friday. Rains and blows—Mostly laying off in office— and "let her drive"
>
> P.M. Ride out with Maj Bell—Get some old apple brandy or Jack—Eve Capt Snyder and I go to town— Lynchburg—and 2nd Brig Hd. Qrs—
>
> …Indulged some in "Apple Jack"—Got pretty lively— In fact, a little unmanned—
>
> That stuff is so deceptive—I've vowed and vowed, and sinned again. Twere better now not to vow. But here I am—ashamed—to know, we both have been foolish— not vicious but too giddy for the rank and place we occupy—The Boys don't see our foolishness—Tis well! Their respect would suffer a little shock! We separate! And soon find our bunks and sleep, and so things go once in a long while. But God forgives—and soon I'll be at Home, and be myself.

By the end of May, Colonel J. K. Robison recovered from his bullet wound and returned, and presumably overindulgence in applejack was greatly reduced. Cormany lauds Robison in a May 31 entry, writing: "O how glad I am that Col Robison has returned. His Fatherly presence is a blessing, but makes me feel my littleness, and see wherein I have been retrograding…"

HOMEWARD BOUND

On June 14, 1865, Colonel John Kincaid Robison delivered a farewell address to his troopers. It was more than two months since

General Robert E. Lee had surrendered at Appomattox, and the men were anxious to leave Virginia and return to the familiar rural hills and villages of their native Pennsylvania. About ninety lucky troopers were fortunate enough to get mustered out, as the army was sending its soldiers home in gradual waves.

The short reading was delivered to the regiment at their evening dress parade. It was quite typical of regimental farewells made across the Union army. Robison's speech featured, as one would expect, the flowery patriotic language of an era that now seems quite antiquated to the modern ear. But, interestingly, it also included a strong urging to give up any "bad habits" that these cavalry troopers might have picked up during months of camp life (perhaps a thinly veiled admonishment for past digressions).

Of course, given a closer examination of the journals of the Civil War years, one cannot help but think "bad habits" probably referred to "whiskey" and "applejack" (along with gambling and perhaps womanizing, though rank-and-file soldiers had little opportunity for the latter).

BACKSLIDIN' SAM

Samuel Cormany may have been overjoyed to have the guiding presence of Colonel Robison returned to the Sixteenth Cavalry, but that in itself was not a total guarantee that John Barleycorn would not still win an occasional round or two. As one of the hapless soldiers still on duty in the Lynchburg area, Cormany wrote on June 27:

> Tuesday. Beautiful day...Dr. Cox and I went to city at 10 a.m...I accosted a Rebel Major who had been drinking some—I took in a fine dinner—Called on Dear Maitland, White, Capt Moss and others—Some 16 of us officers had some "mint julips" [sic]—some too much,

got quite boozy, and made themselves ridiculous—Doc and I put up at a Boarding House for a fine dinner—and quiet. Some got to [sic] high for others of us—But we must not abandon any of our Fellows...about midnight got all hands pretty well regulated, and Doc Cox, and returned to Camp, about 2 ock. A.M. rather ashamed of ourselves for having been drawn into such a crowd of officers and such hilarity.

CHAPTER 16

ONE LAST CHASER
1865

TOASTING COUSIN SALLY ANN

O f course, it took some men longer than others to "get home." Such was the case with a number of the Confederate generals imprisoned at Fort Warren in Boston. Eppa Hunton finally got his freedom in late July, more than three full months after his capture at Saylor's Creek in early April.

Perhaps surprisingly, there were *some* Southern sympathizers in the Boston area, and, upon their release, Hunton and some of his comrades were brought to socialize with some of them. At the Boston area home of the Salter family, a young woman asked Hunton to join her in a wine toast to a "Cousin Sally Ann." Hunton, admittedly thirsty, and more than amenable to the social ritual of a toast, readily agreed. But he also admitted to his youthful hostess that he had no idea who her "Cousin Sally Ann" might be.

The proposer of the toast laughed and almost simultaneously it dawned on Hunton that "Cousin (C) Sally (S) Ann (A)" was a handy way for those sympathetic to "the Cause" to salute the Confederate States of America without incurring the wrath of Bostonians who might not appreciate the sentiments hidden in the acronym.

THE TEETOTALER'S TRIUMPH

There were a few good men who somehow got through the war without so much as a waltz with John Barleycorn. One of these was Elisha Hunt Rhodes, a Rhode Island officer. The war already over for three months, his men were ready to muster out. On Sunday, July 9, 1865, Rhodes—who started the war as a private and finished it as a young colonel—penned in his diary:

> Although I want to go home, yet as I think of the separation from comrades some of whom I have known for more than four years, I cannot help but feeling sad. I trust that I entered the Army with pure motives and from love of country. I have tried to keep myself from evil ways and believe that I have never forgotten that I am a Christian. Thank God no spirituous liquors have ever passed my lips as a beverage, and I feel I can go home to my family as pure as when I left them as a boy of 19 years.

Along similar lines, Samuel K. Miller, a Pennsylvania infantryman stationed in Alexandria, Virginia, in the weeks after Lee's surrender, was frustrated by the unabashed sinfulness displayed by many of his fellow soldiers, writing:

> The soldiers are all complaining and lying about. They say—Why don't the government discharge us and let us go home? Then they will curse and swear and get drunk.

There is nothing too bad for them to say or do. They don't even thank their Heavenly Father for the preservation of their wicked souls to the present time.

Suffice to say, when it came to resisting temptation and praising the Lord, Colonel Rhodes and Private Miller were part of a distinct minority among the hardened veterans who fought on either side during America's bloodiest war.

JEFFERSON DAVIS IN PRISON

After the surrenders of Lee and Johnston, the Federals were faced mostly with minor "mopping up" exercises. However, one crucial goal remaining was to capture Confederate President Jefferson Davis. Still espousing a "fight on" philosophy, Davis had hastily left Richmond on April 2. With Lincoln's assassination a dozen days later, the search for Davis and his entourage intensified. On May 10, near Irwinsville, Georgia, Yankee cavalry troopers captured Davis. He was subsequently sent to a small prison cell at Fort Monroe, Virginia.

Davis would languish in this confinement for two years, but an expected trial for treason never came. During his imprisonment, Davis no doubt was forced to adjust to an existence that was more like that of a monk than a monarch. In fact, in the earliest period of his confinement, Davis was subjected to leg irons for five days. Varina Davis—the former leader's wife—did attempt to brighten her husband's day-to-day life. On November 7, 1865, she wrote to him: "Will you not be permitted to receive books and delicacies? I have procured some very old brandy for you in Charleston, and some good cigars."

Eventually, Davis was moved from his tiny casement to a bigger room with a fireplace. By the fall of 1866, Varina was allowed to visit him and Davis was allowed to receive gifts from friends— including wines, whiskey, fine liquors, and cigars. Although he battled problems with his eyesight, the former leader of the Rebellion also enjoyed short stints of reading and was permitted extended walks—with the promise that he would not attempt to escape.

President Andrew Johnson eventually pardoned Davis on Christmas in 1868.

THE LAST FLAG FLYING

Jefferson Davis's earliest months in prison were elevated somewhat by the knowledge of one Confederate raider still at large—the well-travelled *Shenandoah*. In his memoirs, Davis wrote:

> With General E. K. Smith's surrender [June 2] the Confederate flag no longer floated on the land, but one gallant sailor still unfurled it on the Pacific. Captain Waddell, commanding the Confederate cruiser *Shenandoah*, swept the oceans from Australia nearly to Behring's Straits, making many captures in the Okhotsk Sea and Arctic Ocean.

Commanded by Captain James Waddell (a graduate of the U.S. Naval Academy), the *Shenandoah* was still striking Yankee whaling ships in the summer of 1865, believing—or at least claiming—that they thought the Confederate States were still resisting Northern aggression.

In August, however, a British ship that had sailed from San Francisco with July newspapers provided the *Shenandoah*'s officers with hard evidence. It was no longer possible to deny that the Confederate government (not to mention its armies) had been disbanded and Jefferson Davis imprisoned.

Faced with that sobering news, Captain Waddell began a long journey toward Liverpool, his intention being to "surrender" the ship in a neutral British port. En route, the crew entertained themselves by watching some native Pacific Islanders (whom they had captured from a whaling ship) perform their native dances and songs, while the rebels swilled drams of whiskey.

The scene was quite in line with the ship's bizarre and colorful history. In January of 1865, the ship had docked in Melbourne, Australia, as Captain Waddell needed to make repairs to his ship, plus resupply with provisions and coal. The rebel crew was quite a curiosity to the Aussies, although it took some time to convince the locals that the raider was *not* commanded by Raphael Semmes, the famed captain of the late *Alabama*. At the Melbourne Club, a toast (following one to the Queen of England, of course) was offered to the officers and crew at a cocktail-hoisting event. Deciding that it was too late to go back to the ship, some of the officers continued to carouse around the city into the wee hours of the next morning. At one point during their stay, some officers attended a Shakespearian play and perhaps were amused when a band struck up "Dixie" between acts—the tune eliciting both cheers and boos from Aussies of divided sympathies in the audience.

Although the *Shenandoah* was one of the most successful rebel raiding ships, its operations often were plagued by drunkenness whenever the crew managed to capture alcohol or secure it while in port. When the *Shenandoah* (flying a Russian flag as a ruse, since they were in the icy Sea of Okhotsk) boarded the Yankee whaling ship *Abigail* in late May of 1865, they were delighted to snag some two dozen barrels of whiskey, brandy, and rum.

Predictably, most of the sailors sent to bring the alcohol over to the *Shenandoah* felt an urgent need to taste it first—as did subsequent waves of men sent across. Many of these seadogs overindulged. According to one officer, before this liquid cargo was finally secured, intoxicated men (including some officers) far outnumbered the sober ones. Such incidents, of course, made it easy for enemies of the Confederate Navy to claim the raiders were essentially nothing more than pirate ships.

On November 5, 1865, Waddell finally brought the *Shenandoah* in and, the next day, officially surrendered her to the British in Liverpool. Within a few days, the queen's law officials ruled that the ship's officers and crew were free to go. That many of the crew were of Irish, English, or Scottish nationality did not go unnoticed by British officials—or, for that matter, by a local newspaper which pointed out that some sailors had accents more likely to be heard on the banks of the Clyde than on the banks of the Mississippi.

Regardless of accent, most of the crew likely made a beeline for the pubs of Liverpool; a preferable place from which to contemplate one's adventuresome past or bright future—as opposed to, say, the dank confines of a Yankee prison cell, shackled in leg irons, with charges of piracy pending.

All things considered, it was not the worst way for a sailor to end the war.

EPILOGUE

In the weeks and months following General Lee's and then General Johnston's respective surrenders, true believers in "the Cause" had to swallow a bitter cocktail—one part despair and one part humiliation. As Mary Chesnut wrote in her diary entry of May 16, 1865, bluntly reflecting the zombie-like state of many vanquished Southerners: "We are scattered—stunned—the remnant of heart left alive with us, filled with brotherly hate."

There also was a dash of fear in this "Lost Cause" cocktail, arising partly from their uncertain future made all the more precarious following Lincoln's assassination. Although some rebels, probably even a majority, initially relished the blow struck by "the crazy actor" John Wilkes Booth, soon they watched nervously for newly-appointed President Johnson's next move. As Chesnut—who like many critics of Lincoln's successor could not resist a potshot at the Tennessean's drinking habits—wrote: "We sit and wait until the drunken tailor who rules the U.S.A. issues a proclamation and defines our anomalous position."

Several months later, the combination of depression and apprehension was still front and center in Mary Chesnut's diary:

> We are shut in here—turned with our faces to a dead wall. No mails. A letter is sometimes brought by a man on horseback, traveling through the wilderness made by Sherman. All RR's [railroads] destroyed—bridges gone. We are cut off from the world—to eat out our own hearts.

Alcohol under these circumstances, if one had access to it, was a much-welcomed and valuable commodity—one to be hidden from raiding Yankees, or even desperate friends. In Mary Chesnut's case, she stashed some wine and brandy behind the fire screen of a chimney in her bedroom.

SHERRY COBBLERS AND CHAMPAGNE FRAPPÉS

Still, despite the smothering presence of the blue-clad conquerors ("Yankees hanging over us like the sword of Damocles"), and despite the sudden poverty of even once wealthy and elite families like the Chesnuts, one could spot occasional hints of normalcy. Life trudged on. The celebrated Cassandra of the Confederacy mentions, in her July 26, 1865, entry, a local wedding and its accompanying festivities:

> How Minnie and I baked and brewed for the wedding... It was a quiet midday celebration. The fete was at the Reynolds'... Dr. Lord showed most unhallowed joy when for the first time in many days a sherry cobbler was offered to his sacred lips. "And such sherry!" he murmured, as he sipped. Champagne frappés *I* did not disdain, with a heart grateful for heaven's good gifts.

If not actually "heaven-sent," those sherry cobblers and champagne frappés at a wedding reception must have provided at least a momentary refuge from the realities of the war-ravaged Carolinas. If your homeland is in ruins, the powers of spirit-lifting libations should not be underestimated.

JOHNSON AND GRANT: THE POST-WAR LIBATIONS

Two men in the public spotlight—one famous, one more infamous—never fully shook the public perception that they were "drinking men." The evidence overwhelmingly indicates that Andrew Johnson and U. S. Grant continued to be exactly that in the years immediately following the Civil War.

Johnson's foes—and there were many on both sides of the Mason-Dixon Line—continued to refer to him as "the drunken little tailor" or similarly unflattering monikers. Some of these accusations that the president was a guzzler may have been overblown, given that fervent rebels labeled the Tennessean as a traitor and hardcore abolitionists perceived him to be too *soft* on the conquered Southerners. Johnson was in a no-win situation.

Certainly the feisty Johnson thought these salvos against him were mean-spirited, once defensively bristling: "It is very strange that some men will be abused like the devil for drinking a glass of whiskey and water, while others...may almost roll in the gutters, and not a word is said about it."

THE SWING AROUND THE CIRCLE

Late in the summer of 1866, in an effort to boost his popularity and gain support for his Reconstruction agenda, President Johnson opted for a tour, dubbed "The Swing Around the Circle." Given some of the drinking that went on, Johnson's enemies might have substituted "Swig" for "Swing."

To spearhead his entourage, Johnson enlisted General Ulysses S. Grant, Admiral David Farragut, and General George Armstrong Custer. Johnson was well aware that he could bask in their reflected glory. However, not all the important members of the traveling party were military men. The presence of Henry Chadwick, the proprietor of Willard's Hotel, on the list was a sure sign that the traveling party would not be deprived of top-shelf booze and luxury provisions.

Admiral Farragut was, at best, an extremely cautious imbiber. And—perhaps surprisingly given his proclivity for aggressive and reckless battlefield tactics—the flamboyant General Custer did not ride with Demon Alcohol. As Nathaniel Philbrick, one of Custer's more recent biographers, wrote in *The Last Stand*: "Custer did not drink; he didn't have to. His emotional effusions unhinged his judgment in ways that went far beyond alcohol's ability to interfere with clear thinking."

Ulysses Simpson Grant, however, was a different case altogether.

GRANT GOES DOWN

General Grant still had a tendency to get tripped up by his old nemesis, John Barleycorn. It did not help matters that, due to his fame as a victorious general, there was no short supply of well-wishers and sycophants—including some prominent men—who wanted to drink with the man who had accepted Lee's surrender at Appomattox.

Grant's track record of staying sober when bored, or without at least periodic supervision from his wife Julia, was a checkered one. Since the trip with Johnson involved free lunches and banquets at various stops, there was a constant call for toasts and plenty of fast-flowing spirits. The end result for Grant was predictable.

The claim (some say a dubious one) that Grant tumbled "off the wagon" while on Johnson's "Swing" came from Sylvanus Cadwallader—the former war correspondent—years afterward.

According to Cadwallader, a festively-minded delegation from Cleveland greeted the president's train in New York State with food and, of course, lots of alcohol. Grant allegedly caved to temptation and—since he was notoriously lacking in tolerance—was soon too drunk to function.

In an effort to keep away reporters or curious onlookers who might be astounded to see the Union's most esteemed hero in an intoxicated state, Grant was tossed in an empty railcar where—according to Cadwallader—he passed out on some empty mailbags. Cadwallader and John Rawlins (now a general, but still covering up Grant's episodic smashups, if the story is true) supposedly stood guard to turn back any would-be intruders.

In Cleveland, President Johnson made excuses for Grant's absence, telling the crowd that the victor of Vicksburg and Appomattox was feeling too ill to address them. Grant proceeded by ship to Detroit and wrote to his wife Julia that he was desperately in need of some rest—which certainly was true. However, there was no mention of alcohol to Mrs. Grant.

JOHNSON UNDER FIRE

With Grant sidelined, the "Swing's" major draw was gone—and that was not good news for Andrew Johnson. Later in the tour, Johnson got into shouting exchanges with hecklers, some of whom were demanding that the president "Hang Jeff Davis!" It was somewhat reminiscent of Johnson's botched "speech" at Lincoln's second inauguration, with the pugnacious pol more than eager to berate the audience. Johnson may have been sober (more or less) this time, but he nevertheless appeared combative and undignified. Soon after, the "Swing" was mercifully cut short.

The U.S. Congress impeached Johnson in 1868, but the Senate—by one vote—managed to keep him in the Executive Mansion. According to the presidential bodyguard William Crook, who ran all the way from the Capitol to the White House to deliver the good news, a grateful and teary-eyed Johnson immediately called for whiskey from the cellar. Glasses were filled and passed around, and toasts to Johnson's good luck—for he had definitely dodged a political bullet—were offered in solemn appreciation. A telegraph of congratulations from William Seward also arrived; apparently Seward had wagered on Johnson's acquittal and had won a basket of champagne on what some men might have said were rather long and optimistic odds.

However, nobody was under the illusion that Johnson could get re-elected. He eventually moved back to Tennessee and enjoyed a bit of a political comeback when he was elected to the U.S. Senate in 1874. But he never really got free from the firm grasp of Demon Alcohol. According to an account from John S. Wise, Johnston spoke to a Nashville crowd from a balcony of the city's swanky Maxwell House Hotel, just months before his death. Wise documented:

> It was a pitiful sight to see him standing there, holding on to the iron railing in front of him and swaying back and forth, almost inarticulate with drink.... It was a sight I shall never forget—the bloated, stupid, helpless look of Mr. Johnson, as he was hurried away from the balcony to his rooms by his friends and led staggering through the corridors of the Maxwell House.

GRANT IN THE WHITE HOUSE

Even after Ulysses S. Grant was elected as the eighteenth president of the United States (serving from 1869 to 1877), he was never quite free of the drinking accusations that hounded him from his days as a military man. Grant did not stop imbibing, but he *was* acutely aware of his shaky reputation concerning alcohol. Therefore, the former general took precautions to avoid any serious drinking stints before anyone other than intimate friends or family. The president had no desire to be chastised about his drinking or, for that matter, his penchant for smoking fine cigars.

At the White House dinners, Grant indulged in champagne and other wines—the whiskey-swilling general seemingly a forgotten ghost of his soldierly past. Secret Service agent William Crook recorded that President Grant accumulated a splendid collection of wines and took keen interest in them:

> General Grant particularly loved to have a few friends for dinner.... He chose the wines himself, and gave directions that they should be served at the proper temperature.... General Grant was an open-handed lavish host. I remember one wine bill which impressed me very much at the time—$1,800 for champagne alone.

Crook also told an anecdote about a mishap involving a much-coveted vintage:

> It was brought out for one of the big dinners, and the President went himself, with Henry and Edgar, two of the servants, to have it drawn off into eight large decanters. On the way down, Henry stumbled and fell, breaking the four decanters he was carrying. The President turned and looked at him, but didn't express his feelings further. When they got down-stairs, General Grant said to Beckley, the steward:
> "Get four other decanters and go to the garret and fill them, but don't let Henry go again!"

Despite his obvious interest in fine wines, Grant apparently still—at least on occasions—drank stronger liquors, particularly good brandy. The seldom-circulated "Donaldson Diaries" document some of Grant's alcohol indulgences during his White House years.

Thomas Corwin Donaldson—a prominent man from Ohio—was a close friend to President Rutherford B. Hayes, but he also knew Presidents Grant and James Garfield quite well. He often had access to the White House and was well known to various staffers. In regards to Grant's drinking during his White House years, Donaldson wrote:

> He had many cronies, and I recall a club room where he used to...play a social game of cards...
>
> Sen. Osburn of Fla., once told me that John Francis of Troy, N.Y., went up to the White House during Grant's first term, played poker with a party, got fuddled—was Grant's partner in this perhaps—did it well, and the next day, to his surprise, was appointed Minister to Greece. Is a good hand at poker a qualification for a foreign Minister?

Donaldson also was a friendly acquaintance of Samuel Taylor Suit (he was called "Colonel Suit" in a Kentuckian honorary fashion), a man quite familiar to President Grant and other prominent Washingtonians. Colonel Suit was best known for his whiskey production, but he also created magnificent peach, apple, and cherry brandies from the vast orchards at Suitland, his Maryland estate. Donaldson wrote:

> President Grant seldom spent an evening at home. He went out dining with his friends. Col. S. T. Suit, who knew him well, once told me that he used to meet him in a private club room...and that he had a partial side for some fine French brandy in his (Suit's) house. Sometimes he was very partial to it.

In 1871, delegates from Great Britain and the United States met to work out the damages involving the infamous rebel raider *Alabama* (constructed by the British). President Grant assigned the meetings to Suitland—and one suspects the delegates therefore had ample opportunities to sample Colonel Suit's stellar lineup of liquors.

THE WHISKEY RING

Whiskey—though not whiskey consumed by Grant—did leave some scandalous scars on the great general's legacy in the White House. The Whiskey Ring was a conspiracy in the mid-1870s that allowed the perpetrators—some of them close associates of Grant—to skim millions of uncollected tax dollars that should have gone into government coffers. Although most historians believe Grant had no direct knowledge of the massive fraud, some of his cronies were prosecuted for their involvement.

Grant's U.S. Secretary of the Treasury Benjamin Bristow was the one who uncovered the Whiskey Ring scam and, with bulldoggish tenacity, went after the conspirators at all levels. Initially, Bristow had President Grant's support, but that faded rapidly when the scandal led directly to the White House; Bristow wanted to prosecute Grant's personal secretary and gatekeeper, General Orville Babcock, who apparently assisted the St. Louis-based ring in laundering the take. Babcock—who had been by Grant's side as an aide-de-camp for the last year of the war, including Lee's surrender at Appomattox—was acquitted. That lucky result may have been because Grant himself filed a disposition on Babcock's behalf, emphatically claiming that Babcock was a man of integrity and stellar character. Nevertheless, the scandal forced Babcock to resign, though he managed to avoid prison.

GRANT'S DEATH

Although he was a drinker, it may not have been whiskey (or whiskey ring scandals) that sent Grant to his grave. The general was very fond of tobacco, particularly cigars, and often smoked or chewed half a dozen in a day. Medical experts today recognize that heavy alcohol and tobacco use are oral cancer risks; perhaps unsurprisingly, the sixty-three-year-old former president was diagnosed with throat cancer in 1885.

To add to the dire situation, Grant was essentially bankrupt, having lost most of his savings in an investment scam. The general, in fact, was forced to sell much of his personal Civil War collection in order to pay off some of his more pressing debts.

Mark Twain stepped up to help land the old general a solid publishing contract. Grant—racing against his fading health—set about writing his memoirs. He finished the manuscript just days before his death on July 23, 1885. In his final days, Grant's physicians periodically dosed him with brandy and cocaine to combat the pain.

As for Grant's memoirs, they sold more than 300,000 copies and left his surviving family members with a comfortable financial cushion.

FRIENDLY FOES

In the aftermath of America's bloodiest war, men who fought together were often eager to keep ties. Many regiments held annual or semi-annual reunions. There also gradually emerged occasions when former Confederates and Federals came together to commemorate the common hell endured by men on both sides. Gettysburg was an obvious meeting place for former soldiers to remember the ravages of war, but also to pay homage to the heroic actions of soldiers of both armies.

That alcohol often emerged—both in actual bottle form and in stories from the past—at these rendezvous is well documented.

GENERAL MAHONE AND THE WHISKEY PROMISE

In May of 1887, about one hundred men, most of them former soldiers in the Fifty-Seventh and Fifty-Ninth Massachusetts regiments, journeyed down to Virginia to tour various battlefields where, nearly a quarter-century before, they had once fought and lost comrades. One important stop for the Yankees was Petersburg, where many had taken part in that campaign and some in the particular horror known as the Battle of the Crater, fought on July 30, 1864. These New Englanders were received quite enthusiastically by their Virginian counterparts, and the regimental history of the Fifty-Seventh all but raves about the "Southern hospitality" that greeted them this time around—instead of hot musket and cannon fire.

One of the most distinguished attendees on the rebel side was none other than William Mahone, the former general who reaped much fame for his response to the ill-conceived Federal attack at the crater. Mahone—a railroad investor and politician in his post-war years—could not resist sharing a humorous anecdote with the Massachusetts men, remarking:

> Later on came the flag of truce, and then both sides came on the ground between the two lines to bury the dead. During this flag of truce word came from a surgeon of some Yankee regiment that he would send a bottle of whiskey if I would like it. Of course, I said "Yes," and the doctor went back. Whether he was too slow or the time of truce expired I do not know. I did not get that whiskey. I have not seen the doctor since, but some of your men owe me that bottle of whiskey.

Mahone was no doubt surprised when Dr. Whitman V. White subsequently stepped forward and acknowledged that *he* was the surgeon who had promised the general a bottle of whiskey that day. White had fully intended to deliver the gift of spirits, but, he said, the truce had ended abruptly and anyone venturing out on the field would certainly have been risking another addition to the casualty list.

There is no proof that Dr. White came through with the bottle (some twenty-three years after the fact), but the regimental history states that he and General Mahone soon left the battlefield to dine together—and one must presume a glass or two was hoisted during this reunion.

WHEELCHAIRS AND WHISKEY

The Gettysburg soldier reunions of fifty years and seventy-five years were particularly popular. In 1913, more than 50,000 soldiers (about a fifth of the total were Johnnies, some more than happy to demonstrate the famous "Rebel Yell") converged on the small-but-historic Pennsylvania town for the fiftieth anniversary of the battle to pay homage to past events and to fellow soldiers long deceased. The highest-ranking officer was none other than General Daniel Sickles, the now one-legged former commander of the Third Corps. And, of course, alcohol was along for the ride. Drinks went round on the trains, and toasts abounded when the veterans arrived in Gettysburg.

But for July 3–5, 1938—the seventy-fifth anniversary of the pivotal battle—approximately 1,800 veterans arrived, though most of them were well into their ninth decade of life. Those helping with the event wisely had "a fleet of wheelchairs" at the ready, but apparently most of the old soldiers were considerably sprier than anyone might have anticipated.

There may have been enough wheelchairs on hand, but apparently *not* enough whiskey. According to *Richmond Times-Dispatch* editor Virginius Dabney (one of the reunion's chief proponents): "The Southern contingent was afflicted with a notable thirst, and principally because of this fact the original consignment of five cases of liquor was exhausted almost as soon as it was opened."

Event officials, however, rallied to meet the needs of these "dry" soldiers. According to the *Tar Heel Press*, a plane was dispatched and brought back another twenty-two cases of the amber-colored booze. When those cases were gleefully consumed, liquid reinforcements were apparently called in yet again—enough that when these elderly soldiers began the journey home, they were able to fill up some half-pint flasks to keep them in good spirits.

ALCOHOL AND OPIUM

There were, of course, thousands of Civil War soldiers who headed home and continued to pass round the whiskey jug—some probably to cope with the haunting memories of combat. The label of "Post Traumatic Stress Disorder" from the horrors of the battlefield would not have been in vogue, but there can be no question that many men who witnessed the battlefield slaughter from Shiloh to Cold Harbor were affected by it to varying degrees. There was also the problem of opium addiction, since wounded soldiers were frequently treated with combinations of alcohol and opium (often in the form of laudanum) and, when available, even straight morphine. By the end of the Civil War, some crude hypodermic syringes even appeared in the cases of battlefield surgeons. Opium pills (10 million by one account) were also distributed to inhibit the pain of wounds, but also, surprisingly, for far less serious ailments. In fact, opium addiction after the Civil War was sometimes referred to as "the soldier's disease."

In his 1868 book *The Opium Habit*, Horace B. Day, readily recognized the grim "contribution" of the Civil War to the number of addicted citizens in post-war America, placing the number somewhere between 80,000 and 100,000 (though some estimates are in the 400,000-plus range). Even stressed out civilians indulged in opium during the war; Mary Chesnut was a prime example. She documents her occasional use of the drug, seeking relief from various illnesses and periodic depression. Once, when she witnessed something disturbing during the war years, Mrs. Chesnut wrote:

> I quickly took opium.... It enables me to retain every particle of mind or sense or brains I ever had and so quiets my nerves that I calmly reason and take rational views of things otherwise maddening...

HOOD AND THE SUBSTANCE ABUSE CONTROVERSY

Confederate armies under General John Bell "Sam" Hood suffered some major defeats at Franklin and Nashville in 1864, though it is certainly arguable whether those defeats sped up the Confederate capitulation. Rumors that late in the war Hood may have been under the influence of laudanum—that powerful mixture of alcohol and opium—still result in controversy well into the twenty-first century.

Hood perhaps had reason to seek out something to address his pain. He was wounded at Gettysburg, severely enough that he could not use his left arm. A few months later at Chickamauga, Hood took a bullet in his right thigh, ripping through flesh and shattering bone. In excruciating pain, the big man might have plunged to the ground had not his alert soldiers eased him down from the saddle of his battle-spooked steed. In his memoirs—*Advance and Retreat*—Hood wrote that he was then taken to his brigade hospital where "a most difficult operation was performed by Dr. T. G. Richardson of New Orleans." That surgery, in fact, was an amputation of his right leg, just below the hip.

Hood's personal physician—Dr. John T. Darby—soon arrived to supervise the general's recovery. A graduate of the University of

Pennsylvania, Darby kept daily records. Hood's doctor did use "morphia" to treat Hood, but primarily to induce sleep. Although there definitely were some rocky patches during Hood's recovery, Darby also recorded that, on at least one occasion, the general refused treatment with morphine. Although morphine continued to be part of Hood's treatment for most of October, on the eleventh of that month, Darby noted that he also worked in some doses of alcohol—"a half bottle of sherry wine and three milk punches daily." (Milk punches in the Civil War era typically were laced with whiskey or brandy, something akin to eggnog.)

By November, however, Darby's reports indicated that Hood was sleeping *without* the use of morphine. He also was walking on his crutches. The general was well enough that month to travel to Richmond to be fitted with a prosthesis for his amputated leg. While he was in the Confederate capital, Hood also socialized with Mary Chesnut, as she recorded on December 9, 1863:

> He was lying on a sofa with a carriage blanket throw over him.
>
> Some Durchheimer [a German white wine] still remained in the sideboard, which the general enjoyed with his luncheon. Heavens how he was waited upon! Some cut-up oranges were brought to him.
>
> "How kind people are. Not once since I was wounded have I ever been without fruit, hard as it is to get now."

By March of 1864, Hood was back in the field, attempting—unsuccessfully—to push back Sherman's advances into Georgia.

Did the rumors then jump the tracks in their judgment of Hood's supposed substance abuse? Numerous accounts (the original source published in 1940) seem to simply assume that Hood *must* have needed to continue his use of morphine or laudanum in an effort to cope with the pain of his amputated lower leg and severely injured arm. This alleged dependence on painkillers is often offered up to help explain some of Hood's crushing defeats at Franklin and Nashville at the end of 1864. But Hood's defeats may have had more to do with his temperament than any mind-altering substances. Some modern-day detractors note that Hood was described on the battlefield as "all lion, no fox" (i.e., nobody could question the general's courage, but he probably lacked the finesse to qualify as a renowned military tactician).

In recent years, Stephen M. Hood (one of the general's distant relatives) gamely took up Hood's defense on the subject of substance abuse in the field. In *John Bell Hood: The Rise, Fall, and Resurrection of a Confederate General* and a follow-up titled *The Lost Papers of Confederate General John B. Hood*, Stephen Hood calls into question earlier accounts that Hood was dependent on morphine, alcohol, or both late in the war.

PUSHBACK ON INTOXICANTS

Although Prohibition did not become the law of the land until 1919, the forces behind it were galvanized after the Civil War. The proponents of Prohibition tended to be Protestant in their religious leanings and many of the country's hardcore abolitionists—so unbending on the slavery issue—also proved to be equally uncompromising on the evils of alcohol. Veterans unable to kick alcohol addictions, of course, served as prime examples for those convinced that John Barleycorn must die.

The fifteenth president, James Buchanan—himself a legendary guzzler of whiskey and wine—believed those so zealously crusading for the Prohibition cause were on a fool's errand. "In [Prohibition], I think they will entirely fail," he wrote in an 1867 letter. "Lager beer, especially among the Germans, and old rye will be too strong for them. Still, intemperance is a great curse to our people, but it will never be put down by laws prohibiting the sale of all intoxicating liquors…"

Temperance supporters, however, made some symbolic head-way when former Union General Rutherford B. Hayes took over the White House, after the Whiskey Ring scandal tainted the Grant administration. Although Hayes himself had occasionally imbibed in his youth and during the war, his wife Lucy—soon to garner the sobriquet "Lemonade Lucy" for her refusal to serve alcohol at the White House—was most revered by the "dry" contingent.

AN INCIDENT AT A BANQUET: MEADE SUPPORTS GORDON

The friendships of various generals—even between some men once on opposite sides—is closely chronicled in the years after the war. One such memorable relationship developed between General George Gordon Meade (when Meade served as military governor of Georgia) and former Confederate General John Brown Gordon, who would go on to serve as a U.S. Senator (and later Governor) of Georgia.

As Gordon took particular care to highlight in his post-war memoirs:

> An incident at a banquet in the city of Atlanta illustrates his high personal and soldierly characteristics. The first toast of the evening was to General Meade as the honored guest. When this toast had been drunk, my health was proposed. Thereupon, objection was made upon the ground that it was "too soon after the war to be drinking the health of a man who had been fighting for four years in the Rebel army." It is scarcely necessary to say that this remark came from one who did no fighting in either army. He belonged to that curious class of soldiers who were as valiant in peace as they were docile in war; whose defiance of danger became dazzling after the danger was

past. General Meade belonged to the other class of soldiers, who fought as long as fighting was in order, and was ready for peace when there was no longer any foe in the field.

According to Gordon's account, General Meade was quite outraged by the "bomb-proof warrior's" verbal ambush at the expense of his former adversary. The insulting suggestion was barely uttered before Meade scrambled to his feet, raised his drinking vessel high and declared: "I propose to drink, and drink now, to my former foe, but now my friend, General Gordon, of Georgia."

A SIP OF TOM-AND-JERRY WITH UNCLE JOE

One wintery evening around 1880, two former Confederates—a Captain Edwin Harvie and John S. Wise—paid a call to retired CSA General Joseph Johnston, who was then residing in Richmond. Wise—in his *The End of an Era*—recalled the visit quite vividly:

He sat in his armchair in his library, dressed in a flannel wrapper, and was suffering from influenza. By his side, upon a low stool, stood a tray with whiskey glasses, spoons, sugar, lemon, spice and eggs. At the grate a footman held a brass teakettle of boiling water. Mrs. Johnston was preparing hot Tom-and-Jerry for the old gentleman, and he took from time to time with no sign of objection or resistance. It was snowing outside, and the scene within was very cozy. As I had seen him in public, General Johnston was a stiff, uncommunicative man, punctilious and peppery, as little fellows like him are apt to be. He reminded me of a cock sparrow, full of self-consciousness, and rather enjoying a peck at his neighbor.

Visitors, a warm hearth, and the rounds of Tom-and-Jerry must have lifted the sickly old general to a more gregarious state, as Wise surprisingly found Uncle Joe "communicative as the kettle singing." It was on this particular occasion, in fact, that Wise said General Johnston regaled his visitors with the humorous story of Sherman neglecting to offer the ever-thirsty Breckinridge a second splash of whiskey during the North Carolina surrender negotiations—but also exacting a promise from Wise that he would not make it public while Johnston was alive.

Johnston probably should have downed a few Tom-and-Jerry toddies when he served as an honorary pallbearer at General William T. Sherman's funeral on February 19, 1891, in New York City. By all accounts the weather was dreadful and yet Johnston, in deference to his deceased friend and former foe, refused to wear a hat because he felt it would somehow appear disrespectful. The hatless Uncle Joe caught a serious cold in the inclement conditions, which eventually progressed to pneumonia, resulting in Johnston's own death in Washington, D.C., about a month after Sherman was buried.

A STANDOFF IN ATLANTA: LONGSTREET VERSUS SICKLES

On July 2, 1863, at Gettysburg, it was General Daniel Sickles's ill-conceived advance through the Peach Orchard that led to the smashup of his Third Corps. And it was General James Longstreet's troops that turned back the Yankee forces, inflicting great casualties to the men in blue.

But years later, perhaps surprisingly, the men were friends. In fact, Sickles and Longstreet attended a Saint Patrick's celebration in Atlanta in 1892 where—according to Sickles—both former generals were greeted by a rousing "Rebel Yell." Sickles then proposed a toast to his former enemy and reportedly goaded Longstreet into crooning "The Star Spangled Banner." (Beyond the irony of a former rebel singing such a Yankee song, consider, too, that Sickles many decades before had killed Francis Scott Key's son for allegedly making amorous advances toward Sickles's wife.)

Apparently the toasts at the Saint Patrick's event served as a mere kickoff to some shared drams of whiskey later in the evening, as the two ex-generals—Sickles on crutches—had to help each other back to their respective hotels through the dark streets of Atlanta.

In the course of this spirited carousing and fellowship, Sickles claimed to have suggested that Longstreet owed him an apology for shooting off his leg at Gettysburg. Not to lose the strategic high ground, "Old Peter" quickly retorted that, on the contrary, Sickles should thank *him* for leaving Dan his one remaining leg to stand on. In war memories chiefly dominated by the horror of it all, occasionally—with a drink or two—there was still room for humor to win an occasional skirmish.

Although Longstreet and Sickles must both be considered dedicated drinkers over numerous decades, both men were among the few Civil War generals to live into the twentieth century. Longstreet died in 1904 and Sickles—the infamous "Devil Dan" to his enemies—died in 1914, at the ripe old age of ninety-four.

Apparently alcohol did them no harm when it came to their longevity.

THE DOUBLE-EDGED SWORD

It is easy to argue—and document—the negative effects of alcohol on Civil War era soldiers. Their diaries, letters, and official reports overflow (appropriately) with examples of marches delayed, attacks bungled, and other wrongheaded bravado and stupefied ineptness. Some of these debacles certainly occurred "under the influence."

Those delving into this strange but fascinating nook of Civil War history—this author included—can be somewhat surprised to find that too much alcohol sometimes led to senseless rumbles between regiments on the *same side*. It is also undeniable that too much booze played a significant role in some of the most notorious incidents of the war—such as the burning of cities and towns and private residences.

Yet, alcohol was also a readily available treatment—a much-welcomed painkiller—for those wounded on the field and nursed in the medical tents and hospitals. And who could deny that a stiff batch of holiday eggnog could brighten a soldier's dreary Christmas out in the field, if only temporarily? Hardcore teetotalers excepting, most Civil War soldiers also would have admitted that alcohol could promote camaraderie—even with a captured foe on occasion, when a nip of "the Needful" could serve as the initial peace offering.

The humorous incidents of the Civil War, too—and there were many in between the moments of chaos and adrenaline on the battlefield—cannot be fully explored without encountering the testimony of John Barleycorn. Many of the men who wrote the regimental histories understood this, and gave more than the occasional nod to the use of strong drink and the pursuit of it.

Sometimes even the music of the era reflected the fact that this alcohol-influenced humor was part of the soldierly experience. Even in the twenty-first century, most of us are familiar with the Civil War classic tune *When Johnny Comes Marching Home*. Written by Patrick Gilmore in 1863, the standard version goes like this:

> When Johnny comes marching home again,
> Hurrah, hurrah!
> We'll give him a hearty welcome then,

Hurrah, hurrah!
The men will cheer, the boys will shout,
The ladies they will all turn out,
And we'll all feel gay when Johnny comes
    marching home.

But soldiers well accustomed to a drop of "o be joyful" or "tanglefoot" apparently could not resist adding a mischievous improvisation, irreverently twisting the final line to: "And we'll all drink stone blind, Johnny fill up the bowl!"

A slogan familiar to most soldiers during and after the war was: "*We drank from the same canteen!*" It meant, first and foremost, that regardless of which side they fought for, they understood the mutual hardships they had shared and the slaughter they had witnessed, and somehow—by prayer or blind luck—had dodged the same life-threatening dangers. Now, reading from the relative safety of more than a century and a half later, we have a fairly good idea of what exactly was *in* many of those shared canteens. But given what Johnny Reb and Billy Yank were asked to endure—horrific battles, harsh weather conditions, a slew of deadly diseases, and mind-numbing stints of boredom—who are we to judge them too harshly?

In fact, shouldn't we rather raise a glass in their honor?

ACKNOWLEDGMENTS

The author in pursuit of a finished book sometimes *feels* completely alone, but that's rarely the case. He or she is perhaps more accurately "the point man" on a mission that requires enlightened and visionary leadership and the unwavering support of numerous people.

With that in mind, a sincere thanks to the "soldiers" at Regnery Publishing, especially Alex Novak, Elizabeth Dobak, Lauren Mann, and Loren Long. Their suggestions and tweaks (not to mention patience) helped shape this book into a more interesting and readable history.

Much appreciation to Patrick Egan, Patrick McGeehin, C. M. Goffi, and Robert L. Freeman for reading chapters and putting their shoulders to the wheel in various other situations.

Thanks also to Zachary Schisgal, literary agent and friend, for his work and support on back-to-back projects.

Additional nods to my wife Sally and daughter Jordan for sometimes hearing about the Civil War when perhaps they might have preferred discussing more current topics.

In the age of that all-entangling technical octopus we know as "The Internet," an "old school" writer can nevertheless conduct some productive research in something called a library. Chief among those include the Reeves Library at Moravian College and the libraries at Lehigh University in Bethlehem, Pennsylvania; Trexler Library at Muhlenberg College in Allentown, Pennsylvania; and the Skillman Library at Lafayette College in Easton, Pennsylvania. Farther afield, the Musselman Library at Gettysburg College in Gettysburg, Pennsylvania also provided valuable insight for this book.

Finally, how does one applaud soldiers of the past? Their fascinating diaries and journals and their compelling, heartfelt letters home invariably left me shaking my head and wondering, "Good God, how did they endure it?"

BIBLIOGRAPHY

Adams, Charles Francis, Jr., and Henry Adams. *A Cycle of Adams Letters, 1861–1865.* (*Vols. 1–2*). Edited by Worthington Chauncey Ford. Boston: Houghton Mifflin Company, 1920.

Alexander, Edward Porter. *Fighting for the Confederacy: The Personal Recollections of General Edward Porter Alexander.* Edited by Gary W. Gallagher. Chapel Hill: University of North Carolina Press, 1989.

Anderson, John. *The Fifty-Seventh Regiment of Massachusetts Volunteers in the War of the Rebellion.* Boston: E. B. Stillings & Company, 1896.

Avary, Myrta Lockett. *A Virginia Girl in the Civil War, 1861–1865: Being a Record of the Actual Experiences of the Wife of a Confederate Officer.* New York: D. Appleton and Company, 1903.

Axelrod, Alan. *The Horrid Pit: The Battle of the Crater, the Civil War's Cruelest Mission*. New York: Carroll & Graf Publishers, 2007.

Barber, Lucius W. *Army Memoirs of Lucius W. Barber, Company D, 15th Illinois Volunteer Infantry*. Chicago: J.M.W. Jones Stationary and Printing, Co., 1894.

Bellard, Alfred. *Gone for a Soldier: The Civil War Memoirs of Private Alfred Bellard*. Edited by David Herbert Donald. Boston: Little, Brown and Company, 1975.

Billings, John D. *Hardtack and Coffee: Or the Unwritten Story of Army Life*. Boston: George M. Smith & Co., 1887.

Booth, George Wilson. *A Maryland Boy in Lee's Army: Personal Reminiscences of a Maryland soldier in the War Between the States*. Omaha: University of Nebraska Press, 2000.

Boulard, Garry. *The Swing around the Circle: Andrew Johnson and the Train Ride That Destroyed a Presidency*. New York: iUniverse, Inc., 2008.

Bowers, John. *Stonewall Jackson: Portrait of a Soldier*. New York: HarperCollins Publishers, Inc., 1990.

Bradley, Mark L. *The Astounding Close: The Road to Bennett Place*. Chapel Hill: University of North Carolina Press, 2000.

Bridges, Hal. *Lee's Maverick General: Daniel Harvey Hill*. Lincoln: University of Nebraska Press, 1961.

Brinton, John H. *Personal Memoirs of John H. Brinton, Civil War Surgeon, 1861–1865*. New York: Neale Publishing Company, 1914.

Brown, G. Campbell. *Campbell Brown's Civil War: With Ewell and the Army of Northern Virginia*. Edited by Terry L. Jones. Baton Rouge: Louisiana State University Press, 2001.

Bruce, Susannah Ural. *The Harp and the Eagle: Irish-American Volunteers and the Union Army, 1861–1865*. New York: New York University Press, 2006.

————. *Chickamauga and Chattanooga: The Battle that Doomed the Confederacy.* New York: HarperCollins Publishers, Inc., 1992.

Buchanan, James and William Frederic Worner. *Letters of James Buchanan.* Lancaster, PA: Lancaster County Historical Society, 1932.

Butler, Benjamin F. *Butler's Book: Autobiography and Personal Reminiscences.* Boston: A. M. Thayer, 1892.

Cadwallader, Sylvanus. *Three Years with Grant.* Edited by Benjamin P. Thomas. New York: Alfred J. Knopf, 1955.

Carter, Arthur B. *The Tarnished Cavalier: Major General Earl Van Dorn, C.S.A.* Knoxville: University of Tennessee Press, 1999.

Catton, Bruce. *Grant Takes Command.* Edison, NJ: Castle Books, 2000.

Chaffin, Tom. *Sea of Gray: The Around-The-World Odyssey of the Confederate Raider Shenandoah.* New York: Hill and Wang, 2006.

Chesnut, Mary Boykin, Isabella D. Martin, and Myrta Lockett Avary. *A Diary from Dixie, as Written by Mary Boykin Chesnut, Wife of James Chesnut, Jr., United States Senator from South Carolina, 1859–1861, and Afterward an Aide to Jefferson Davis and a Brigadier-General in the Confederate Army.* New York: D. Appleton and Company, 1905.

————. *The Private Mary Chesnut: The Unpublished Civil War Diaries.* Edited by C. Vann Woodward and Elisabeth Muhlenfeld. New York: Oxford University Press, 1984.

Christ, Lynda Lasswell, ed. *The Papers of Jefferson Davis. (Vol. 1).* Baton Rouge: Louisiana State University Press, 1971.

Coddington, Edwin B. *The Gettysburg Campaign: A Study in Command.* New York: Charles Scribner's Sons, 1968.

Collins, Darrell L. *Major General Robert E. Rhodes of the Army of Northern Virginia.* New York: Savas Beatie LLC, 2008.

Collins, R.M. *Chapters from the Unwritten History of the War Between the States: Or the Incidents in the life of a Confederate in Camp, on the March, in the Great Battles, and in Prison.* St. Louis: Nixon-Jones Printing, 1868.

Connolly, James A. *Three Years in the Army of the Cumberland: The Letters and Diary of Major James A. Connolly.* Edited by Paul M. Angle. Bloomington: Indiana University Press, 1959.

Cormany, Rachel and Samuel Cormany. *The Cormany Diaries: A Northern Family in the Civil War.* Edited by James C. Mohr. Pittsburgh: University of Pittsburgh Press, 1982.

Cornelius, Steven. *Music of the Civil War Era.* Westport, CT: Greenwood Publishing Group, 2004.

Cozzens, Peter. *This Terrible Sound: The Battle of Chickamauga.* Urbana and Chicago: University of Illinois Press, 1996.

Crook, William H. *Through Five Administrations: Reminiscences of William H. Crook, Body-guard to President Lincoln.* New York: Harper and Brothers, 1910.

Davis, William C. *Duel Between the First Ironclads.* New York: Doubleday & Company, Inc., 1975.

———. *A Taste for War: The Culinary History of the Blue and Gray.* Lincoln: University of Nebraska Press, 2003.

———. *Battle of Bull Run: A History of the First Major Campaign of the Civil War.* Garden City, NY: Doubleday & Company, Inc., 1977.

———. *The Battle of New Market.* Garden City, NY: Doubleday & Company, Inc., 1975.

Dawson, Francis W. *Reminiscences of Confederate Service, 1861–1865.* Edited by Bell I. Wiley. Baton Rouge: Louisiana State University Press, 1980.

Day, Horace B. *The Opium Habit: With Suggestions as to the Remedy.* New York: Harper & Brothers Publishing, 1868.

Delaney, Norman C. *John McIntosh Kell of the Raider Alabama.* Tuscaloosa: The University of Alabama Press, 1973.

DeLeon, Thomas Cooper. *Four Years in Rebel Capitals*. New York: Collier Books, 1962.

Dooley, John. *Confederate Soldier, His War Journal*. Washington, DC: Georgetown University Press, 1945.

Douglas, Henry Kyd. *I Rode with Stonewall*. Chapel Hill: University of North Carolina Press, 1940.

Dufour, Charles L. *Gentle Tiger: The Gallant Life of Roberdeau Wheat*. Baton Rouge: Louisiana State University Press, 1957.

Early, Jubal Anderson. *War Memories: Autobiographical sketches and narrative of the War Between the States*. Bloomington: Indiana University Press, 1960 (originally published 1912).

Engle, Stephen D. *Don Carlos Buell: Most Promising of All*. Chapel Hill: University of North Carolina Press, 1999.

Evans, Robert G. *The 16th Mississippi Infantry: Civil War Letters and Reminiscences*. Oxford: University Press of Mississippi, 2002.

Fite, John Amenas, and Rebrovick John Fite. *Memories of Col. John Amenas Fite: Seventh Tennessee Infantry, Confederate States of America: born February 10, 1832, died August 23, 1925*. North Charleston, SC: CreateSpace, 2015.

Forney, John W. *Anecdotes of Public Men (Vols. 1–2)*. New York: Harper & Brothers, 1873.

Foster, Samuel T. *One of Cleburne's Command: The Civil War Reminiscences and Diary of Capt. Samuel T. Foster, Granbury's Texas Brigade, CSA*. Edited by Norman D. Brown. Austin: University of Texas Press, 1980.

Fremantle, Arthur J. L. *The Freemantle Diary: Being the Journal of Lieutenant Colonel James Arthur Lyon Fremantle, Cold Stream Guards, of his Three Months in the Southern States*. Edited by Walter Lord. Boston: Little, Brown and Company, 1954.

Gladstone, Thomas H. *The Englishman in Kansas: Or Squatter Life and Border Warfare*. New York: Miller & Co., 1857.

Goodwin, Doris Kearns. *Team of Rivals: The Political Genius of Abraham Lincoln.* New York: Simon & Schuster, 2005.

Gordon, John B. *Reminiscences of the Civil War.* Baton Rouge: Louisiana State University Press, 1993.

Gordon, Lesley J. *General George E. Pickett in Life & Legend.* Chapel Hill: University of North Carolina Press, 1998.

Goree, Thomas J. *Longstreet's Aide: The Civil War Letters of Major Thomas J. Goree.* Edited by Thomas W. Cutrer. Charlottesville: University Press of Virginia, 1995.

Gragg, Rod. *Confederate Goliath: The Battle of Fort Fisher.* New York: HarperCollins Publishers, Inc., 1991.

Grant, U. S. *Memoirs and Selected Letters.* New York: Library of America, 1990.

Gwynne, S. C. *Rebel Yell: The Violence, Passion, and Redemption of Stonewall Jackson.* New York: Scribner, 2014.

Haley, John W. *Rebel Yell & the Yankee Hurrah: The Civil War Journal of a Maine Volunteer.* Camden, ME: Down East Books, 2014.

Haskell, John Cheves. *The Haskell Memoirs.* Edited by Gilbert E. Govan and James W. Livingood. New York: G. P. Putnam's Sons, 1960.

Hay, John. *Inside Lincoln's White House: The Complete Civil War Diary of John Hay.* Edited by Michael Burlingame and John R. Turner Ettlinger. Carbondale: Southern Illinois University Press, 1999.

Hayes, Rutherford B. and Charles Richard Williams. *Diary and Letters of Rutherford Birchard Hayes, Nineteenth President of the United States.* Columbus: Ohio State Archaeological and Historical Society, 1922.

Hearn, Chester G. *The Capture of New Orleans 1862.* Baton Rouge: Louisiana State University Press, 1995.

Hitchcock, Frederick. *War from the Inside.* Philadelphia: Press of J. B. Lippincott, 1904.

Hitchcock, George A. *"Death Does Seem to Have All He Can Attend To"*: *The Civil War Diary of an Andersonville Survivor.* Jefferson, NC: McFarland & Company, Inc., Publishers, 2014.

Hitchcock, Henry H. *Marching with Sherman*: *Passages from the Letters and Campaign Diaries of Henry Hitchcock.* New Haven: Yale University Press, 1927.

Hoehling, A.A. & Mary Hoehling. *The Last Days of the Confederacy*: *An Eyewitness Account of the Fall of Richmond, Capital City of the Confederate States.* New York: The Fairfax Press, 1981.

Holmes, Oliver Wendell, Jr. *Touched with Fire*: *Civil War letters and diary of Oliver Wendell Holmes, Jr., 1861–1864.* Boston: Harvard University Press, 1947.

Hood, John Bell. *Advance and Retreat*: *Personal Experiences in the United States & Confederates States Armies.* New York: Da Capo Press, 1993.

Hood, Stephen M. *John Bell Hood*: *The Rise, Fall and Resurrection of a Confederate General.* El Dorado Hills, CA: Savas Beatie LLC, 2013.

———. *The Lost Papers of Confederate General John B. Hood.* El Dorado Hills, CA: Savas Beatie LLC, 2015.

Hoogenboom, Ari Arthur. *Rutherford B. Hayes*: *Warrior and President.* Lawrence: University Press of Kansas, 1995.

Horwitz, Tony. *Midnight Rising*: *John Brown and the Raid That Sparked the Civil War.* New York: Henry Holt and Company, 2011.

Hotchkiss, Jedediah. *Make Me a Map of the Valley*: *The Civil War Journal of Stonewall Jackson's Topographer.* Dallas: Southern Methodist University, 1973.

Hughes, Nathaniel Cheairs, Jr. *The Battle of Belmont*: *Grant Strikes South.* Chapel Hill: University of North Carolina Press, 2000.

Hunton, Eppa. *The Autobiography of Eppa Hunton.* Richmond: William Byrd Press, 1933.

Jackson, Isaac. *"Some of the Boys…"*: *The Civil War Letters of Isacc Jackson, 1862–1865*. Edited by Joseph Orville Jackson. Carbondale: Southern Illinois University Press, 1960.

Jackson, Oscar Lawrence. *The Colonel's Diary*: *Journals Kept Before and During the Civil War by the late Colonel Oscar L. Jackson*. Sharon, PA: Library of Congress, 1922.

Jones, Terry L. *Lee's Tigers*: *The Louisiana Infantry in the Army of Northern Virginia*. Baton Rouge: Louisiana State University Press, 1987.

Jordan, David M. *"Happiness Is Not My Companion"*: *The Life of General G.K. Warren*. Bloomington: Indiana University Press, 2001.

Kampfoefner, Walter D. and Wolfgang Helbich. *Germans in the Civil War*: *The Letters They Wrote Home*. Chapel Hill: University of North Carolina Press, 2009.

Keeler, William Frederick and Anne Elizabeth Dutton Keeler. *Aboard the USS Monitor*: *1862*: *The Letters of Acting Paymaster William Frederick Keeler, Anne Elizabeth Dutton Keeler*. Annapolis: U.S. Naval Institute, 1962.

Kennett, Lee. *Marching Through Georgia*: *The Story of Soldiers & Civilians During Sherman's Campaign*. New York: HarperCollins Publishers, Inc., 1995.

Key, Thomas Jefferson and Robert J Campbell. *Two Soldiers*: *The Campaign Diaries of Thomas J. Key, C.S.A., and Robert J. Campbell, U.S.A.* Chapel Hill: University of North Carolina Press, 1938.

King, Alvy L. *Louis T. Wigfall*: *Southern Fire-Eater*. Baton Rouge: Louisiana State University Press, 1970.

Kohl, Lawrence Frederick and Margaret Crosse Richard. *Irish Green and Union Blue*: *The Civil War Letters of Peter Welsh, Color Sergeant, 28th Massachusetts*. New York: Fordham University Press, 1986.

Lankford, Nelson. *Richmond Burning*: *The Last Days of the Confederate Capital*. New York: Viking, 2002.

Lasswell, Mary, ed. *Rags and Hope: The Recollections of Val C. Giles, Four Years with Hood's Brigade, Fourth Texas Infantry, 1861–1865*. New York: Coward-McCann, Inc., 1961.

Lawson, Albert. *War Anecdotes and Incidents of Army Life: Reminiscences from Both Sides of the Conflict Between North and South*. Cincinnati: E. H. Beasley & Co., 1888.

Lee, Elizabeth Blair. *Wartime Washington: The Civil War Letters of Elizabeth Blair Lee*. Edited by Virginia Jeans Laas. Urbana and Chicago: University of Illinois Press, 1991.

Livermore, Thomas L. *Days and Events, 1860–1866*. Boston: Houghton Mifflin Company, 1920.

Logan, Kate Virginia Cox. *My Confederate Girlhood: The Memoirs of Kate Virginia Cox Logan*. Edited by Lily Logan Morrill. New York: Arno Publishing, 1980.

Lyman, Theodore. *Meade's Headquarters 1863–1865: Letters of Colonel Theodore Lyman from The Wilderness to Appomattox*. Edited by George R. Agassiz. Boston: The Atlantic Monthly Press, 1922.

Martin, Samuel J. *General Braxton Bragg, CSA*. Jefferson, NC: McFarland & Company, 2011.

Marvel, William. *Burnside*. Chapel Hill: University of North Carolina Press, 1991.

———. *Lee's Last Retreat: The Flight to Appomattox*. Chapel Hill: University of North Carolina Press, 2002.

McCorkle, John and Oswald S. Barton. *Three Years with Quantrill: A True Story Told By His Scout*. Norman, OK: University of Oklahoma Press, 1914.

McGuire, Hunter, and George L. Christian. *The Confederate Cause and Conduct in the War Between the States*. Richmond: L. H. Jenkins, 1907.

McNeely, Patricia G., Debra Reddin van Tuyll, and Henry H. Schulte. *Knights of the Quill: Confederate Correspondents and their Civil War Reporting*. West Lafayette, IN: Purdue University Press, 2010.

Meade, George Gordon. *The Life and Letters of George Gordon Meade, Major-General, U.S. Army. (Vol. 2)* New York: Charles Scribner's Sons, 1913.

Miller, Samuel K. *The Soul of a Soldier: The True Story of a Mounted Pioneer in the Civil War.* Edited by Myron M. Miller. Bloomington, IN: Xibris Corp., 2011.

Morgan, Sarah. *The Civil War Diary of Sarah Morgan.* Edited by Charles East. Athens: The University of Georgia Press, 1991.

Mosby, John S. *The Memoirs of Colonel John S. Mosby.* Bloomington: Indiana University Press, 1959.

Nash, Howard P., Jr. *Stormy Petrel: The Life and Times of General Benjamin F. Butler, 1818–1893.* Madison, NJ: Fairleigh Dickinson University Press, 1969.

Nichols, James Moses. *Perry's Saints: Or, the Fighting Parson's Regiment in the War of the Rebellion.* New York: D. Lothrop, 1886.

Olsen, Bernard E., ed. *Upon the Tented Field.* Red Bank, NJ: Historic Projects, Inc., 1993.

Opdycke, Emerson. *To Battle for God and the Right: The Civil War Letterbooks of Emerson Opdycke.* Edited by Glenn V. Longacre and John E. Haas. Urbana and Chicago: University of Illinois Press, 2003.

Osborn, Thomas Ward. *The Fiery Trail: A Union Officer's Account of Sherman's Last Campaigns.* Edited by Richard Harwell and Philip N. Racine. Knoxville: The University of Tennessee Press, 1986.

Parker, Thomas H. *History of the 51st Regiment of Pennsylvania Volunteers.* Philadelphia: Higginson Book Company, 1869.

Parks, Joseph Howard. *General Leonidas Polk, C.S.A.: The Fighting Bishop.* Baton Rouge: Louisiana State University Press, 1962.

Patrick, Marsena Rudolph. *Inside Lincoln's Army: The Diary of Marsena Rudolph Patrick, Provost Marshal General, Army of the Potomac*. Edited by David S. Sparks. New York: Thomas Yoseloff, 1964.

Patterson, Edmund DeWitt. *Yankee Rebel: The Civil War Journal of Edmund DeWitt Patterson*. Chapel Hill: University of North Carolina, 1966.

Pember, Phoebe Yates. *A Southern Woman's Story*. New York: G. W. Carleton & Company, 1879.

Perry, James M. *A Bohemian Brigade: The Civil War Correspondents*. New York: John Wiley & Sons, Inc., 2000.

Pfanz, Donald. *Richard S. Ewell: A Soldier's Life*. Chapel Hill: University of North Carolina Press, 1998.

Philbrick, Nathaniel. *The Last Stand: Custer, Sitting Bull, and The Battle of the Little Bighorn*. New York: Viking, 2010.

Piston, William Garrett and Richard W. Hatcher III. *Wilson's Creek: The Second Battle of the Civil War and the Men Who Fought It*. Chapel Hill: University of North Carolina Press, 2000.

Porter, Horace. *Campaigning with Grant*, New York: Century Company, 1897.

Putnam, Sallie Brock. *Richmond During the War: Four Years of Personal Observation*. Lincoln: University of Nebraska Press, 1996.

Rawle, William Brooke. *History of the Third Pennsylvania Cavalry, 1861–1865*. Philadelphia: Franklin Printing Company, 1905.

Reardon, Carol. *Pickett's Charge in History & Memory*. Chapel Hill: University of North Carolina Press, 1997.

Rhea, Gordon C. *The Battles for Spotsylvania Court House and the Road to Yellow Tavern, May 7–12*. Baton Rouge: Louisiana State University Press, 2005.

Rhodes, Elisha Hunt. *All for the Union: The Civil War Diary & Letters of Elisha Hunt Rhodes*. New York: Knopf Doubleday Publishing Group, 2010.

Robertson, James I., Jr. *The Civil War Letters of General Robert McAllister*. Baton Rouge: Louisiana State University Press, 1998.

Rodick, Burleigh Cushing. *Appomattox: The Last Campaign*. Gaithersburg, MD: Old Soldier Books, 1987.

Roe, Alfred Seelye. *The Thirty-Ninth Massachusetts Volunteers, 1862–1865*. Worcester, MA: Regimental Veteran Association, 1914.

Rollins, Richard, ed. *Pickett's Charge! Eyewitness Accounts*. Redondo Beach, CA: Rank and File Publications, 1994.

Ruffin, Edmund. *The Diary of Edmund Ruffin*. Edited by William Kauffman Scarborough and Avery O. Craven. Baton Rouge: Louisiana University Press, 1972.

Russell, William Howard. *My Diary North and South*. London: Bradbury and Evans, 1865.

Sears, Stephen W. *For Country, Cause, and Leader: The Civil War Journals of Charles B. Haydon*. Boston: Houghton Mifflin Harcourt, 2016.

Schofield, John M. *Forty-Six Years in the Army*. New York: The Century Company, 1897.

Schultz, Duane. *Quantrill's War: The Life and Times of William Clarke Quantrill, 1837–1865*. New York: St. Martin's Press, 1996.

Shelden, Rachel. *Washington Brotherhood: Politics, Social Life, and the Coming of the Civil War*. Chapel Hill: University of North Carolina Press, 2013.

Sheridan, Philip Henry. *Personal Memoirs of P.H. Sheridan, General United States Army*. New York: Charles L. Webster & Company, 1888.

Sherman, William T. *Memoirs of General William T. Sherman, by himself*. New York: D. Appleton and Company, 1875.

Siegel, Alan A. *Beneath the Starry Flag: New Jersey's Civil War Experience*. Piscataway, NJ: Rutgers University Press, 2001.

Silverman, Jason H., Samuel N. Thomas Jr., and Beverly D. Evans IV. *Shanks: The Life and Wars of General Nathan George Evans.* Boston: Da Capo Press, 2002.

Small, Abner R. *The Road to Richmond: The Civil War Letters of Major Abner R. Small of the 16th Maine Volunteers.* Edited by Harold Adams Small. New York: Fordham University Press, 2000.

Smith, Jean Edward. *Grant.* New York: Simon & Schuster, 2002.

Sneden, Robert K. *Eye of the Storm.* Edited by Charles F. Bryan Jr. and Nelson D. Lankford. New York: Simon & Schuster, 2002.

Sorrel, Gilbert Moxley. *Recollections of a Confederate Field Officer.* New York: The Neale Publishing Company, 1905.

Stackpole, Edward J. *Chancellorsville: Lee's Greatest Battle.* Harrisburg, PA: The Stackpole Company, 1958.

Stephens, George E. *A Voice of Thunder: The Civil War Letters of George E. Stephens.* Urbana-Champaign: University of Illinois, 1997.

Stoddard, William Osborn. *Inside the White House in War Times.* New York: C.L. Webster & Company, 1890.

Stone, Dewitt Boyd. *Wandering to Glory: Confederate Veterans Remember Evans' Brigade.* Columbia: University of South Carolina Press, 2001.

Stowe, Harriet Beecher. *Uncle Tom's Cabin; or Life among the Lowly.* Boston: John P. Jewett & Co., 1852.

Strother, David Hunter. *A Virginia Yankee in the Civil War: The Diaries of David Hunter Strother.* Edited by Cecil D. Eby Jr. Chapel Hill: University of North Carolina Press, 1998.

Swanberg, William A. *Sickles the Incredible.* New York: Ace Books, 1956.

———. *First Blood: The Story of Fort Sumter.* New York: Longmans, 1960.

Sword, Wiley. *Shiloh: Bloody April.* Dayton: Morningside Bookshop Press, 2001.

Symonds, Craig L. *Stonewall of the West*: *Patrick Cleburne and the Civil War*. Lawrence: University Press of Kansas, 1997.

Taylor, Richard. *Destruction and Reconstruction*: *Personal Experiences of the Late War*. Edited by Charles P. Roland. Waltham: Blaisdell Publishing Company, 1968.

Tiball, Eugene C. *"No Disgrace to My Country"*: *The Life of John C. Tiball*. Kent, OH: The Kent State University Press, 2002.

Trobriand, Regis de. *Four Years with the Army of the Potomac*. Boston: Ticknor and Company, 1889.

Trudeau, Noah Andre. *The Last Citadel*: *Petersburg, Virginia, June 1864–April 1865*. Baton Rouge: Louisiana State University Press, 1991.

Tucker, Phillip. *Pickett's Charge*: *A New Look at Gettysburg's Final Attack*. New York: Skyhorse Publishing, Inc., 2016.

Upson, Theodore F. *With Sherman to the Sea*: *The Civil War Letters Diaries & Reminiscences of Theodore F. Upson*. Edited by Oscar Osburn Winther. Bloomington: Indiana University Press, 1958.

Vandiver, Frank E. *Jubal Early's Raid. General Early's Famous Attack on Washington in 1864*. New York: McGraw-Hill Book Company, Inc., 1960.

Wainwright, Charles S. *A Diary of Battle*: *The Personal Journals of Colonel Charles S. Wainwright, 1861–1865*. New York: Harcourt, 1962.

Walker, Gary C. *Hunter's Fiery Raid Through Virginia's Valleys*. Gretna, LA: Pelican Publishing, Inc., 1989.

Ward, Andrew. *River Run Red*: *The Fort Pillow Massacre in the American Civil War*. New York: Viking, 2005.

Welles, Gideon. *Diary of Gideon Welles (Vols. 1–3)*. Boston: Houghton Mifflin, Riverside Press, 1911.

Werstein, Irving. *Kearny the Magnificent*: *The Story of General Philip Kearny, 1815–1862*. New York: The John Day Company, 1962.

Williams, T. Harry. *P.G.T. Beauregard*: *Napoleon in Gray*. Baton Rouge: Louisiana State University Press, 1955.

Will-Weber, Mark. *Mint Juleps with Teddy Roosevelt*: *The Complete History of Presidential Drinking*. Washington, D.C.: Regnery Publishing, 2014.

Wilson, Suzanne Colton. *Column South*: *With the Fifteenth Pennsylvania Cavalry from Antietam to the Capture of Jefferson Davis*. Edited by J. Ferrell Colton and Antoinette G. Smith. Flagstaff, AZ: J.F. Colton & Co., 1960.

Wise, John S. *The End of an Era*. New York: Houghton Mifflin, 1899.

Wood, William Nathaniel. *Reminiscences of Big I*. Edited by Bell Irvin Wiley. Jackson, TN: Jackson McCowet-Mercer Press, 1956.

INDEX